Assessment for an Evolving Business Education Curriculum

National Business Education Association Yearbook, No. 45

2007

Editor
Marcia L. Bush
Lincoln, California

Associate Editor
Kimberly A. Schultz
Kirkwood Community College
Cedar Rapids, Iowa

Published by

National Business Education Association
1914 Association Drive
Reston, VA 20191-1596
(703) 860-8300 • Fax: (703) 620-4483
www.nbea.org

TABLE OF CONTENTS

Part III. Assessment and the Impact of Technology

Part IV. Assessment Data as a Focus

Part V. Assessment of Subject Matter Competence

Part VI. Assessment of Program Effectiveness

PREFACE

Assessment in business education at all levels validates what students are learning and provides proof of student competence. As the business education curriculum continues to evolve in the 21st century, it is clear that assessment is a critical component. Business educators, as leaders, consider assessment to be a definite professional responsibility, understand the importance of standards, develop skills using multiple strategies, incorporate the use of technology, and utilize assessment data for continuous improvement.

The *2007 Yearbook* is divided into six parts; four parts represent a continuum for business educators wishing to improve their skills in assessing student progress, an additional part looks at the assessment of subject matter competence, and a final part addresses the assessment of program effectiveness.

Part I Introduction to Assessment Fundamentals is presented as a course. Chapter 1, Assessment 101, establishes a common language to be shared and understood by all business educators. Assessment fundamentals are the foundation for developing sound assessment practices.

Part II Assessment Practices becomes a checklist that business educators can use to verify their own assessment strategies. Each chapter addresses an important assessment component. Chapters 2-6 present a complete range of effective practices beginning with providing student feedback, moving to reflecting on effective teaching, supporting and reinforcing academics, determining student outcomes in the content areas, and selecting appropriate assessment methods.

Part III Assessment and the Impact of Technology looks at the emerging advantages of technology as an assessment companion. Chapter 7 features online assessment strategies and resources. Chapter 8 emphasizes the emerging role of the delivery of instruction from remote locations and solutions for student assessment.

Part IV Assessment Data as a Focus raises the important questions about gathering and analyzing data for a variety of purposes. Chapter 9 illustrates how assessment data can drive instructional decisions. Chapter 10 takes on the challenge of compiling assessment data from multiple measures to verify and celebrate student achievement. Chapter 11 looks at assessment data as feedback to guide professional development plans for business educators.

Part V Assessment of Subject Matter Competence addresses two important cornerstones of the business education profession. Chapter 12 addresses the assessment of research and how research can be utilized by business educators. Chapter 13 discusses business education subject matter competency and features the requirements for business education licensure in three states.

Part VI Assessment of Program Effectiveness provides guidance and resources for business educators as they seek to prepare for the evaluation of their programs. Chapter 14 addresses assessment methods for determining program effectiveness that provide reportable program outcomes.

The *2007 Yearbook* represents an enormous contribution on the part of 27 authors who stepped forward to contribute their expertise to this business education publication. In every case this work was accomplished above and beyond already full professional and personal schedules.

Sincere appreciation is extended to 27 reviewers who provided the important professional feedback for each and every chapter to make this refereed publication possible as well as to Janice Harder, Chair, and members of the Publications Committee for their valuable oversight from the beginning theme to the final publication.

Finally, very special commendations to Susan O'Brien who provided much-needed assistance throughout the process and who skillfully contributed the amazing finishing touches to produce a quality publication.

Marcia Bush, Editor
Retired Educational Consultant
Lincoln, California

Kimberly Schultz, Associate Editor
Kirkwood Community College
Cedar Rapids, Iowa

ACKNOWLEDGMENTS

The following individuals graciously contributed their time and talents to review manuscripts for *Assessment for an Evolving Business Education Curriculum*.

Marcia Anderson	Linda McGrew
Lori Braunstein	Bridget O'Connor
Julie Chadd	Kay Orrell
Judy Clark	Donna Redmann
Tena B. Crews	Anne Rowe
Janice C. Harder	Jim Rucker
Donna Henderson	Judith Sams
William Hoyt	Mona Schoenrock
Colleen Hunt	Rebecca Seher
Susan Jaderstrom	Bonnie Sibert
Sheryl Piening Keller	Sue Sydow
Dennis Krejci	Cheryl Wiedmaier
Anne Mace	Dawn Woodland
Melinda McCannon	

Assessment 101

Nancy D. Zeliff
Northwest Missouri State University
Maryville, Missouri

How long has it been since today's business educator has taken a testing and measurement class? Has every business educator even taken a course in assessment? This author did not have *Assessment 101* as an undergraduate student. It was more than ten years later in the final courses of a doctoral program when a formal assessment course was taken.

This chapter serves as crash course in *Assessment 101* for all business educators. Topics that will be explored include definitions and examples of assessment and measurement, a discussion on validity and reliability of assessment measures, and a look at the purposes of assessment. Sit down, take out a notebook and a number two pencil, put on your freshman beanie—it's time to go back to *Assessment 101* to revisit the important basics of measuring student growth and achievement.

ASSESSMENT

Evaluating student growth and achievement is what assessment is all about. Business educators use varied means of assessment to best identify the skills and competencies students have achieved in all domains of learning. These three domains include the cognitive, affective, and psychomotor domains (Linn and Gronlund, 2000). The cognitive domain includes "thinking" or outcomes based upon student knowledge. The affective domain assesses a student's behavior and attitudes. The psychomotor domain assesses a student's motor skills.

A student of assessment will find a language unique to this field of study. Types of assessment include traditional, alternative, performance, authentic, high stakes, benchmark, formative, and summative.

Traditional Assessment

Traditional assessment has long included objective test questions. Objective tests consist of multiple choice or true-false questions, which allow a business educator to assess lower-level cognitive skills. Short-answer and essay questions are other examples of questions used in traditional testing, which help measure higher levels of the cognitive domain. Essay questions can either be restricted or open-ended. Restricted essay questions include parameters within which students must respond. An example of a restricted essay question would read, "Describe the three forms of business and an advantage and disadvantage of each." Open-ended essay questions ask the student to respond to a prompt and justify the answer by assigning a judgment or value to the answer. Modifying the example used above, an open-ended essay question would read, "Which of the three forms of business organization would you select to form your own business? Justify your selection." Objective testing strategies are usually employed in high-stakes testing.

Alternative Assessment

Business educators use alternative assessment to best measure the affective domain and the higher levels of the cognitive domain. Student behaviors and attitudes can be measured by anecdotal records and observations. Longitudinal growth shown through reflections and portfolios can be assessed. Human relations skills can be assessed through observations made by supervisors in cooperative work experiences and by peers with individual or group tasks and assignments. Self-assessment is another alternative assessment format that provides the learner with assessment information not available with traditional evaluation methods.

Performance Assessment

Common to business education, performance assessment measures the psychomotor domain where the student demonstrates competence by actually carrying out a skill or task. In keyboarding, business educators use a checklist to observe a learner's keyboarding technique. Another example would be observing a student perform varied tasks on a multi-line telephone and recording the student's performance on an evaluation instrument.

Performance assessment can also be used to assess a student's achievement of the cognitive domain. To best measure a student's ability to format a block business letter, the business educator has the student format a block business letter. To best assess the student's ability to complete a job interview, a mock interview with a human resource manager is completed. Simulations where students complete work-flow activities, set priorities, and work in team environments also are excellent ways to assess student achievement in the cognitive and affective domains. Although a multiple-choice or true-false assessment could assess the student's knowledge of formatting a block business letter, interview skills, and office procedures, these traditional assessments would not adequately assess a student's skill and competence attainment. Performance assessments are the best ways to assess the skills chosen to be assessed.

Authentic Assessment

Authentic workplace tasks bring authenticity to business classrooms and should be an integral part of assessing business students. Authentic assessment is a form of performance assessment that involves real-world tasks and activities rather than contrived projects from textbooks and workbooks. These authentic tasks allow students to use their business skills and knowledge in a real-world context. Both the classroom teacher and external evaluators can assess authentic tasks performed by students. School district patrons may provide feedback to school personnel on the student-developed school district Web page. If FBLA members present a PowerPoint presentation to the local Chamber of Commerce, for example, the Chamber members can provide feedback to the presenters about their presentation skills and the information shared. If a mass mailing is produced by business students for a community service group, the service group can later report to the students the return rate of the mailing. Students will have pride in their work knowing that these projects are used by external audiences and will value the feedback provided by stakeholders outside of the school (Zeliff and Schultz, 1998).

High-Stakes Testing and Assessment

A driver's license written test to a 16-year old; the SAT or ACT to a high school student; the PRAXIS to a pre-service teacher candidate; or the GRE to a prospective graduate student are examples of high-stakes testing. These examinations, when passed, allow the test taker to obtain a desired license or certification or be admitted to a program or college. If these examinations are not passed upon the first sitting, then the exam is taken again and again until the desired test score or outcome is obtained. Licensure or admittance is not granted until the desired score is met—indeed high stakes to each test taker.

Benchmark Assessments

Benchmark tests or assessments are provided by agencies, institutions, or vendors who have designed testing systems that coordinate with state and industry standards and are administered to assess student progress. The purpose of benchmark tests are to "provide both accurate information about how well students are progressing toward mastery of standards and useful diagnostic feedback to guide instruction and improve learning" (Herman & Baker, 2005, p. 1). The delivery format of benchmark tests can be via the Web, on CDs, or in customized testing programs. Reports generated from student results can be customized for a variety of stakeholders— students, teachers, administrators, and parents (Herman and Baker, 2005). Examples of benchmark tests in computer and information processing would be the Computer Science AP exam, IC³ certification, MOS certification, or A+ certification.

Most state educational agencies either develop their own state benchmark tests or use national exams. The Department of Elementary and Secondary Education in Missouri (2006) utilizes the Missouri Assessment Program (MAP) test to measure student progress towards the state standards. Many other states use the National Assessment of Educational Progress or NAEP (Institute of Education Sciences, 2006). Benchmark tests are useful when they are aligned to standards, are mapped to content, are fair, have utility, and are feasible. Aligning to state standards and mapping to content are very important and both commitments must be met. It is not enough that benchmark tests meet state standards, but they must assess the most important content. It is not feasible, however, to align the benchmark tests to all standards and contain all content—the test would be too long and complicated for students.

To be fair to all test takers, benchmark tests need to allow accommodations for students with disabilities that mirror the accommodations they receive with other testing. These tests should also be routinely reviewed to be bias-free for special populations who may take the test. Benchmark tests have high utility when they can provide stakeholders timely feedback that is meaningful and usable to improve teaching and learning. Teachers and administrators need to be able to administer benchmark exams when it is timely for their class or school district.

Diagnostic measures to improve student learning are an important element of effective benchmark tests. Feedback provided to students usually includes national percentile rankings and elements of a given subject that were assessed. For example, with mathematical testing, a student's ability with number relationships or problem solving can be diagnostically analyzed for specific feedback. In language arts testing, a student's ability with sentence structure or writing strategies can be profiled. Finally, benchmark testing needs to be worth the time and money educational institutions invest. If the results help improve student learning, then they are useful and worthy of use (Herman and Baker, 2005).

Formative Assessment

Formative assessment is "learn as you go." Business educators utilize formative assessment daily with questions asked of students during class lecture and discussion, 3-minute writes, journal or blog entries, performance events such as timed writings or formatted business documents, and chapter quizzes. Chappuis (2005) indicates that formative assessment helps a student answer three questions: "Where am I going? Where am I now? and How can I close the gap?" (p. 1).

In order for students to know where they are going, it is important for them to share the learning outcomes. Some school districts require the day's objective be visible to students, so that when they enter the classroom, students clearly know the purpose of the day's lesson and activities. Another way that students can identify where they are going is for the business educator to share a scoring guide as a project is assigned. Showing an exemplary finished project is another way to guide students to the direct outcome (Chappuis, 2005).

Self-assessment allows a student to ask, "Where am I now?" Self-assessment can be completed with scoring guides, checklists, blog entries, or reflections. Students may be required to submit a scoring guide or checklist with the student's perception of his or her performance. Reflections or blog entries reveal what a student has perceived he or she has learned and is informative to the business educator in identifying content that needs to be retaught (Chappuis, 2005).

Chappuis (2005) provides strategies for helping students "close the gap" between where they are and where they need to be. Identifying the gap in what is to be mastered can be achieved with the use of strategies that include scoring guides, reflections, and revisions. If a student in accounting is to prepare an income statement and is unsure of the sections to include, he or she could look at the scoring guide for guidance. Scoring guides identify the criteria on which student work is evaluated and describes the requirements of an assignment. A scoring guide used to evaluate an income statement, for example, would list the required sections and accounts of an income statement. Therefore, the student could deduce from the scoring guide that expenses are recorded on the left side of the income statement and proceed with completing the income statement correctly.

After a mock job interview, a business student could think through the questions asked and be assigned to write a self-reflection to his/her responses to those questions. Answers to reflective questions such as "Did I anticipate the questions that would be asked?" or "Did I substantiate my responses with behaviors and experiences?" or "Did I in turn ask appropriate questions of the interviewer?" provide students the opportunity for important reflection.

While reflections are an end in the evaluation process, revisions allow students to correct misinterpreted or incorrect knowledge or skills. In a keyboarding class, students may be allowed to revise graded documents until they are correct, allowing them to proofread in teams, polish editing skills, and identify what they have learned. When an accounting student works with a simulation, a mid-cycle audit of the transactions and accounting records can reveal inaccuracies. It is imperative they correct these inaccuracies so that the ending financial records report true and factual information.

Each time this author reads about, writes about, or uses formative assessment, an advertising jingle is remembered. An early Wonder Bread television advertisement stated its bread was made with fortified flour containing minerals and vitamins that were important for a child's diet in the "the formative years." Formative assessment is very important to students in their diet of learning and mastering knowledge and skills. How else will students identify the intended outcome, assess where they are at a given point in the learning process, and complete additional practice and learning to meet their objectives?

Summative Assessment

While formative assessment is completed throughout the learning process, summative assessment is completed as a "summary" or assessment of the end result. In a personal finance class, a unit exam over four chapters related to money management and budgeting would be a summative assessment. A comprehensive final exam at the end of a semester economics class is another summative assessment. Another example of a summative assessment is the evaluation of the pre-service teacher completed at the end of the student teaching experience.

Lambrecht (2000) indicates that summative assessments are often "high-stakes testing" completed at the end of programs or experiences. If summative assessments are positive, then graduation, certification, admittance, or licensure often is the result. If summative assessments are not positive, then remediation is often needed.

Learners are not the only recipients of summative assessments. School districts and college or university programs undergo accreditation, which results in a visiting team assessing all components of that program or organization. If accreditation is not achieved, elements of the program or organization that need improvement are identified and become the focus of reorganization and change.

There are a variety of assessment measures used in the formative or summative manner. A business educator can select from traditional, alternative, performance, or authentic assessment to identify skills and competencies achieved by students. High-stakes testing and benchmarks usually are created by agencies and institutions and have state, industry, or national use.

MEASUREMENT

A ruler measures one foot or 12 inches. On the ruler, increments of one-eighth are marked for each inch. One who uses the ruler can accurately measure the length or height of an object and have as a result of that measurement a quantitative measure. Measurement, when used with the assessment process, has a quantitative measure or outcome that serves as the standard or measure of knowledge and skill. A gymnast who scores a 9.4 on the balance beam has been measured with standards of skill and difficulty. When the next gymnast scores a 9.65, that measure or score is easily identified as being "higher" than the 9.4 score. Methods of interpreting scores of measurement are by norm-referenced and criterion-referenced methods.

Linn and Gronlund (2000, p. 32) describe measurement as "the process of obtaining a numerical description of the degree to which an individual possesses a particular characteristic." Measurement is just a score or point that answers the question "how much?" No evaluation or assessment is associated with the measurement. Loyal fans of an undefeated basketball team that lost by 25 points would assess the game from many angles to explain the loss to a lesser team. Yet, the victorious team who beat the undefeated team by 25 points may dwell only on the measure of winning by "25 points." A measure then, by itself, is not what's important. The "big picture," or what the measure *means* is what is important.

Convert the basketball example into a business classroom. A student sees a 72 on a returned exam in a personal finance class, notes the score, and tucks the paper away in a folder. The 72 is a measure, a rather meaningless measure if it is not used with other facts or assessment measures. The 72 might mean "earned 72 points out of 80 points," which is 90%, or an "A." The 72 could also mean, "earned 72 points out of 100," or 72%, only a "C." The 72 could be huge drop in performance from the previous formative assessment, and the business educator and student should evaluate why this drop has occurred. The 72 could also be a big improvement that would warrant a different perspective. Finally, the 72 could mean that the student scored above the 72nd percentile. A measure alone is nearly meaningless; quantifiable scores and data used in assessment are just one of several ways to assess student learning and achievement.

Norm-Referenced Measurement

Norm-referenced scores are compared in a ranking to other students' measures who have taken the same assessment (Gronlund, 2006). Standardized examinations that are summative in nature such as the ACT, SAT, MFAT, and PRAXIS share norm-referenced results, which allow the test takers to see how they measure against others who have taken the same test. Norm-referenced results are commonly used as evaluative measures in school district evaluations or college and university program accreditation reviews.

State and federal funding can also be tied to results of norm-referenced assessments. Missouri public universities and colleges receive additional state dollars when students perform above the 50th percentile on nationally-normed examinations (Northwest, 1997). This "funding for results" incentive serves as a measure of the institution's effectiveness. A given group of students can be exceptional in a given year and score well on norm-referenced examinations. In contrast, test scores can decline because students may not be as academically gifted. In addition, the norm itself may increase, contributing to the inability to meet institution's assessment measures. When reviewing norm-referenced results, business educators must explain these anomalies to stakeholders and identify the reasons why students may or may not have met assessment expectations. Measurements and scores are useful to a point, but assessment of both students and programs need to involve multiple measures to accurately and adequately measure student growth and achievement.

Criterion-Referenced Measurement

Using district, state, or national standards as the gauge, criterion-referenced measures are commonly used in formative and as well as summative assessments. Gronlund (2006, p. 28) identifies criterion-referenced measures as those "description[s] of the learning task a student can and cannot perform." Formative assessments in business courses use curriculum standards as the criterion for instruction and assessment. A unit on income taxes is common in a Personal Finance class and is aligned to local, state, or national standards. The formative assessment in such a unit is the completion of a 1040EZ.

Summative assessments are used at the end of instruction in "certifying mastery or assigning grades" (Gronlund, 2006, p. 8). When students receive their summative score or grade, they know how they fare against a set of standards in a course or in their chosen field or discipline. These scores may determine whether the student passes the class, is accepted in an honor society, or earns certification.

Many examinations on the state or national level provide both criterion- and norm-referenced statistics. Business education majors at Missouri universities must meet a prescribed measure on the criterion-referenced PRAXIS—once called the national teacher exam (Missouri, 2004). However, the administration is primarily interested in the norm-referenced results, because the results provide evidence of the institution's effectiveness.

Measurement is a quantifiable measure or score. Interpretation of measures can be norm-referenced where ratings or comparisons are made to other learners' outcomes. Criterion-referenced scores are used to measure student outcomes when compared to standards and content of a given field or discipline.

VALIDITY AND RELIABILITY

Gronlund (2006) identifies basic concepts that are essential to assessment. The first two and most important two are validity and reliability. The importance of validity and reliability are evident in the discussion for each that follows. The use of scoring guides is a means by which to increase the reliability, both internally and among raters. Increased validity can be reached by monitoring the construction and administration of evaluation methods.

Validity

Validity refers to the degree to which an assessment measures what is intended to be measured (Gronlund, 2006). To best assess a student's ability to format a block business letter, a business educator asks the student to do just that—prepare a block business letter. A performance or authentic assessment is used. An authentic assessment with high validity would be to require a student to compose, key, and format a block business letter to a college or university inquiring about scholarships or programs to study. To add reliability in assessing student work, a scoring guide or rubric would be used to evaluate that block business letter. The business educator does not assess the student's knowledge and skill of formatting a block business letter with five multiple choice questions. Rather, the student is asked to perform the task with word processing and a keyboard—which is highly valid.

Other highly valid assessments that business educators use would be the completion of journal entries and financial statements in an accounting class, rather than using objective quizzes and examinations based on these tasks. Business educators can require students in a multimedia class to evaluate Web pages for soundness of design elements and navigational ease by using criteria on a checklist, rather than quizzing them with multiple choice questions about design and navigation. Finally, business educators should require students in a Personal Finance class to complete a checking account reconciliation in its entirety, rather than have the students "fill in the blanks" on a reconciliation problem that has been begun but is not quite complete. To achieve validity, require that students "just do it." When you want to assess a student's ability to complete a task or perform a skill, performance and authentic assessments are highly valid assessment measures (Zeliff and Schultz, 1998).

Reliability

Reliability is the degree to which the assessment provides consistency in what it measures. Herman and Baker (2005) discuss inter-rater reliability as consistency of assessment of a student's skill by more than one evaluator. Higher inter-rater reliability is reached when scoring guides are used by *all* evaluators and the criteria on those instruments are descriptive, clear, and varied in degrees. Subjective performance events such as writing, speaking, and fine arts performances have more inter-rater reliability among judges and evaluators when scoring guides are used.

An assessment could have insufficient reliability if a student's performance varies significantly when assessed with the same criteria on more than one occurrence. Therefore, internal reliability or consistency (Herman and Baker, 2005) must be monitored. Gronlund (2006) indicates that internal consistency can be increased when assessment questions are constructed correctly and assessments are administered under similar environments and conditions. Objective tests of multiple choice or true-false questions are highly reliable. Specific outcomes are expected on each completion of these questions.

Multiple measures will result in higher validity and reliability; however, it is interesting to note that many standardized and high-stakes tests utilize objective examinations. Although objective examinations are more reliable, higher validity is reached with performance testing. Some states utilize both in their state tests. Missouri (2006) utilizes both performance and objective testing in its state MAP program. The "constructed response" sections of the state tests are evaluated by trained evaluators who are Missouri educators. In the early years of MAP testing, outside evaluators in other states were used. To reduce costs and improve the time involved in evaluating these performance tests, trained Missouri teachers now serve as evaluators. Utilizing both objective and performance testing, however, is not always feasible.

An interesting relationship exists, therefore, with validity and reliability. Highly valid measures such as performance events can be less reliable both among test takers and among evaluators. Highly reliable measures such as objective tests using multiple-choice and true-false questions can be less valid. Business educators should use evaluation tools that enable them to reach both validity and reliability; the use of scoring guides is one such evaluation tool.

Scoring Guides

Scoring guides, or rubrics, are excellent instruments to use in assessing students. Scoring guides prove to be reliable instruments both internally and among multiple evaluators. These instruments are best used to assess performance and authentic tasks, which are highly valid assessments.

Loveland (2005) outlines the benefits of using scoring guides to both students and teachers. Students clearly know what is expected to reach success, because the scoring guides list specific guidelines before the assignment is completed and provide feedback when the assignment is scored. Self-assessment is also possible when students see the criteria specifically stated on the scoring guides. Teachers benefit from using scoring guides because subjective grading is reduced, as is time needed to score assignments. Students are more satisfied with grading results when scoring guides are used, and the guides serve as roadmaps to what is expected of students.

Other stakeholders benefit from the use of scoring guides as well: administrators and parents can clearly see what is being taught and evaluated (Loveland, 2005). Developing scoring guides becomes easier with use and experience. Varied Web and print resources aide business educators in developing scoring guides and building one's library of usable instruments.

Using valid and reliable assessments is important in assessing students. Validity ensures that the goal of the assessment is met, and reliability ensures that there is consistency among evaluators and with several uses of the assessment. Using nontraditional performance assessment leads to higher validity. Scoring guides are just one assessment measure to ensure inter-rater reliability is met. Sound test construction and administrative functions will ensure internal reliability.

PURPOSES OF ASSESSMENT

If a student were asked the purpose of assessment, he/she would undoubtedly respond quite differently from a business educator. Students see assessment as a requirement in a class, for admission to college, or a means to earn a license or certificate. It often is a superficial, one-time view of assessment. However, business educators hold a more in-depth, longitudinal view of assessment.

Gronlund (2006) identifies a variety of purposes of assessment that include motivating students, assigning grades, certifying mastery of district and course objectives, diagnosing learning difficulties or giftedness, placing students in appropriate learning environments, providing career guidance, evaluating programs and institutions, improving instruction, and assessing teacher effectiveness. Lambrecht (2000) states that the ultimate purpose of assessment is to promote quality instruction.

Formative assessments provide students and business educators with "snapshots" or daily/weekly reports on how students are progressing toward district or state standards. When assessment outcomes are positive, business educators can reflect that sound instructional strategies were employed to guide students to achievement. If assessment outcomes do not meet expectations, then an assessment of how the content was taught and re-tooling and re-teaching must take place.

Diagnostic testing classifies students for special education services, remediation, or placement in advanced placement courses or accelerated educational programs. Aptitude assessments or interest inventories can guide students and business educators towards career or educational choices.

Summative assessment data is often used in district and college and university program evaluations where norm-referenced scores on state or national assessments serve as indicators of the efficiency and success of educational efforts. Because the measures are quantitative in nature, multiple measures should be used in district and program evaluations to better assess the overall effectiveness of the learning environment provided to students.

Initially, it is easy to state that assessment is primarily administered for students to know how they have achieved. However, assessment strategies are for students, business educators and all educational stakeholders. Many days, business educators drive home from school while thinking through their school day and pondering, "Why did so many students struggle with that part of the exam?" It's clear to see that assessment is often just as purposeful to business educators in evaluating their teaching effectiveness as it is in evaluating their students' growth and achievement.

SUMMARY

Evaluating student growth and achievement is what assessment is all about. Types of assessments that can be used include traditional, alternative, performance, authentic, high stakes, benchmark, formative, and summative. A quantifiable measurement or score does not reveal all elements and often is a snapshot of one aspect of what the student knows and can do. Assessment is accurate and meaningful if multiple measures of assessment are used.

Business educators need to be fully prepared to assess students in multiple ways and interpret what those measures and assessments reveal. Business education knowledge and skills can best be assessed through highly valid authentic and perform-ance assessments utilizing scoring guides and other assessment instruments that contribute to higher reliability of the assessment process. Traditional assessment with objective questions has its place among business assessment practices. Traditional assessment is often used with high stakes testing completed in a summative assessment that is norm-referenced and used for certification, licensure, or admittance to programs. Criterion-referenced testing is often used with formative assessments that assess student achievement.

Assessment is used to provide information on student growth and achievement to not only the students, teachers, and administrators but to other stakeholders including parents, state and federal educational agencies, and prospective employers. Assessment is the best feedback to students to assess their attainment of competencies and is also useful to teachers to assess their teaching effectiveness.

With this crash course in *Assessment 101,* business educators can now complete a self-assessment of the assessment strategies used in their teaching and move towards the development of a plan to utilize a variety of assessment measures to best assess their students' growth and achievement.

REFERENCES

Chappuis, J. (2005). Helping students understand assessment. [Electronic version]. *Educational Leadership, 63,* 39-43. Retrieved December 8, 2005, from the Academic Search database.

Gronlund, N. E. (2006). *Assessment of student achievement* (8th ed.). Boston, MA: Pearson Education Inc.

Herman, J. L., & Baker, E. L. (2005, November). Making benchmark testing work. [Electronic version]. *Educational Leadership 63,* 48-54. Retrieved March 17, 2006, from the Wilson Web database.

Institute of Education Sciences. (2006). *The nation's report card.* Retrieved August 1, 2006, from http://nces.ed.gov/nationsreportcard/about/national.asp

Lambrecht, J. J. (2000). Characteristics of good assessment. In J. Rucker (Ed.), *Assessment in business education,* (Yearbook No. 38, pp. 25-38). Reston, VA: National Business Education Association.

Linn, R. E., & Gronlund, N. E. (2000). *Measurement and assessment in teaching* (8th ed.). Upper Saddle River, NJ: Prentice-Hall, Inc.

Loveland, T. (2005). Writing standards-based rubrics for technology education classrooms. [Electronic version]. *Technology Teacher, 65,* 19-22. Retrieved December 8, 2005, from the Academic Search database.

Missouri Department of Elementary and Secondary Education. (2004, September). *Educator certification.* Retrieved August 1, 2006, from http://www.dese.mo.gov/divteachqual/teachcert/PraxisAreas.html

Missouri Department of Elementary and Secondary Education. (2006, June). *Student assessment.* Retrieved August 1, 2006, from http://www.dese.mo.gov/divimprove/assess/index.html

Northwest Missouri State University. (1997). *Information and analysis.* Retrieved August 1, 2006, from http://www.nwmissouri.edu/mqa/cat4_app.html

Zeliff, N., & Schultz, K. (1998). *Authentic assessment in action: Preparing for the business workplace.* Little Rock, AR: Delta Pi Epsilon.

Provide Student Feedback to Define Quality Work

Dianna Briggs
University of Northern Iowa
Cedar Falls, Iowa

Teachers make an impact on student learning by providing timely and quality feedback. This feedback involves constructive suggestions on "work done, skills acquired, and emerging capabilities" (Milton, 2000). As a result, teachers influence learning by guiding students toward their learning goals. This chapter provides a review of types of feedback, feedback in the assessment process, and resources for giving feedback.

TYPES OF FEEDBACK

Teachers ask questions, read student work, monitor student body language, and listen to student comments to gain feedback. Based on the response received from their students, teachers make instructional decisions. Similarly, students need feedback to make decisions regarding their own learning.

Feedback that is continuous, constructive, relevant, timely, specific, and sincere offers students a greater opportunity to successfully reach their learning goals. Feedback can be positive or negative, but according to Connellan (2003), providing no feedback is "the least motivating response you can make to any action" (p. 89). Therefore, teachers should focus on giving feedback that motivates and guides students through the learning process.

Continuous Feedback

For the student who earns a low grade, some direction is essential as to what he or she needs to demonstrate before moving to the next set of concepts. Providing continuous feedback can help keep a student focused on the goal, and if necessary, help the teacher redirect the student back to the desired path of learning.

For some students, continuous feedback could mean a daily checklist or notes from the teacher. A means of providing feedback to the class as a whole could involve the use of *data collecting forms* such as a Plus/Delta. Teachers ask students to respond to a Plus/Delta sheet on a large chart: they identify what went well on the Plus side of the sheet and what could go better on the Delta side. This focuses the discussion on improvement rather than on lack of success.

Another method of providing continuous feedback is through the use of *guided practice*. Guided practice helps a student know how to progress through an assignment or activity. Students are allowed class time to work on the assignment with the teacher available for assistance. During this time, the teacher identifies students who need assistance.

Hargrove (2005) gives the example of a personal trainer who uses a show-and-tell approach with a client. By consistently reinforcing the correct form, while critiquing the wrong moves, the individual learns where and how to improve. Ken Blanchard in *Whale Done!* states, "We need to. . .catch them doing things better, if not exactly right, and praise progress" (p. 37). This is the ongoing feedback teachers need to provide students.

Constructive Feedback

Feedback to students should cover positive aspects as well as areas needing improvement. When a student is doing something wrong, a teacher has the choice of stopping the wrong behavior with a negative comment or offering a positive suggestion leading to the preferred behavior. Milton (2000) states that providing constructive feedback to students is probably one of the most useful things teachers can do for student learning. Teachers should, therefore, try to focus on improvement and success.

Kellough and Kellough (2003) caution teachers to carefully gauge responses to students' answers. The way that a teacher responds can determine the student's subsequent participation. If a teacher encourages, probes for further information, and provides positive reinforcement, students are more likely to remain actively engaged. However, Kellough and Kellough (2003) recommend using strong praise sparingly to keep students thinking creatively. Strong praise may prevent creative thinking if students become satisfied with their current performances and do not strive to reach beyond that level.

An obstacle that both teachers and students need to overcome is the tendency to dwell on errors. A student obviously needs to know what prevented him or her from reaching a desired outcome. Concentrating on how better to reach the outcome rather than on the error that prevented achievement helps the student redirect his or her efforts in a positive manner.

Relevant Feedback

Students need to receive relevant feedback that helps them progress through each instructional activity. Praising past performance is appreciated, but students need information that is tied to their current learning goals to help them continue to grow. Consequently, feedback should be focused on what is happening throughout a course, with reference to a clear sense of what the course is trying to prepare them to "do" in the future, after the course is over (University of Oklahoma, 1999).

When the guidance provided makes sense to the student in terms of his or her learning goals, the feedback becomes a springboard for further discussion, progress, and learning. Students are more willing to complete an activity, search out additional information, or perform at a higher level when their efforts are recognized, and recognized in a manner that makes sense to them.

For example, in a high school computer class, two of the students are seniors. One is planning to attend college the following year and the other is planning to apply at a local business as a clerical worker. The college-bound senior may be more motivated if he or she knew how a spreadsheet and its corresponding chart is used in a college report. The business-bound senior may be more motivated if he or she knew how a spreadsheet is used to record daily business activities. The end use, although similar, is different, and the feedback should reflect this difference whenever appropriate.

Timely Feedback

Imperato (1998) states that feedback delayed is feedback denied. The teacher shouldn't wait until the assignment, project, or course is completed to provide information to students regarding performance. Some projects require considerable time to grade. If this is the case, break the assignment down into parts and provide feedback on each part, rather than waiting until the entire assignment is completed. The instructor can decide whether or not to provide a grade for each individual checkpoint, or wait to provide the grade after completion. In either case, the student has the opportunity to make adjustments prior to submitting the final project.

Providing feedback along the way is particularly important if an assignment builds on a previous assignment. Students need corrective feedback on the first assignment before they can begin working on the next assignment, or the same errors will continue. For this reason many accounting instructors provide checkpoints for students as they are working on a simulation. These checkpoints provide the feedback students need to continue through the simulation.

There is a difference between timely feedback and rushed feedback (Imperto, 1998). Giving corrective feedback too soon can deprive students of self-discovery and prevent learning. Sometimes allowing students to work through a situation is the best teaching method. A debriefing session immediately following the situation is an opportunity for the student to assess the situation and determine the success of his or her actions. The instructor faces the challenge of allowing the student time to work through the assessment without interrupting or offering answers. Students who get timely feedback not only learn content, but also practice problem solving.

Kang, Oah, & Dickinson (2003) found that participants who received feedback for every session completed significantly more work units than participants who received feedback every fourth session. Consequently, students who receive timely feedback should be able to make needed adjustments and improve their overall performance.

Specific Feedback

For feedback to be effective, "it must focus on the specific observations about current behaviors" (MDA Leadership, 2006). This means that feedback must be directed to the specific actions being observed. Frequently, a teacher will roam around the room while students are working and say, "Good job!" moving on to the next student to repeat the all-too-familiar phrase again and again. The phrase becomes meaningless unless the student knows specifically what he or she is doing well. If a teacher wants to use praise effectively, "Good job!" should be followed by, "on finding the right answer," or "on trying different approaches to find the solution." This way, the student knows what was considered good and should be repeated.

Sincere Feedback

Students respond to feedback in a number of ways. If they do not feel that the words are sincere, rarely will they take the information seriously, and they act accordingly. Teachers frequently overuse certain expressions to respond to students as a result of habits they've formed. If a teacher uses the word "super" every time a student answers a question or completes a paper, the word no longer holds meaning for the students—it becomes noise to them.

Teachers must not only vary what they say to a student, they must be sure that the delivery of the feedback is sincere. This is evidenced through the tone of voice as well as the volume level. Eye contact can help the student to know the information is specific for them and that the teacher is sincere. Body language is also an important factor. Praising a student for a great performance while standing aloof with arms crossed and yawning sends a mixed message.

All types of feedback are important to both students and teachers. With all of the daily activities teachers are required to complete, teachers can easily lose sight of the importance of feedback. However, maintaining a conscientious effort to provide students with continuous, constructive, relevant, timely, specific, and sincere feedback provides students with the information needed for success in the classroom.

FEEDBACK IN THE ASSESSMENT PROCESS

Assessment can be ongoing (formative) to determine student performance on a continuum, or culminating (summative) to identify what the student has learned. Both types of assessment provide the opportunity for teachers to inform students of their progress. The manner in which this feedback is provided can be formal or informal, depending on the given situation and the amount of feedback necessary.

Formative vs. Summative

Formative assessments are meant to suggest actions for change (Lenze and Warner, 1995). They can be the checkpoints to help guide and redirect students toward their final goal. Winninger (2005) states that testing can be a type of formative assessment, as it provides feedback to both the student and teacher regarding learning progress, with the goal of improving learning and instruction.

Formative assessments assist the teacher in helping students determine their performance at various stages of the project. These smaller targets (or checkpoints) allow students to progress in a systematic manner toward the final assessment. These assessments, therefore, become formative feedback to students.

Responses provided on assignments or activities that build toward the final assessment can be written, oral, or nonverbal. Some examples of this formative feedback include notes written on student work, verbal responses to student answers in class discussion, anecdotal records, observation notes, checklists, ratings, quizzes, and facial expressions.

Summative assessments given at the end of the chapter, unit, project, or course are more comprehensive in nature. These are the final evaluations that assess the student progress after completion of the assignment, test, or project. Summative feedback, therefore, is provided after the final assessment and includes comments provided to students regarding their overall performance.

Formal vs. Informal

Much of the feedback teachers provide is informal and ongoing. Teachers assess student interaction with one another during large group discussions, small group projects, and as individuals on a daily basis. This feedback can be a brief visit with a student to see how he or she is feeling about the project, and then providing reassurance that the student is on the right track. Feedback can also be a quick note written on the top of a paper to encourage the student to keep going in the same direction. Sometimes feedback can be in the form of a gesture or facial expression. Since this type of feedback is more spontaneous, it lacks documentation or proof that the message was conveyed.

Formal feedback involves scheduled activities that provide documentation. Examples include keeping structured anecdotal records, ratings, checklists, observation forms, scores, and grades. These documents can help teachers provide more formal feedback that assist in determining student performance. Some examples of documentation are provided in the section titled "Resources—Tools of the Trade." These feedback tools become the basis for working with a student to identify strengths, determine areas needing improvement, and establish learning goals.

Both formative and summative feedback contribute to the progress of student learning. Feedback, regardless of whether it is formal or informal, helps guide performance.

RESOURCES—TOOLS OF THE TRADE

To increase teacher accountability, and in some cases to speed up the assessment process, teachers would be wise to develop a variety of tools to document student performance and provide feedback. Through the use of multiple and varied assessments and feedback tools, teachers are better able to accommodate all student learning styles.

Assessment tools need to address the various targets and proficiency levels established according to a students' learning goals. A few examples of tools that teachers can use to provide feedback to students include observation forms, journals, quick-writes, reflections, checklists, rubrics, rating scales, review activities, portfolios, individual or group conferences, and student performances. Each tool can and should be adapted to meet the needs of diverse learners.

Observation Forms

An observation form should include the details of the observation such as the date, time, topic, and situation. The form can be created to identify areas of success, things to think about, and comments for future success as shown below. This could be a half or full sheet depending on the amount of information needed. Table 1 depicts a sample observation form.

Table 1. *Observation Form*	
Student's Name: _____	
Observed Activity _____Date/Time_____	
Area of success:	Things to think about:
General comments:	

The observation form is used for the recording and the subsequent evaluating of a teacher's observation (Callahan, Clark, and Kellough, 2002, p. 341). This documentation of a student's learning process provides proof of the student's capabilities and behaviors and can be shared during conference settings such as a parent/teacher conference.

Journals

An informal, formative assessment can be in the form of a journal. Having a student keep a journal about various topics, including their own learning, can help teachers communicate with students in a timely and sincere format. If a teacher chooses to use this activity, the success of the feedback comes in the quality of comments provided in response to the students' thoughts and ideas. This can be time consuming, but perhaps one of the more rewarding means of both providing and gaining quality feedback. Teachers need to determine the topic, format, length, and frequency of the journal entries prior to assigning this activity.

An additional benefit of journal writing is the opportunity created for helping students develop writing skills. Fulkert, in his 2000 NBEA Yearbook chapter, states that "implementing the use of personal journals or learning logs gives students another opportunity to use creative writing integrated with problem solving, leadership, synthesis thinking, and other skills desired by the corporate world" (p. 86). The teacher would need to establish the criteria required for both the writing skills and the content.

Quick-Writes

At any time during a class period, teachers can have students do a quick-writing activity. The intent of this type of writing is to provide feedback to the teacher, but it can also give feedback to the student. Examples include Snowball, Ticket/Passport In/Out the Door, and Dear Abby.

Snowball activity. The Snowball requires students to write a response to one of the preprinted questions or statements on a white piece of paper such as "What are you still wondering about?" The students each write a brief response, sharing their opinions before wadding the paper into a ball and throwing it into a central space in the room. Students then go get a snowball from the pile and respond to a second question printed on their snowball. Students will inevitably read a peer's response to the first question before answering the second question and returning the snowball to the pile. This continues for each of the questions on the paper. The sheets can have only one question or up to four. Through the process of answering the questions and seeing others' opinions, students realize, by using a safe, anonymous method, that they are not alone in their thoughts or ideas.

Effective tools such as the Snowball activity allow students to identify what they feel comfortable about, as well as what they are still struggling with or do not understand.

Ticket/Passport and In/Out the Door. Another example of a quick-write is the ticket or passport in the door at the beginning of class or out the door at the end of class. The teacher asks students to identify in writing what they understood or what may still be unclear. Students are asked to complete a question such as "What is still muddy for you?" These tickets or passports are collected by the teacher and used either as a springboard for that day's lesson or to determine what needs to be clarified as part of the next lesson.

Dear Abby. A third quick-write example is the use of a Dear Abby letter. Students write a short letter to a fictional Abby about a content area they want to have clarified (Gibbs, 1995, p. 235). These activities need to be done without identifying factors such as names or student ID numbers, to give students the freedom to ask questions without fear of criticism.

The student responses in any writing activity can serve the teacher by identifying areas needing additional instruction. These short writing activities not only provide feedback to the teacher, but help the students to work on their writing skills.

Reflections

Reflection writing is generally more time consuming than the quick-writes discussed above. In a reflection, a student might discuss the process undertaken to complete the assignment as well as the quality of his or her level of performance. The instructor can provide feedback in the form of written comments on the reflection or request a brief conference to discuss the student's comments. If the student's reflection is truly thoughtful about the assignment or the performance, generally written comments that support the reflection are used. If the student's reflection is tenuous or contains inaccuracies, a conference can be used to guide the student back on course.

Bush and Timms (2000) state that students must take responsibility for their own learning, evaluate their progress, and set individual goals for achievement (p. 103). Asking students to practice self-reflection on their performance encourages them to take ownership of their own learning. Quality self-assessments enhance learning and performance. Students need to be able to provide an honest appraisal of what they believe was done well, what was done less than their best, and what could be improved.

Checklists

One common tool in assessing students is a checklist. The student can use the checklist to determine his or her progress through an assignment—to know what has been accomplished and what is left to complete. The teacher can also see at a glance if each student is progressing as expected. The checklist shown in Table 2 can be used for this kind of informal feedback.

Table 2. *Sample Checklist (A)*
Group Project Checklist
_____ 1. Select a project leader
_____ 2. Review project requirements as a group and assign tasks
_____ 3. Develop timeline to complete assignments

In this instance, the students would be responsible for checking off items as they are completed. This type of checklist is helpful as an organizer for the students as well as a means of continual feedback on their progress toward completing the assignment. The checklist does not, however, provide feedback regarding the quality of work. Teachers who use this type of checklist will typically use it in addition to other feedback and assessment tools.

The checklist also can be used as a summative assessment for assigning points, or including an evaluative comment for each step of the assignment. This checklist could be completed by the student, the teacher, or both. There are numerous Web sites available to help teachers create checklists. One such site, http://pblchecklist.4teachers.org/, is quite helpful and creates professional looking checklists with minimal effort.

A portion of a sample checklist that asks students to assess their own performance in creating a project is illustrated in Table 3:

Table 3. *Sample Checklist (B)*		
Project Self-Assessment		
Name: _____ Date: _____		
Category:	**Completed:**	
	Yes No Maybe	
Appearance	❑ ❑ ❑	Fonts were used in a consistent manner
	❑ ❑ ❑	Titles and headings are easy to distinguish from text
	❑ ❑ ❑	Text and graphic areas appear balanced
	❑ ❑ ❑	Graphics are clear, easy to see, and appropriate
Organization	❑ ❑ ❑	Ideas are organized in a logical order
	❑ ❑ ❑	Topics are fully explained

Using a checklist with just a *yes* or *no* will work in many situations. However, adding an option for *maybe* or *almost* allows students to reflect that an effort has been made but perhaps not to the level of the teacher's expectation.

Rubrics

One method of providing specific feedback is the use of *rubrics*. Rubrics come in many designs, but the most effective are those that clearly explain what is required— what is at the top of the scale, what is acceptable, and what misses the mark. Rubrics should allow the instructor room for comments to clarify the score as needed. These comments help the student identify what specifically caused him or her to earn a specific score. In the example provided below, a student receiving a "1" in the category Writing/Organization might receive a comment identifying words that caused confusion or a comment identifying the part of the project that was incomplete. Therefore, the student not only knows the category score, but what specifically in the project produced that score.

A rubric is one of the best tools for providing feedback to students regarding their performance on projects and activities. If designed properly, rubrics identify the expected behavior, as well as define various levels of performance for each criterion. The descriptors in each category should be consistent across the rating scale and be tied to the learning objectives. These descriptors should include both the objective and subjective issues related to the project. For example, students may have ten slides created for a presentation as required, but might not do quality work on the slides. Including subjective expectations reduces the opportunity for students to expect full credit for minimum quality.

Callahan, Clark, and Kellough (2005) clarify the difference between a checklist and a rubric. They explain that rubrics show the degrees for the desired characteristics, while checklists usually show only the desired characteristics. A concern about rubrics is the amount of time it takes to create a good rubric, identifying all of the degrees for desired characteristics. There are various Web sites available to assist teachers in constructing a rubric. The Web site rubistar.4teachers.org provides many samples of rubrics and helps teachers to easily create their own rubrics.

Table 4 is an example of two characteristics being scored using a rubric.

In this example, the first characteristic is open to a student scoring anywhere from 5 to 0, where the second characteristic allows only a 5, 3, 1, or 0. Both provide the details to the students to know how their work was scored without having to use a complete descriptor in every column.

Rating Scales

Rating scales can be developed quickly and are similar to rubrics. Students are provided a listing of the characteristics being evaluated with a scale, usually 1-5, with

Table 4. *Sample Partial Rubric*

Category	5 (Beyond Expectations)	4	3 (Average Performance)	2	1 (Minimal Effort)	0 (Try Again)
Writing/ Organization	The details are well organized, easy to under-stand, and show creativity in explaining information; easily answers all questions		Details are in a logical order, with clear descriptions; is easy to follow and understand		Details may be incom-plete or in no obvious order; some confusion as to meaning	Details are missing and the content is difficult to understand; the product does not answer questions
Spelling, Mechanics, and Proofreading	No spelling or word usage errors; capi-talization & punctuation are correct		1 error in spelling, word usage errors, capitalization, or punctuation		No more than 3 spelling, word usage, capitaliza-tion, and/or punctuation errors	More than 3 spelling, word usage, capitaliza-tion, and/or punctuation errors

1 meaning *poor* and 5 meaning *good*. This is a quick method of scoring student work that provides feedback to the student as to strong points or areas of strength. However, the rating scale does not help the student to know why each characteristic was scored as it was. To give effective feedback, the scorer should write comments to help the student understand the rating.

Tables 5 and 6 show portions of rating scales used to provide feedback to students regarding performance. The sample rating scale in Table 5 uses a 1-5 scale.

Students could score a 1, 2, 3, 4, or 5. These scales use a continuum to allow for deviation from having to score an exact number in a category; instead, the scale allows for marking at any point along the scale.

Table 5. *Sample Rating Scale (A)*

Presentation Scale				
Poor		OK		Great
Preparation	1	2	3	4	5
Eye Contact	1	2	3	4	5
Voice Quality	1	2	3	4	5

Table 6. *Sample Rating Scale (B)*				
Presentation Scale				
	Poor	OK		Great
Preparation	___ ___	___ ___	___ ___	___ ___	___
Eye Contact	___ ___	___ ___	___ ___	___ ___	___
Voice Quality	___ ___	___ ___	___ ___	___ ___	___

Continuum scales allow for flexibility in scoring, but should also be accompanied by comments for the student.

Review Activities

Using review activities is common practice for teachers who want to provide a variation in the daily routine while helping students to prepare for an upcoming assessment. Often these activities take the form of a game, take considerable preparation time, and usually take the majority of or all of the class period. However, review activities do not have to be so time consuming. Short activities can accomplish the same goal and be inserted throughout the instructional time period.

Quick reviews that require only note cards and a list of questions are easier to prepare and require much less time to implement. For example, the teacher needs one note card per student with a question and correct answer written on each. Have the first student begin by asking a question from his or her note card of a second student. Have the second student answer the question and then ask a third student a question. This continues through the "chain" until each group member has answered and then asked a question. The questions are related to the topic of study and help all students hear the questions and answers. If a student does not know the answer, the student can ask for help before continuing the sequence.

This is an engaging, active review for the students and is an informal assessment for the teacher to determine student understanding. Through this informal assessment activity, the teacher has helped students to understand their own level of understanding and perhaps the need to be better prepared for the upcoming formal assessment.

Another version of this type of questioning is the activity "Who Is…?" Using note cards or strips of paper, students are given first an answer, and then an unrelated question. The first student reads his or her question, e.g., "Who is (meaning, which person in the room represents) one of the consumer rights?" The student with the correct answer to that question written on his or her card would respond, "I am the Right to be Informed." This student would then ask the question written on his or her card. This continues around the room until all questions have been asked and answered, ending with the student who read the first question. This activity is also known as "Around the World."

Again, this is an informal assessment that provides the students with a varied means of reviewing for the formal assessment and provides the teacher with an idea of where students may still be unsure of content.

Portfolios

An effective means of assessing student work is through the use of portfolios. Callahan, Clark, and Kellough (2002) suggest that "student self-assessment should be planned as an important component of the assessment program" (p. 344). Students can maintain portfolios of their work and then use rating scales, checklists, rubrics, and other tools to self-assess their progress. Portfolios can serve as a means for teachers to evaluate student performance, and the portfolio can provide students with continual feedback of their performance as they reflect on the artifacts selected.

If done correctly, the student has provided a reflection to demonstrate his or her learning or progress for each artifact. Sometimes these reflections are all-encompassing, so that the teacher provides feedback through notes written on sticky notes placed throughout the portfolio, or in a response sheet given back to the student. At other times, these reflections are the basis of a conference between the student and the teacher.

Individual or Group Conferences

Depending on the work being required, teachers might opt for individual conferences with their students. An example may be in a class where group projects have been assigned. After the groups have been determined and have begun working, the teacher can meet with students individually or as a group to discuss any concerns, questions, and progress. In this manner, the teacher provides feedback from observations of individual and group interaction.

Student Performances

When students are asked to perform, feedback can be provided by the teacher, peers, or external viewers. One key method of feedback for a performance is nonverbal feedback.

While presenting skits, performances, oral presentations, or various projects, students are frequently searching for approval from their audience. This approval, or feedback, can be given by audience members through maintaining good eye contact, smiling, or even nodding. A frown can indicate displeasure or lack of understanding. If peers are yawning, talking, or engaging in other activities, the feedback can be perceived as being negative. Although this type of feedback is informal, it is very powerful to the students and can supersede any formal feedback provided.

Teachers have a wide variety of resources available from which to select a means of providing feedback to students. Any tool selected should be tailored to meet the needs of individual students and designed according to their learning goals.

SUMMARY

Feedback needs to be continuous, constructive, relevant, timely, specific, and sincere. Students need to know what their expectations and have a means of meeting those expectations. Teachers should help students learn to be reflective participants in the assessment of their own performance and learning.

Teachers can have an impact student learning by keeping students well informed throughout the learning process. Information can be provided formally or informally, but should be in a clear manner to eliminate any miscommunication.

Teachers who take the time to create effective tools to use for feedback are providing their students with documented information regarding performance. These tools can come in various formats and offer both the teacher and the student feedback for a more accurate view as to how the student can more fully reach his or her own potential.

REFERENCES

Blanchard, K., Lacinak, T., Tompkins, C., Tompkins, C., & Ballard, J. (2002). *Whale done! The power of positive relationships*. New York: The Free Press.

Bush, M., & Timms, M. (2000). Rubric- and portfolio-based assessment: Focusing on student progress. In J. Rucker (Ed.), *Assessment in business education*, (*Yearbook* No. 38, pp. 103-120). Reston, VA: National Business Education Association.

Callahan, J., Leonard, C., & Kellough, R. (2002). *Teaching in the middle and secondary schools* (pp. 338-347). New Jersey: Merrill Prentice Hall.

Connellan, T. (2003). *Bringing out the best in others!* Austin: Bard Press.

Fulkert, R. (2000). Authentic assessment. In J. Rucker (Ed.), *Assessment in business education*, (*Yearbook* No. 38, pp. 71-90). Reston, VA: National Business Education Association.

Gibbs, J. (1995). *Tribes, a new way of learning and being together*. California: Center Source Systems, LLC.

Hargrove, K. (2005). What makes a "good" teacher "great"? *Gifted Child Today Magazine 28*(1), 30-31.

Hernandez, A. (2005). *Formative assessment and feedback*. Retrieved October 26, 2005, from San Diego State University, College of Education Web site: coe.sdsu.edu/eet/articles/formeval/start.htm.

Imperato, G. (1998). *How to give good feedback*. Retrieved October 19, 2005, from http://pf.fastcompany.com/magazine/17/feedback.html.

Kang, K., Oah, S., & Dickinson, A. (2003). The relative effects of different frequencies of feedback on work performance: A simulation. *Journal of Organizational Behavior Management, 23*(4), 21-53.

Kauchak, D., Eggen, P., & Carter, C. (2002). *Introduction to teaching, becoming a professional* (pp. 353-363). New Jersey: Merrill Prentice Hall.

Kellough, R., & Kellough, N. (2003). *Secondary school teaching* (pp. 28-35 & 231-232). New Jersey: Merrill Prentice Hall.

Lenze, L., & Warner, M. (1995). Summative evaluation and formative feedback. *Encyclopedia of educational technology*, (Vol. 1, pp. 1-4). San Diego, California: San Diego State University.

MDA Leadership. *Give feedback that gets results: Specific, timely, balanced and actionable*, Retrieved January 22, 2006, from www.mdaleadership.com/Leadership-Give_feedback.asp.

Milton, J. (2001). *Feedback to students*. Retrieved November 18, 2005, from lts.rmit.edu.au/renewal/assess/faq_feedback.doc.

University of Oklahoma (1999). *Ideas on teaching, feedback and assessment: Educative assessment*. Retrieved November 18, 2005, from University of Oklahoma, Instructional Development Program Web site: www.ou.edu/idp/tips/ideas/feedback2.html.

Vos, H. (2000). How to assess for improvement of learning. *Engineering Education*, *25*(3), pp. 227-233.

Winninger, S. (2005). Using your tests to teach: Formative summative assessment. *Teaching of Psychology, 32*(3), pp. 154-166.

Reflect on Effective Teaching

Diane Fisher, Sharon E. Rouse, and Lajuan Davis
University of Southern Mississippi
Hattiesburg, Mississippi

All teachers will reflect on effective teaching by remembering the one teacher who made a real difference for them in the classroom. Reflecting on the teaching/learning process can yield valuable information to the teacher who wishes to improve his or her classroom effectiveness. In his book, *The Courage to Teach*, Palmer (1998) states that "good teachers . . . are able to weave a complex web of connections among themselves, their subjects, and their students so that students can learn to weave a world for themselves" (p. 11). This chapter will address six dimensions of effective teaching, including planning and preparation, managing the classroom environment, providing quality instruction, assessing student outcomes, pursuing professional responsibilities, and engaging in reflective practice. In addition, standards for the teaching profession for each dimension will be presented along with examples of how business educators might assess their own effectiveness.

PLANNING AND PREPARATION

The first dimension of effective teaching, planning and preparation, directs the educator to take great care in aligning instruction with preset, effective pedagogical standards. Although the practice of aligning teaching and learning to standards can be a challenging one, standards alignment instills a quality in both the teaching and learning processes that may otherwise not be present or apparent.

Standards for Instruction

Authors Brown and Wiedmaier (2003) advise that planning for instruction is one of the most important steps in the teaching process. The first step in the planning process entails the identification of national, industry, state, and local standards. The *National Standards for Business Education* (NBEA, 2001) provides an impetus for teachers to plan their courses. These standards, along with state curriculum standards, provide a framework for teachers to follow when developing lessons. Once the required standards are identified, a syllabus is constructed to provide an outline of the course content. The course content includes unit planning that contains the overall goals and objectives for each unit in the course. The unit plan is broader than a daily lesson plan and provides an overview of what will be taught in the unit. Once the unit plan is created, the individual lesson plans will become the focus of the planning process. With this precise planning, teachers are empowered to guide student learning outcomes as they strive to prepare the students to reach their greatest potential. Students become engaged in learning when lessons are thoughtfully planned and aligned with accepted standards that add substance and quality to the curriculum.

Standards for the Teaching Profession

Just as instructional standards serve as the important planning and preparation component to guide student learning, national standards for the teaching profession also provide the foundation for identifying excellent teaching. The Interstate New Teacher Assessment and Support Consortium (INTASC) Standards and the National Association of Business Teacher Education (NABTE) Standards, both performance-based sets of standards, report what teachers should know and be able to do in order to teach effectively.

INTASC standards. INTASC standards are principles to follow in the formation of pedagogical practices for both new and experienced teachers. The premise behind the design of INTASC standards is that "teaching is complex and requires performance-based standards and assessment strategies" (Limback & Mansfield, 2002, p. 52). The INTASC standards, on which many state standards are based, include ten principles that have three areas of competencies effective teachers should possess—knowledge, dispositions, and performance (INTASC, 1992). For example, INTASC Standard 7: Planning Instruction states that the teacher plans and manages instruction based upon knowledge of subject matter, students, the community, and curriculum goals.

NABTE standards. The NABTE standards "reflect emerging trends in teacher education and incorporate NBEA's *National Standards for Business Education*" (NBEA, 2005, p. 2). NABTE provides the standards document as a "guide in developing up-to-date, high-quality business teacher education programs" (p. 3). Like the INTASC standards, the NABTE standards are performance-based and describe what business teachers should know and be able to do. Comparable to INTASC Standard 7: Planning Instruction, the NABTE standard for planning and preparation indicates that the business teacher creates, analyzes, revises, and implements curricula to prepare students for a dynamic and rapidly changing world.

Planning and preparation is the first and one of the most important dimensions of effective teaching. Utilizing performance-based standards as a guide in the planning and preparation process helps ensure an element of quality in the educational environment for both teachers and students.

MANAGING THE CLASSROOM ENVIRONMENT

After planning and preparation has successfully occurred, the effective teacher must further ensure successful learning by providing students with a classroom environment that is conducive to learning. If one were to write all the characteristics of a favorite teacher, one would discover that many of the responses would fall into the classroom environment category (R. McNeese, personal communication, 2005). In a study conducted by Stitt-Gohdes (2001), researchers concluded that students "prefer a friendly learning situation where a warm, personal relationship is established and maintained between instructor and student" (p. 143). Furthermore, students prefer a hands-on environment that is real-world-based in order for instruction to be considered *effective* (Stitt-Gohdes, 2001).

Rader (2003) states that "effective classroom management occurs when a teacher consistently prepares well-planned lessons and materials; provides a positive supportive atmosphere for learning; establishes and reinforces classroom procedures and rules; and deals quickly and firmly with distractions and inappropriate student behaviors" (p. 81). Classroom management strategies include the creation of a classroom management plan in which procedures of order are established. These procedures for completing routine tasks avoid the loss of instructional time and allow work to be completed in an organized manner. Constructing a discipline plan that includes rules, consequences, and rewards is an essential component of classroom management.

Providing a learning environment in which all students can feel safe and learn is a hallmark of an effective teacher. Implementing classroom management is vital to teachers being able to provide quality instruction.

PROVIDING QUALITY INSTRUCTION

McKeachie (2002) purports that instructional methods used to present materials in the classroom have an effect on student learning and warrant attention and exploration. When selecting instructional methods, teachers must consider students' learning styles and meet students' learning needs in order to foster critical thinking. Numerous methods of instruction exist. Some methods are more effective than others and may require an instructor to utilize his or her advanced thinking and preparation skills in order to properly integrate this instruction into the classroom.

Identifying Learning Styles

Some business educators use instructional methods with which they are familiar. For example, many teachers adhere to the standby methods of teaching via straight lecture, while students take notes or complete in-class worksheets, or teachers provide students with teacher-created activities to be completed in groups. Teachers must, however, consider the differences in student learning styles when choosing appropriate methods of instruction for the classroom. Students should be presented with a variety of learning activities that appeal to students' learning needs. In simple terms, students' learning styles may be visual, auditory, or kinesthetic, or a combination of these styles. Visual learners require pictures, written instructions, and other visual aids to stimulate learning; auditory learners enjoy lectures, reading, and note taking; while kinesthetic learners must have hands-on activities to actively engage in learning. Instructional methods that address various learning styles include lecture/central presentation, discussion, Socratic instruction, cooperative learning, and problem-based learning (McEwen, 2003; McKeachie, 2002).

By successfully identifying students' learning styles and providing instruction that satisfies students' learning needs, teachers can encourage students to think. Educators who work to improve classroom instruction and thinking processes of students must continually strive to explore and utilize effective instructional strategies in the classroom.

Effective Instructional Strategies

Research has shown that an individual teacher can have a powerful effect on his or her students, even if the school does not (Marzano, Pickering, & Pollock, 2001). Because the classroom teacher is the most important factor affecting student learning, teachers' employing effective instructional strategies can affect student learning.

Researchers at Midcontinent Research for Education and Learning (McREL) identified nine categories of instructional strategies that have a significant effect on student achievement. Part of the primary focus of a major study conducted by McREL researchers was "to identify those instructional strategies that have a high probability of enhancing student achievement for all students in all subject areas at all grade levels" (Marzano et al., 2001, pp. 6 – 7). These nine instructional categories are listed in Table 1.

The following subsections feature brief discussions of the nine different McREL instructional categories presented in Table 1.

Identifying similarities and differences. Asking students to identify similarities and differences increases their understanding of the subject matter. Students can identify similarities and differences through tasks that involve comparisons, classifications,

Table 1. *Instructional Strategies for Student Achievement*
Categories of Instructional Strategies That Affect Student Achievement
1. Identifying similarities and differences 2. Summarizing and note taking 3. Reinforcing effort and providing recognition 4. Homework and practice 5. Nonlinguistic representations 6. Cooperative learning 7. Setting objectives and providing feedback 8. Generating and testing hypotheses 9. Questions, cues, and advance organizers
Note. From *Classroom Instruction That Works: Research-based Strategies for Increasing Student Achievement* (2001) by Robert J. Marzano, Debra Pickering, and Jane E. Pollock.

metaphors, and analogies. Additionally, graphic and symbolic representations of similarities and differences via use of the Venn diagram, for example, enhance student understanding of the content (Marzano et al., 2001). Students studying a banking unit in a personal finance class can use a Venn diagram to discover the similarities and differences between checking and savings accounts.

Summarizing and note taking. McKeachie (2002) suggests that summarizing requires students to delete, substitute, and keep information. Therefore, students must analyze the information at a deep level. When taking notes, students must determine what is important. Verbatim note taking remains the least effective method of taking notes. Notes should be considered a work in progress, should be used as study guides for tests, and should be as comprehensive as possible.

Reinforcing effort and providing recognition. Researchers Marzano et al. (2001) state that research on effort shows that many students do not realize the importance of believing in effort and those students can alter their beliefs to include an emphasis on expending effort. Providing recognition for attainment of goals not only enhances achievement, but stimulates motivation. Furthermore, a set of studies reviewed by Marzano et al. (2001) suggests that simply demonstrating an added effort enhances student achievement. Teachers can help students make the connections between effort and achievement by sharing personal stories of achievements or discussing examples of famous athletes,' entertainers,' or social leaders' success stories.

Homework and practice. Homework and practice are powerful instructional tools that provide students with opportunities to refine and extend their knowledge.

Practice is necessary to master a skill. Completing homework assignments provides students with some practice. The amount of homework assigned to students in the elementary, middle school, high school, and college levels should vary. Various research study results have been compiled and yield the recommended total minutes per day for homework as follows: primary level, 10 – 30 minutes; upper elementary, 30 – 90 minutes; middle school, 50 – 120 minutes; high school, 60 – 180 minutes; and college, 120 minutes of homework for every 60 minutes spent in class.

Nonlinguistic representations. Creating nonlinguistic representations helps students understand content in a whole new way. Types of nonlinguistic representations include students' being guided in creating graphic representations such as *webs* or descriptive pattern organizers, producing physical models of the element(s) being studied, generating mental imagery or pictures, and even drawing pictures of items that will lead to students' increasing their knowledge (Marzano et al., 2001). Students in a desktop publishing class could use a storyboard to plan a brochure they are creating. The storyboard (nonlinguistic representation) serves as a model or plan and helps the students develop details for the design elements. Another example of nonlinguistic representation in the business education classroom is the use of webs or mapping while brainstorming related ideas for a human relations topic.

Cooperative learning. Cooperative learning is a flexible and powerful grouping strategy. The need for cooperative learning is evident in today's rapidly changing information-based and high-technology economy where the norm in the workplace is interaction. Kagan (1994) states, "Because cooperative teamwork, interaction, and communication will characterize the workplace of the future, it is imperative that our classrooms include not only individualistic and competitive interaction, but also cooperative interaction" (p. 2). The three most important outcomes of cooperative learning are academic gains, especially for minority and low achieving students, improved race relations, and improved social and affective development among all students. Organizing groups based on ability levels should be done sparingly and groups should be kept small in size with three to four members (McKeachie, 2002).

Setting objectives and providing feedback. Instructional goals target the elements that students should focus on and should be general enough to provide some flexibility. Goals should not be too specific so students can adapt them to their personal needs and desires. Teachers writing lesson plans for a unit on the job search process will want to establish objectives that students can adapt to their own needs. For example, teachers can present multiple activities for a lesson on creating a résumé and allow students to choose whichever activity they feel is the most effective and realistic. Marzano et al. (2001) report that feedback should be corrective and well-timed (e.g., immediately after a test-like situation), and specific to standards (e.g., utilizing a rubric to which the students have access). Research shows that feedback can be the single most powerful enhancer of achievement, and students can effectively supply some of their own feedback.

Generating and testing hypotheses. Generation of hypotheses and student testing can be accomplished from a deductive or inductive standpoint and are powerful cognitive operators. Students should be asked to clearly explain their hypotheses and their conclusions, preferably in writing. If students are studying accounting, for example, they could be asked to formulate a hypothesis that would explain what would happen if a change in the balance sheet or income statement occurred. Students can be engaged in generating and testing hypotheses through problem solving, decision making, investing, or participating in experimental inquiry (Marzano et al., 2001).

Questions, cues, and advance organizers. Cues, questions, and advance organizers help students recall information that they already know about a topic. Cues and questions help set the stage for learning by giving students a hint about what they are going to experience. Waiting briefly before accepting responses from students has the effect of increasing the depth of students' answers. Questions are effective learning tools even when asked before a learning experience. Advance organizers "are designed to bridge the gap between what the learner already knows and what he/she needs to know before he/she successfully learns the task at hand" (Marzano, et. al, 2001, p. 117).

Examples of types of advance organizers are those that 1) describe new content to which students are to be exposed 2) present information to students in story format 3) skim information before reading and 4) use graphic organizers such as concept maps. For example, a business education teacher could tell students a personal story about his or her first job interview as an advance organizer on the job search topic. Additionally, a graphic organizer or web could be used to help students generate new ideas about obtaining credit in a personal finance unit (Marzano et al., 2001).

Including activities that will lead students to master the objectives set forth in the lesson plan is a goal of quality instruction. The instructional strategies used to guide the learning process are important elements to help teachers and students connect the subject matter to successful student outcomes.

ASSESSING STUDENT OUTCOMES
Now that a firm idea of the appropriate inclusion of teaching strategies in the classroom setting is established, assessing student outcomes is the next step in the process of developing optimal teaching strategies. Assessing student outcomes provides a means of determining teacher effectiveness. When students are invited into the learning process, the teacher provides the hook at the beginning of class, thereby setting the stage for assessments (Ainsworth & Christinson, 1998). Two elements of assessing student outcomes are the use of peer evaluation and self-evaluation—students learning from students and students taking responsibility for their own learning. Used along with rubrics, or scoring guides, these two methods of assessing outcomes are addressed in the following section.

McKeachie (2002) purports that using peer evaluation in the classroom benefits both the students being taught and the students doing the teaching. When students have to actually prepare to teach material, they engage in more in-depth study, analysis, and, thus, retention of the subject matter. The students being taught feel less threatened by the peer teacher and more comfortable about questioning, responding to questions, and sharing ideas or concepts that promote learning. Successful peer evaluation helps students learn to function in collaborative work environments. Students who evaluate their own work using teacher-provided rubrics or checklists also feel safer and less threatened during the process, thereby feeling more empowered in their learning. Self-evaluation should take place before the writing assignment is turned in to the instructor, allowing students to learn proofreading skills and to practice thinking skills. Research shows that in many cases students are more critical of themselves and their writing than their instructors are, so the use of self-evaluation techniques can help save the instructors grading time, in addition to producing a better quality of student work.

Rubrics are used with evaluation methods to provide evidence that standards have been met and the degree to which they have been met. Specificity is critical in rubric creation. When rubrics are used, expectations are clearly defined and understood, and the grading process is no longer a mystery to students. Another benefit of using rubrics is that the students' personal responsibility increases and the quality of their work improves. Rubrics offer additional benefits to teachers through the alignment of instructional objectives, activities, and performance tasks. Utilizing effective performance tasks keeps the focus on the targeted standards and provides evidence that the standards have been met. Therefore, the assessment of student learning is more objective, consistent, and fair (Ainsworth & Christinson, 1998). Because the use of rubrics helps students to feel secure, they can then reflect on what was learned and assist in setting a direction for future learning.

For assessing student outcomes, peer evaluation and self-evaluation used with rubrics are important elements of effective teaching; they lessen the teacher's grading load while improving the student's quality of work.

PURSUING PROFESSIONAL RESPONSIBILITY

Assessing student outcomes to determine teacher effectiveness is only one way in which that effectiveness can be reviewed and improved. Another avenue for improving teacher effectiveness is to give teachers professional responsibility for lifelong learning. The term *professional responsibility* evokes different thoughts for different individuals. Although some individuals equate professional responsibility with sponsoring student organizations in order to develop students' and workplace skills, the term can have much broader implications. For example, professional responsibility would entail participating in professional development activities to promote lifelong learning, networking with peers in the same and related professions, attending in-service training, engaging in work-experience placements, sponsoring student organizations, and attaining additional professional certification or licensure. Whatever phrase one chooses for describing professional responsibility, the important aspect of this component is that educators continue to learn and grow in every possible capacity to enhance their own lives as well as the lives of their students by improving their learning outcomes (Scott, 2003; Gandy & Green, 2003).

ENGAGING IN REFLECTIVE PRACTICE

Effective teachers take the time to engage in reflective practice. Rather than teach the same subjects the same way, day after day, year after year, these teachers use their reflections to guide them to new and better ways of teaching. Effective teachers seek to identify factors that contribute to a student's experience and experiment with alternate ways of teaching based on feedback from students. These are the teachers who apply research to their instruction and identify categories of teaching strategies that have a strong, positive effect on student achievement (Marzano, et al., 2001). The importance of teachers engaging in post-teaching reflection should not be ignored. Engaging in this process is vital to the success of an effective educator.

Post-Teaching Reflection

Reflective practice includes the process of post-teaching reflection. In an effort to direct post-teaching reflection, Danielson (1996) outlines questions that may be posed at the end of a lesson or unit. These questions may serve as a reflective guide to determine levels of student achievement or if instructional plans need changing. These questions are presented in Table 2.

Table 2. *Post-Teaching Reflection Questions*

Categories of Instructional Strategies That Affect Student Achievement

1. As I reflect on the lesson, to what extent were students productively engaged?

2. Did the students learn what I intended? Were my instructional goals met? How do I know, or how and when will I know?

3. Did I alter my goals or instructional plans as I taught the lesson? Why?

4. If I had the opportunity to teach this lesson again to the same group of students, what would I do differently? Why?

5. Can I provide several samples of student work on this assignment? This work should reflect the full range of student ability in my class and include feedback to provide to students on their papers.

Note. Adapted from *Enhancing Professional Practice: A Framework for Teaching* (1996) by Charlotte Danielson.

As INTASC (1992) Standard 9: Reflection and Professional Development states, "The teacher is a reflective practitioner who continually evaluates the effects of his or her choices and actions on others (students, parents, and other professionals in the learning community) and who actively seeks out opportunities to grow professionally" (p. 31). Examples of effective reflection for business educators include the use of reflective journaling and freewriting.

Journaling. Journaling is a common method of recording events over a period of time and later reflecting on those events. While guidelines exist to develop reflective thinking through journals, an entry might include the recording of date and time, sequence and details of the experience, and analysis of the experience (Taggart and Wilson, 2005). Taggart and Wilson (2005) maintain that "more learning is derived from reflecting on an experience than from the experience itself" (p. 77). Reflective journaling promotes growth in the critical analysis of teaching.

Freewriting. Freewriting is nonstop writing that is usually private. By writing nonstop for a given period of time—10 to 15 minutes—words flow onto paper or screen and thinking improves. The use of freewriting in reflective practice can provide a beginning to getting thoughts on paper and transforming the thoughts into clear and organized ideas for better teaching practices (Elbow, 2000). For example, at the conclusion of teaching a unit on job interviewing skills, the business educator could sit and freewrite about what elements of the unit were effective, which elements were not effective, and record ideas for future improvement of the unit.

Nature of Reflective Thinking

According to Taggart and Wilson (2005), research provides evidence of the hierarchical nature of reflective thinking to include three levels: technical, contextual, and dialectical. The technical level, the initial level, can be categorized as reaction in which novice teachers might reference past experiences and focus on content and skill. The contextual level examines the relationship between theory and practice and communicates their significance to student growth. Dialectical reflective thinking, the highest level, "deals with the questioning of moral and ethical issues related directly and indirectly to teaching practices" (Taggart & Wilson, 2005, p. 4).

For an educator to explore his or her level of reflective thinking, the *Profile of Reflective Thinking Attributes* created by Germaine Taggart (2005) is provided in Table 3.

Table 3. *Profile of Reflective Thinking Attributes*				
4 = Almost always 3 = On a regular basis 2 = Situational 1 = Seldom				
When confronted with a problem situation,				
1. I can identify a problem situation	4	3	2	1
2. I analyze a problem based upon the needs of the student	4	3	2	1
3. I seek evidence that supports or refutes my decision	4	3	2	1
4. I view the problem situation in an ethical context	4	3	2	1
5. I use an organized approach to problem solving	4	3	2	1
6. I am intuitive in making judgments	4	3	2	1
7. I creatively interpret the situation	4	3	2	1
8. My actions vary with the context of the situation	4	3	2	1
9. I feel most comfortable with a set routine	4	3	2	1
10. I have strong commitment to values (e.g., all students can learn)	4	3	2	1
11. I am responsive to the educational needs of students	4	3	2	1
12. I review my personal aims and actions	4	3	2	1
13. I am flexible in my thinking	4	3	2	1
14. I have a questioning nature	4	3	2	1
15. I welcome peer review of my actions	4	3	2	1
When preparing, implementing, and assessing a lesson,				
16. Innovative ideas are often used	4	3	2	1
17. My focus is on the objective of each lesson	4	3	2	1
18. I feel there is no one best approach to teaching	4	3	2	1
19. I have the skills necessary to be a successful teacher	4	3	2	1
20. I have the knowledge necessary to be a successful teacher	4	3	2	1
21. I consciously modify my teaching to meet student needs	4	3	2	1
22. I complete tasks adequately	4	3	2	1
23. I understand concepts, underlying facts, procedures, and skills	4	3	2	1
24. I consider the social implications of so-called best practice	4	3	2	1
25. I set long-term goals	4	3	2	1
26. I self-monitor my actions	4	3	2	1
27. I evaluate my teaching effectiveness	4	3	2	1
28. My students meet my instructional objective when evaluated	4	3	2	1
29. I use a journal regularly	4	3	2	1
30. I engage in action research	4	3	2	1

Note: From *Promoting Reflective Thinking in Teachers,* (pp. 39–40), by G. L. Taggart and A. P. Wilson, 2005, Thousand Oaks, CA: Corwin Press. Copyright 1996 by G. Taggart. Reprinted with permission.

To reach an overall score, tally the number of times each indicator is circled and multiply by the indicator number. Add all the subtotals to reach an overall score and use the following scale to determine the level of reflection.

Technical level = Below 75
Contextual level = 75-104
Dialectical level = 105-120

After completing the profile, determine what level of reflection was most evident. Growth in reflection can be assessed by establishing a baseline with the information gathered in self-evaluation of reflective thinking attributes (Taggart and Wilson, 2005).

Engaging in post-teaching reflection provides educators with an avenue to grow as effective teachers. By discovering their level of reflective thinking, educators are empowered to make the necessary link between theory and practice.

SUMMARY

Whether one is a beginning or veteran teacher, effective teaching begins with teachers being able to weave themselves, their subject knowledge, and their students into a web that is highlighted by quality teaching and learning. Effective teachers plan and prepare units and lessons thoroughly. Teaching and learning activities are aligned with educational standards. Students are provided with a safe, orderly, and organized learning environment. Most of all, effective teachers provide quality instruction, accurately assess students outcomes, and participate in activities that promote lifelong learning. Reflecting on these effective teaching practices can tell teachers what has been learned, what changes need to take place, and what improvements need to be made to ensure more effective teaching and learning.

REFERENCES

Ainsworth, L., & Christinson, C. (1998). Rubrics: *An assessment model to help all students succeed*. White Plains, NY: Dale Seymour Publications.

Brown, H. F., & Wiedmaier, C. D. (2003). Planning for instruction. In M. H. Rader (Ed.), *Effective methods of teaching business education in the 21st century*. (Yearbook #41, pp. 46 – 62). Reston, VA: National Business Education Association.

Danielson, C. (1996). *Enhancing professional practice: A framework for teaching*. NJ: ASCD.

Elbow, P. (2000). *Everyone can write: Essays toward a hopeful theory of writing and teaching writing*. New York: Oxford University Press.

Gandy, J. M., & Green, D. (2003). Sponsoring student organizations. In M. H. Rader (Ed.), *Effective methods of teaching business education in the 21st century*. (Yearbook #41, pp. 298 – 313). Reston, VA: National Business Education Association.

Interstate New Teacher Assessment and Support Consortium [INTASC]. (1992). *Model standards for beginning teacher licensing and development*. Washington, DC: Council of Chief State School Officers. ED 369 767.

Kagan, S. (1994). *Cooperative learning*. San Clemente, CA: Kagan Publishing.

Limback, E., & Mansfield, R. (2002). *Student teacher assessment: A multidimensional process. Delta Pi Epsilon Journal, 44*(1) 50 – 58.

Marzano, R. J., Pickering, D. J., & Pollock, J. E. (2001). *Classroom instruction that works: Research-based strategies for increasing student achievement*. Alexandria, VA: ASCD.

McEwen, B. C. (2003). Providing for students' learning styles and differences. In M. H. Rader, (Ed.), *Effective methods of teaching business education in the 21ˢᵗ century*. (Yearbook #41, pp. 63 – 79). Reston, VA: National Business Education Association.

McKeachie, W. J. (2002). *Teaching tips: Strategies, research, and theory for college and university teachers*. 11ᵗʰ ed. Boston: Houghton Mifflin Company.

National Business Education Association (2005). *Business teacher education curriculum guide and program standards*. Reston, VA: Author

National Business Education Association. (2001) *National standards for business education*. Reston, VA: Author.

Palmer, P. J. (1998). *The courage to teach*. San Francisco, CA: Jossey-Bass Inc.

Rader, M. H. (2003). Managing the classroom and technology lab. In M. H. Rader (Ed.), *Effective methods of teaching business education in the 21ˢᵗ century*. (Yearbook #41, pp. 80 – 92). Reston, VA: National Business Education Association.

Scott, J. C. (2003). Lifelong professional development. In M. H. Rader (Ed.), *Effective methods of teaching business education in the 21ˢᵗ century*. (Yearbook #41, pp. 314 – 318). Reston, VA: National Business Education Association.

Stitt-Gohdes, W. (2001). Business education students' preferred learning styles and their teachers' preferred instructional styles: Do they match? *Delta Pi Epsilon Journal, 43*(3) 137 –151.

Taggart, G. L., & Wilson, A. P. (2005). *Promoting reflective thinking in teachers*. Thousand Oaks, CA: Corwin Press.

Assessment to Support and Reinforce Academics

Lana Carnes and Janna P. Vice
Eastern Kentucky University
Richmond, Kentucky

The importance of assessing the impact of academic programs has been well established publicly among accrediting agencies, governing bodies, legislators, alumni, and employers (Roberson, Carnes, & Vice, 2002). Businesses today demand a worker who is highly literate as well as technically competent. This chapter addresses the development of English, mathematics, social studies, and science skills that routinely occur in the context of educating students for the business world, and it provides examples of various strategies to use when core academic teachers and business teachers collaborate to assess across the curriculum. This chapter focuses on how business courses enhance core academics, the role of assessment in business education programs in relation to high stakes testing, and the value of involving external evaluators to validate the business curriculum.

ASSESSING COLLABORATIVELY ACROSS THE CURRICULUM

Business educators today are recognizing the critical need to verify the academic skills reinforced in business education courses (Stapleton, 2005; Warner, 2005; Wayne, Conder, & Davis, 2005). To avoid the risk of program or course elimination due to high-stakes academic testing, business educators must work collaboratively across all curricula to demonstrate that business classes include and strengthen core academic content. This section discusses strategies for collaboration, a collaborative assessment process, and alignment of assessment measures.

Strategies for Collaboration

Business teachers can serve in a train-the-trainer role to share valuable insight with other teachers regarding assessment methods that align core academic expectations across the curriculum. In this role, business teachers should consider the following collaborative methods (Carnes, Jennings, Vice, & Wiedmaier, 2001):

- Encourage fellow business teachers to stress in all business courses the importance and relevance of English, mathematics, social studies, and science skills.

- Provide leadership and direction to faculty who are willing to collaborate on projects promoting integration of curriculum.

- Assist faculty in developing written assignment guidelines and their corresponding checklists and rubrics designed to provide structure, direction, and standardization for collaborative writing assignments.

- Serve as a facilitator for teachers who may be unfamiliar or uncomfortable with the course content being integrated.

- Conduct professional development sessions to clearly define learning objectives and student learning outcomes.

- Design a collaborative assessment process to evaluate students' performances.

Collaborative strategies benefit instructors of business classes and core content classesas well as students. In statewide initiatives in Florida and Kentucky, collaborative projects between business, career and technical education, and core content providers achieved the following results: higher test scores on statewide high-stakes tests, higher student retention rates, increased communication among teachers, fewer discipline problems in classrooms, and more engaged students due to real-world activities (Bedard, 2005; Wayne, Conder, & Davis, 2005). Business teachers must be willing to collaborate with other disciplines to create learning experiences, align curriculum, design assessment measures, and use assessment data to improve instruction (Policies Commission for Business and Economic Education, 2005).

Collaborative Assessment Process

One of the first steps in designing the collaborative assessment process is to map the business education and academic standards, visually identifying where learning objectives are being taught or reinforced. Carnes, Awang, and Robles (2004) describe how mapping can be effective as an interdisciplinary tool to show what skills are covered in which courses. Skills that might be included in the mapping are communication, computer applications, problem solving, and quantitative ability. Once teachers collaboratively identify the skills, knowledge, and abilities they want students to develop, instructors then determine the learning opportunities that should be included in an individual class or program. Table 1 depicts a partial sample of a mapped business program.

Table 1. *Sample Mapped Business Program*

Communication Skill	International Business	Management	Marketing
Listening	Identify basic words and phrases used in business throughout the world.	Listening to a prescribed dialogue, and determine the demonstrated leadership style.	Participate in a role play to determine the customer's "given" problem.
Speaking	Practice making introductions following cultural rules.	Practice interviewing from the business side of the table.	Perform a radio spot for a product.
Writing	Write a report detailing etiquette rules to follow when on a business trip to a given country.	Given a sample review form, prepare a performance review for your teacher.	Write a paper defining and describing the elements of a marketing mix.

Cross-walking can also be effectively used to find the connections between academic and business standards. Business teachers can work with core content teachers to provide learning activities to reinforce and support academics as shown in the partial example in Table 2.

Alignment of Assessment Measures

Once the cross-referencing process is complete, teachers can work collaboratively to articulate objectives that define overarching expectations; articulate learning outcomes; construct assignments; develop instructional methods; determine the tools to be used to assess the performance; create scoring rubrics; determine when the assessment will occur (i.e., formative and summative); and decide who will assess the results, analyze and interpret the results, communicate the interpretations, implement the changes, reassess the results of the changes, and communicate the results of the changes.

The cross-walk process described above is a valuable tool for aligning assessment. A collaborative assessment process helps to standardize evaluation processes within multiple-section courses or across multiple-discipline courses. Using predetermined

Table 2. *Sample Core Content and Business Standards Map*				
Business	**Language Arts**	**Mathematics**	**Social Studies**	**Science**
Accounting	Write a letter to accompany a set of financial statements.	Create a personal budget using a spreadsheet.	Write an article persuading peers to manage money more effectively.	Develop a financial plan for a medical research proposal of your choice.
Business Law	Write a feature article on an ethical dilemma such as music piracy.	Prepare a report on the financial aspects of music piracy.	Give an oral report on the social and legal issues surrounding music piracy.	Research ethical issues surrounding producing, buying, and marketing counterfeit drugs.
Career Development	Write a cover letter and resume for a job you might like.	Research salaries and living expenses of specific jobs in towns where you would like to live.	Write an editorial for your local newspaper responding to a current, local employment issue.	Identify scientific careers, and research those that might be of interest to you.

checklists or rubrics built on learning outcomes can promote assessment alignment. The nature of the collaborative process involving teachers and administrators helps to increase communication and credibility for all parties involved. Through this communication, teachers understand what is being taught and what expectations exist in other classes. Areas that need more learning opportunities can also be identified and strengthened.

Aligning business courses with core content courses is essential for continued business and technical education growth and vitality. Using collaborative strategies for curriculum design, assessment, and the alignment of assessment measures, business teachers and core content teachers can become valuable partners to support and reinforce academics.

ENHANCING CORE ACADEMICS

In the current No Child Left Behind (NCLB) environment, business educators must work collaboratively with core content teachers to promote the reality that basic entry-level skills are the same in all industries (Warner, 2005). In the four areas of core content—English, mathematics, social studies, and science—business classes provide opportunities for students to apply and build upon learning gained in a core content classes (Carnevale & Desrochers, 2003). Specific examples follow for integrating English and mathematics into the business curriculum.

English Components Found in the Business Classroom

- English skills are enhanced in business classes through work on grammar, mechanics of writing, or the composition of documents. English teachers and business teachers working together can assess the progress students are making through portfolio entries, shared assignments, and the use of common rubrics. For example, beginning in 2007 and 2008, Kentucky will require a technical writing entry in each student's portfolio that focuses on units of study based on a student's area of interest. This requirement will provide an excellent way for core content teachers to work with business teachers in creating and facilitating the technical writing assignment. Ideas for technical writing assignments include the following: Choose a computer application program that would benefit teachers, the whole student body, the yearbook staff, or student organizations. Write an article for the school newspaper describing the application and its benefits.

- In a memo to all employees, explain how a lack of personal financial skills can affect the workplace and lead to stress. Encourage employees to share their ideas regarding effective money management and offer solutions to help employees relieve stress in the workplace.

- Create a Web page for your student organization. Narrow the focus of the topic of your page by focusing on an aspect of the organization that people may not be aware of by highlighting individual or group achievements.

- Write a policy statement for an employee manual explaining ethical and unethical uses of computers and information. Your policy should include ethical practices regarding e-mail and Internet usage.

- Research the issues surrounding counterfeiting electronic and digital products. Write a newsletter article to argue for a better understanding among students in your school regarding the basic issues of software and music piracy.

Mathematics Components Found in the Business Classroom

Students can benefit from business classes that apply mathematics skills. One area in which to integrate applied mathematics is personal finance. In fact, legislators in several states are mandating that financial literacy be taught in secondary schools, and business instructors are accepting the challenge (Glenn, 2005). In accounting, business mathematics, and computer applications classes, students can design spreadsheets; create budgets; understand basic financial planning; reconcile checkbooks; learn about insurance, taxes, and credit; and analyze their personal finances. Activities involving calculating interest and service charges on credit card accounts, loans, and purchases will provide information students need while reinforcing mathematics skills.

Business teachers can also reinforce mathematics skills by obtaining employment mathematics tests from local industries and integrating similar problems into business classes. Applied mathematics skills such as determining percentages, using decimals, converting decimals to fractions, calculating salaries using straight time and over time, and applying mathematics to solve problems could easily be addressed in accounting, computer applications, and electronic office classrooms. Suggestions for creating student interest and incorporating mathematics skills into business classes while minimizing class time and grading time include the following:

- Begin each class with a warm-up exercise depicting a common mathematics scenario.

- Require students to maintain a mathematics journal—randomly collect the journals to grade.

- Invite a business executive to discuss workplace employment testing and mathematics expectations to encourage student interest and participation.

RESPONDING TO HIGH-STAKES TESTING

Establishing Student Learning Outcomes
Business educators must respond to high-stakes testing and increased accountability measures in order to retain viable programs and to ensure student enrollment in business courses. An accreditation agency for postsecondary business programs, the Association to Advance Collegiate Schools of Business (AACSB) International, adopted new standards that recognize the importance of assessment in the continuous improvement of curriculum and student performance based on specific, predetermined learning outcomes. This approach to assessment focuses on student learning rather than on instruction to answer the question, "How do we know if they've learned the material or concepts presented?" This student-centered, learner outcome approach to assessment also supports Polomba and Banta's (1999) definition of assessment as a systematic collection, analysis, and use of information about academic courses designed for the purpose of improving student learning and development.

With this approach, the main focus of assessment is unquestionably to support and reinforce academics through improved student learning. Assessment becomes an integral part of curriculum planning to be used in instruction rather than merely a report placed on the shelf to collect dust. The assessment plan includes a guide to establish student learning outcomes, to assess collaboratively with business educators and core content teachers, and to involve external evaluators in the assessment process.

No Child Left Behind: Compatible with Business Education

The No Child Left Behind Act (NCLB) that became law in 2002 was designed to ensure student learning by raising overall achievement indices, closing the achievement gap, and measuring performance through statewide testing (U. S. Department of Education, 2005). The second phase of the NCLB requirements extended to high schools, requiring all teachers of core academic subjects to meet highly qualified requirements, and increasing high school assessments on an annual basis (Bush, 2005). NCLB calls for "improving the quality of secondary education, ensuring that every student graduates from high school, and ensuring that every student graduates prepared to enter college or the workforce with the skills to succeed" (Glenn, 2005, p. 12).

These goals are in perfect harmony with those of business education. However, in some schools, the push to assess core content has resulted in a push to pressure students to enroll in more traditional academic courses at the expense of courses in career and technical education. Business educators must show how their classes further the goals of NCLB in order to be players in school reform. A strong assessment plan, based on integrated learning dimensions, incorporates clearly written assignments with real-world application, uses multiple measures to evaluate learning outcomes, involves teachers throughout and across program areas, and involves professionals in the workplace. This is a way to validate the importance of business education in a school's curriculum.

Maki (2004) defines assessment as "intellectual curiosity about what and how well students learn," (p. 2). Assessment is the means of answering those questions of curiosity about the work of educators, including how educators know what students are learning, and how well students apply their skills and knowledge across their business programs, their core curricula, and their business careers.

Developing a Comprehensive Assessment Plan

Defining dimensions of learning. Assessment extends inquiry about student learning beyond student achievements in individual courses to their achievement over time (Alverno College Institute, 2000; Maki, 2004). Integration of the three domains of learning—cognitive, psychomotor, and affective—are critical to creating learning outcomes. All three domains must be evaluated for assessment to support and reinforce academics. As described by Anderson and Krathwohl (2001), the cognitive domain is the development of intellectual abilities including knowledge, comprehension, application, analysis, synthesis, and evaluation. The psychomotor domain is the development of physical movement, coordination, and sets of skills. The affective domain is the development of values, attitudes, soft skills, and commitments.

When business educators consciously design their courses to include the three domains of learning, the results seem naturally to fit the conceptual, project-based reality of business courses. For example, a faculty member designing a business communication report writing assignment might first look at the cognitive skills students need to use in writing the assignment, including writing principles, organizational patterns, communication strategies, and writing mechanics. The psychomotor skills might include integrating computer skills in order to word process the report and create graphics. The affective skills might include the student's approach to work, attention to detail, professionalism exhibited, deadline management, and work ethic shown.

Business classes lend themselves naturally to integrating the domains of learning based on their authentic context; use of cases, simulations, and real-life situations; and their emphasis and reinforcement of core content (Policies Commission for Business and Economic Education, 2005). Now more than ever, business educators have a challenge to demonstrate how business education reinforces the domains of learning in core content courses to survive and flourish in the NCLB environment (Glenn, 2005; Beddard, 2005; Stapleton, n.d.; Plank, 2001).

Creating a learning outcomes matrix. For a student's performance to be effectively assessed, a student must be engaged in learning. Developing a learning outcomes matrix helps students understand the teacher's expectations of them, places the ownership of learning on the students, and positions students to take responsibility for their learning (Maki, 2004). The matrix may be developed for a specific course or a program of study and includes (a) course/program objectives, (b) student learning outcome statements, (c) assignments, and (d) the assessment method.

Course/program objectives are the overarching expectations for students—what students should be able to do after completing them. Examples of course objectives might be that students will develop effective oral communication skills, students will develop team skills, and students will understand the role personal finance plays in career success.

Learning outcome statements indicate how a teacher knows whether a student has met a learning objective. The learning outcome statement describes what a student should produce or demonstrate to meet the overarching expectation for the course or program. The statements should rely on active verbs, align with course or program standards, and be measurable. Examples of learning outcomes statements might include (a) students will deliver an effective team oral report using PowerPoint, (b) students will perform as a member of a team to complete a primary research project, and (c) students will create a realistic personal budget.

The assignment section of the matrix describes the exercises, homework, tests, and assignments faculty give to help students meet the learning objectives. The assessment section of the matrix describes how the assignment will be measured. A learning outcomes matrix such as this helps the teacher design the course to meet course and program objectives, serves to validate the content of the course and assessment methods, may be used to standardize or integrate course content, can be used as a communication tool to let parents know the class or program expectations, and most importantly, helps students understand what they can expect to learn. A partial example of a learning outcomes matrix created for a business communication class is provided in Table 3.

Table 3. *Partial Sample of Assessing Learning Outcomes*

ASSESSING LEARNING OUTCOMES FOR BUSINESS COMMUNICATION		
Objective (Overarching Expectation)	Learning Outcome Statement (How Will We Know?)	Assessment (How Do We Evaluate?)
Demonstrate effective communication principles for oral presentations using appropriate technology.	Deliver an effective oral report using PowerPoint.	Checklist completed by peers, instructor, and outside evaluator.

Using checklists. After articulating student learning objectives and outcomes, many teachers decide to measure progress using something other than a standardized test or multiple-choice exam (Roberson, Carnes, & Vice, 2002; Vice & Carnes, 2002). Evaluating assignments, projects, and presentations may require a checklist or scoring guide (rubric), especially when multiple faculty will be evaluating the same learning objectives in different settings. Teachers must work together to decide what constitutes quality performance in their projects or programs. One example of a collaborative scoring guide for oral presentations is provided in Table 4.

Building skills through assignments. Business educators must prepare students with appropriate skill levels to access quality jobs with expanding skill demands (Carnevale & Desrochers, 2003). Business educators also have the challenge of responding to a variety of technological, global, economic, and demographic changes, including a potential decline in labor force growth at the same time as a rise in skill expectations (Kesten & Lambrecht, 2005). Using business as an authentic context for learners, business educators have the opportunity to design relevant assignments that build skills and prepare students to enter the workplace. Additionally, business educators recognize the high priority they must place on developing critical-thinking skills within a business context (Kesten & Lambrecht, 2005). Focusing attention on the learning domains and student learning outcomes will help teachers design assignments that maximize student performance. Using real-world examples is effective in business assignments and leads to applied learning. (Policies Commission for Business and Economic Education, 2005).

Table 4. *Partial Sample Oral Presentation Scoring Guide*

	Weak 1	Average 2	Good 3	Excellent 4
Audience Rapport				
Adapted to a specific audience				
Maintained eye contact; did not read				
Introduction				
Demanded audience's attention				
Stated purpose clearly				
Body				
Supported statements with facts				
Used questions for effective transitions				
Conclusion				
Summarized major points				
Ended with memorable statement				
Organization				
Kept the message SIMPLE				
Was coherent, easy to follow				
Visual Aids				
Used large font/type (at least 24)				
Audience did not "see one thing and hear another."				

Recent ethical violations provide excellent cases for problem solving and critical thinking across disciplines in business and other core content areas. Spain & Carnes (2005) describe a sample case focusing on Martha Stewart that led to a weeklong, multidiscipline ethics awareness week. The faculty committee developed the case, providing students background information regarding Martha Stewart's company and the ethical violations on which she was convicted. The objective of the case was to provide opportunities for students to

- observe that the actions of one individual can have significant short-term and long-term repercussions

- scrutinize the corporate code of ethics and its viability

- examine the importance of good personal decision making and accountability

- consider the importance of organizational culture in determining values and corporate responsibility

- develop a checklist of trouble signs needed in making personal or corporate decisions

- discuss the long-term financial, management, and marketing implications of the original decision to sell the stock and the continued decision to defend her actions.

Discussion questions were designed for specific disciplines including marketing, management, general business, accounting, finance, corporate communication, and computer information systems. Suggestions for incorporating these questions into classroom instruction and assignments were provided to the faculty in each subject area. Some examples of the assignments created using the case include are the following:

- Compare the written codes of ethics of major corporations to identify differences and similarities. Develop a list of common ethical behaviors/issues that the codes address and apply those issues to the ethical decisions students face.

- Develop guidelines for MSO that address the media's questions about the future leadership and health of the company.

- Discuss/debate how Stewart should have/could have communicated her role in the stock transactions to perhaps avoid a trial and conviction.

- Discuss how Stewart's ethical dilemma and conviction has affected her personal/ professional credibility.

- Write a letter to the stockholders of Martha Stewart Omnimedia, Inc., assuring them that the company will continue to be a viable company.

Spain and Carnes indicated that the highlight of the week was a student-led debate of the ethical issues surrounding Martha's trial and conviction. Such cases provide critical-thinking opportunities beyond traditional multiple-choice tests or objective quizzes.

Sending students into the business world is another way to expand a student's comfort level and his/her professional development. A student who participates in a primary research project interviewing business executives learns firsthand how to schedule and prepare for the interview, conduct the interview, and follow-up the interview in a professional manner. The student develops writing skills through preparing the interview guide, writing the analytical report, and preparing an oral presentation. A student also gains valuable content knowledge regarding current business issues.

One particularly important topic to a student is personal financial literacy. A student could interview an executive regarding this topic and be motivated to develop his or her personal finance skills when hearing how important these skills are to workplace success. Entering the workplace for interviews such as this provides an important avenue for a student to begin networking with professionals. The interviewed executive's participation in the assessment process would add further credibility to both the assignment and the student's performance outcome evaluation.

INVOLVING EXTERNAL EVALUATORS

In addition to being accountable to national agencies, state government, high-stakes assessment, and accrediting agencies, business educators must also be accountable to the business community, which depends on educators to prepare highly trained employees. The call for more rigorous education emphasizing school accountability focuses on student performance (Policies Commission for Business and Economic Education, 2005). Business educators must equip students to enter the workforce. Therefore, for assessment to be meaningful and valued, the focus and content of the assessment must be seen as relevant. According to Glenn (2005) "Business, career, and technical education promote 'relevance.' When education is relevant, students are engaged and they remain in school" (p. 12).

How can schools ensure that their curriculum focuses on relevant skills? Glenn (2005) says that schools need to maximize the use of business advisory boards to determine the exact skills students need and to provide the real-world experiences that make education relevant and useful. Robert F. Sexton (2005), Executive Director of the Prichard Committee for Academic Excellence in Kentucky, called for more involvement from business leaders to help address school reform. Cooper and Cliatt (2000) promote viewing the increased involvement of the business community in all aspects of education and assessment as an opportunity.

Assess Student Performance in the Classroom

External evaluators (i.e., business professionals) can be used to assess student performance in the classroom, can participate in research that is applied to the classroom, and can offer implications for curriculum design. Using an external evaluator helps schools learn whether the established student-learning goals are relevant, and whether student performance is at an acceptable quality level for employment.

How can educators engage external evaluators in the learning process in a manner that supports and reinforces academics? Vice and Carnes (2005) describe that in one business communication program, executives visited the classroom to formally review the oral presentations of over 1,500 business students, participating in more than 500 teams.

As evaluators, professionals validate the rigor and relevance of established student-learning goals. They can provide feedback for the instructor, students, and administrators as to whether student performance is *excellent, good, average,* or *needs considerable improvement* to meet their expectations for entry-level positions. The following examples are ways to involve external evaluators in the classroom:

- Invite visiting executives to observe and assess students' oral presentations. Students use appropriate presentation technology and work as a team. Executives can evaluate both the team and the individual performance.

- Ask the evaluator to assign a real-world business case (e.g., engaging the students in a problem-solving exercise resulting in a written document) and assist in assessing the student outcomes.

- Engage executives in the classroom through students' writing cold-call letters of inquiry to business leaders—asking leaders' advice (e.g., "Imagine you were just now starting your career. What do you wish someone had told you?").

Apply Research in the Classroom

External evaluators can also be used in the continuous improvement process of business education programs through the sharing of applied research. Instructors can use the executives' assessment of all students to identify trends of student performance that reflect areas for needed improvement. This feedback then can be used to modify instruction. For example, if an executive remarked that both formal and informal presentation skills should be developed, the instructor could change the course content accordingly—informal presentation skills could be developed through the use of a two-minute elevator speech assignment or a role-play of impromptu scenarios an employee might encounter at a business gathering, conference, or when walking to and from the parking lot.

Employers' views are commonly sought through surveys or interviews. Their opinions regarding topics such as resume preparation or job skills are then incorporated into classroom instruction. For example, an executive might indicate that some students had difficulty in carrying on a professional conversation not directly related to the interview questions. The next semester more emphasis could be placed on students reading secondary data prior to the interview so that their knowledge base of the subject was more developed, and they felt comfortable discussing side issues related to the topic.

Executives can also evaluate students' affective or "soft" skills regarding the professionalism students demonstrate outside the classroom. While these soft skills are essential for success, they are difficult to assess in a classroom environment. One way to assess these soft skills is to require students to interview a business executive at the executive's work site. After the interview, the executive could complete a survey giving his/her perceptions of the student's professional skills. As shown in Table 5, the executive could assess the extent to which the student met the executive's expectations for an entry-level employee based on (a) the student's telephone call to schedule the interview, (b) the student's conduct and demeanor in conducting the interview, and (c) the student's follow-up process after the interview.

Table 5. *Partial Sample of Outside Evaluator's Scoring Guide*			
EXECUTIVE'S ASSESSMENT OF STUDENT INTERVIEWER'S PROFESSIONAL SKILLS			
Place a check in the column indicating your opinion of the student's professionalism level.			
Professionalism Exhibited by the Student When He/She. . .	**Expectation for Entry-Level Employee**		
	Failed to Meet	**Met**	**Exceeded**
Telephoned to Schedule the Interview			
• Used appropriate telephone protocol			
• Suggested date provided adequate advance notice			
Conducted the Interview			
• Used appropriate non-verbal communication			
• Demonstrated friendliness, was relaxed			
Followed Up with the Interview			
• Sent a thank-you letter within 24 hours			
• Paid attention to detail and accuracy in composing & formatting letter			

The executive's responses could then be incorporated into classroom instruction regarding professionalism and protocol with executives in any course teaching this objective.

Design Curriculum

Advisory councils, which are generally comprised of alumni and area employers, have a special interest in helping schools build programs of excellence. Advisory councils can participate in formal surveys, focus groups, or curriculum review committees. The council could provide feedback as to the relevance and importance of each core course topic. Changes in curriculum would occur based upon the council's recommendations.

Through the use of external reviewers, teachers ensure relevant content, rigorous standards, and continuous revision of curriculum.

SUMMARY

With NCLB and high-stakes assessment focused on traditional college prep academic courses, business educators face the great challenge of being viewed as important players in school reform. Business educators must validate the importance of business education in the school's curriculum. They must collaborate with other disciplines to ensure that the business curriculum incorporates the core curriculum included in the state and national assessments. Through this collaboration, business teachers must develop a comprehensive, valid, and reliable assessment program that clearly defines desired student-learning outcomes and designs assessment tools to determine whether students achieve established outcomes. Business educators must be willing to engage external reviewers to ensure the curriculum is relevant and the standards are sufficiently rigorous to produce the quality of employee that employers need in order to meet the demands of the global workforce of the 21st century.

REFERENCES

Alverno College Institute. (2000). *Ability-based learning program*. Milwaukee, Wisconsin: Author.

Anderson, L. W., & Krathwohl, D. R. (Eds.). (2001). *A taxonomy for learning, teaching, and assessment: A revision of Bloom's taxonomy of educational objectives*. New York: Longman.

Bedard, S. (2005). Establish a connection between CTE and NCLB. *The balance sheet*, November/December 2005. Retrieved November 14, 2005 from http://balancesheet.swlearning.com/1105/11050.html

Bush, G. W. (2005, March 4) President Bush's fiscal year 2006 proposed federal budget for education. Missouri PTA Federal Ticker. Retrieved January 3, 2006, from http://www.mopta.org/ticker/default.htm

Carnevale, A. P., & Desrochers, D. M. (2003). *Standards for what? The economic roots of K-16 reform*. Princeton, New Jersey: Educational Testing Service. Available online at www.ets.org/research/publeadpubs.html

Carnes, L., Jennings, J., Vice, J., & Wiedmaier, C. (2001, Spring). The role of the business educator in a writing-across-the-curriculum-program. *Journal of Education for Business*, 216-219.

Carnes, L., Awang, F., & Robles, M. (2004). Assessing office and business information systems programs: A case study. *Information Technology, Learning, and Performance Journal*, 22 (1), 1-7.

Cooper, A. A., & Cliatt, K. (2000). Business and education: A partnership for successful assessment. In J. Rucker (Ed.), *Assessment in business education* (*Yearbook* No. 38, pp. 121-131). Reston, Virginia: National Business Education Association.

Glenn, J. (2005). A Seat at the NCLB table: How business education furthers NCLB goals. *Business Education Forum*, 60(1), 9-14.

Kesten, C., & Lambrecht, J. J. (2005). Business educators' assessments of trends, assumptions, and actions affecting practice in the field. *Business Education Forum*, 60(1), 44-49.

Maki, P. (2004). *Assessing for learning*. Sterling, Virginia: American Association for Higher Education.

Plank, S. B. (2001). A question of balance: CTE, academic courses, high school persistence, and student achievement. *Journal of Vocational Educational Research*, 26(3). Retrieved November, 6, 2005, from http://scholar.lib.vt.edu/ejournals/JVER/v26n3/

Policies Commission for Business and Economic Education. (2005). *Policy statement # 76: This we believe about business education as core academic content.* Retrieved November 6, 2005, from http://www.nbea.org/curfpolicy.html

Polomba, C.A., & Banta, T. W. (1999). *Assessment essentials : Planning, implementing, and improving assessment in higher education.* San Francisco: Jossey-Bass, Inc.

Roberson, M., Carnes, L., & Vice, J. (2002). Defining and measuring student competencies: A content validation approach for business program outcome assessment. *The Delta Pi Epsilon Journal, XLIV*(1), 13-24.

Sexton, R. F. (2005, October 31). Business leaders' plan for education gets an A. *Lexington Herald* (Lexington, Kentucky) p. A9.

Spain, J. W., & Carnes, L. (2005). Strategies for teaching business ethics across the curriculum. *Business Education Forum, 60*(2) 31-33.

Stapleton, J. (Spring, 2005). Keeping business education relevant: A contextual curriculum to sustain secondary business education programs. *Online Journal for Workforce Education and Development.* Retrieved November 6, 2005, from http://wed.siu.edu/Journal/vol1num1/vol1num1.php#keeping

U. S. Department of Education. (2005, April 7). *Secretary Spellings announces more workable, "common sense" approach to implement No Child Left Behind law.* Retrieved January 3, 2006, from http://www.ed.gov/news/pressreleases/2005/04/04072005.html

Vice, J., & Carnes, L. (2005). Assessing communication skills of first-generation college graduates. In K. Martell & T. Calderon (Eds.), *Assessment of student learning in business schools: Best practices each step of the way.* Tallahassee, FL: Association of Institutional Research and AACSB International.

Vice, J., & Carnes, L. (2002). Integrating assessment into teaching practices: Using checklists for business writing assignments. *Business Education Forum, 56*(3), 36-38.

Warner, C. (2005). Thinking anew. In H. C. Sobehart (Ed.), *Leadership in a time of change: Women Administrators Conference 2004 monograph* (p.5). Pittsburgh, PA: Duquesne University School of Education Leadership Institute. Retrieved November 6, 2005, from http://www.aasa.org/conferences/women/2004_WC_monograph.pdf

Wayne, S., Conder, S., & Davis, R. (2005) Promoting and positioning business and marketing education. *KBEA Journal,* 22-2.

Determine Student Outcomes in the Content Areas

Wayne Moore and Stephen J. Woytowish
Indiana University of Pennsylvania
Indiana, Pennsylvania

One could review the historical nature of the integration of standards into the educational system to see that standards are here to stay. In 1983, a report from the National Commission on Excellence in Education entitled *A Nation at Risk* defined excellence to mean several related things:

> At the level of the individual learner, it means performing on the boundary of individual ability in ways that test and push back personal limits, in school and in the workplace. Excellence characterizes a school or college that sets high expectations and goals for all learners, then tries in every way possible to help students reach them. Excellence characterizes a society that has adopted these policies, for it will then be prepared through the education and skill of its people to respond to the challenges of a rapidly changing world. Our Nation's people and its schools and colleges must be committed to achieving excellence in all these senses (National Commission on Excellence in Education, 1983).

The education reform movement has received broad support at the national and state levels from government officials, federal and state agencies, educational policymakers and many educators (Saxe, 2003). This movement has resulted in the passage of the No Child Left Behind Act (NCLB), which mandates that schools must increase accountability and improve student performance (Davila-Medrano, 2003).

This concept of standards-driven education has evolved and now includes standards for most academic subjects at the elementary, middle school, and secondary grade levels.

The difference in standards-based education two decades later is the inclusion of testing and assessment to measure the success of students achieving standards set by individual states. Many practicing educators also view standards as a method of determining student outcomes. Although standards had been a major component of education, there were no penalties if goals were not met. It is difficult to understand how slowly the United States has moved toward the original goal of providing all students with a challenging curriculum and finding ways to ensure that they all achieve excellence.

In business education, teaching to standards has always been something to which teachers were accustomed. Most states have established a set of academic standards that identify the level of success students need to acquire at each grade level to meet the goals of NCLB, but not all states have laid out specific standards for business education (Rader, 2005). In addition, academic standards set the condition as to what needs to be taught, but not the teaching strategy to teach the content. What this means to business education is the necessity to integrate business standards with other curriculum areas to provide opportunities for student assessment that involves multiple standards. This chapter describes the mapping of instructional practices and techniques for designing assessment tasks with multiple purposes, both of which are necessary to determine student outcomes in the content areas.

MAPPING INSTRUCTIONAL PRACTICES

The process of mapping instructional practices is not new. Mapping can be seen as an element of reflective practice, where an educator evaluates the elements of instruction (e.g., technology use, national or state standards) or any combination of resources, and whether those practices work best for the students. Reflective practice encourages educators to critically examine what went well in the lesson, what did not go well, and what would be changed if the lesson were to be re-taught.

Reflective practice and current legislation dictate that "standards are essential for educational reform, as they are used to develop and standardize curriculum, establish benchmarks for student performance, provide the basis for formative and summative assessment, and guide instructional practices" (Bernauer, 1999; Ogawa, Sandholtz, & Martinez-Flores, 2003). Many practicing educators also view the acceptance of standards, both in instruction and assessment, as a method of determining student outcomes for the courses they teach.

Standards-Based Instruction

In the current era of standardized testing and teacher accountability, one cannot ignore the role played by various types of standards. At the broadest level, standards should guide instruction and provide benchmarks for student achievement. Content and performance standards establish the bar for measuring success and specify what students need to do to demonstrate their knowledge and skills (Lee, 2003). Additional variations of standards include curriculum standards, which specify what teachers must teach, rather than what students must learn (Sweeney, 1999) and delivery standards, which specify what educators must know and do (Brandt, 2003). Educators look toward professional associations (such as ISTE or NBEA) as the source for national standards. While NCLB is a federal mandate, state standards may vary and are set forth by the various state departments of education.

NBEA standards. Standards for business education have been in existence since 1985. In that year, the National Business Education Association published a document entitled *Standards for Excellence in Business Education.* Curriculum and delivery standards were set forth as they were traditionally accepted at that time. An example, "Each faculty member possesses a minimum of a baccalaureate degree from an accredited teacher education program" (p. 39), is a far cry from today's student achievement competency standards.

The process standards set forth in 1985 were replaced by content and performance standards when the National Business Education Association published the *National Standards for Business Education*, which first appeared in 1995 and was revised in 2001. Content and performance standards focus on specific measurable outcomes for learning processes (Lee, 2003).

The 2001 revision shows evolution from the 1995 —publication—from a skills focus in 1995 to a conceptual focus in 2001 (Jacobsen, Heth, Prigge, & Braathen, 2003). The current national standards emphasize more critical-thinking and problem-solving strategies than in the past (Parker & Forde, 2000; Glenn 2001). The 1995 *Standards* were revised by separate task forces in 11 content areas: accounting, business law, career development, communication, computation, economics and personal finance, entrepreneurship, information technology, international business, management, and marketing (Glenn, 2001; National Business Education Association, 2001).

The *National Standards* are intended to be used by school administrators, curriculum writers at the state and local levels, and teachers who seek to develop or improve their business education curricula (Cochrane, 2001). The *Standards* specify the business skills and knowledge that the students are expected to possess at each level of education from elementary through postsecondary education (Ten great reasons to support the *National Standards for Business Education*, 2002).

State standards. When comparing state standards for the business content areas to those standards set forth by the National Business Education Association, Rader (2005) reports that 11 states have no specific standards for business education. Among the 39 remaining states that have adopted business education standards, 16 states' standards are not at all similar to NBEA *Standards*; 16 states' standards are somewhat similar; 5 states' standards are very similar; and 2 states' standards are identical to the NBEA standards.

Rader (2005) lists the following states as those that have not adopted business education standards: Illinois, Kansas, Maine, Maryland, Massachusetts, Minnesota, New Jersey, New Mexico, Ohio, Pennsylvania, and Wyoming. One of the states without adopted standards is Pennsylvania. In the Commonwealth of Pennsylvania, Chapter 13 of the Academic Standards for Career Education and Work are listed as proposed (Pennsylvania Department of Education 2006). Chapter 13 lists four subchapters: Career Awareness and Preparation; Career Acquisition (Getting a Job); Career Retention and Advancement; and Entrepreneurship.

In the 501 school districts that constitute the Commonwealth of Pennsylvania, each district makes decisions about the fulfillment of mandated standards. Business education is not a mandated curriculum within the commonwealth; content commonly found in the business education area can be found in other academic standards chapters. For example, Pennsylvania Chapter 3, Academic Standards for Science and Technology has subchapters 3.6 (Technology Education) and 3.7 (Technological Devices). These subchapters include such topics as Information Technology, Computer Operations, Computer Software, and Computer Communications Systems.

A state-by-state evaluation of business education content standards is outside the scope of this chapter. It is recommended that readers become more familiar with the standards in their respective states.

No Child Left Behind. With the passage of *No Child Left Behind* (NCLB), states are required to set clear and high standards for what students in each grade should know in each core academic subject, and they are required to measure each student's progress toward those standards (Leckrone & Griffith, 2006).

Elements of this legislation have been beneficial in establishing the goal of improved student achievement and in providing information and options for parents (Leckrone & Griffith, 2006). There is no doubt that the impact of NCLB upon education, funding, and instruction is profound. Assessments of learning have received much attention in the wake of NCLB, and a widespread concern about the effectiveness of public education has emerged (McNamee & Chen, 2005). If the educator can focus on how NCLB can assist students in the classroom, there are advantages for public education. The commonly accepted practice of using various types of assessments (e.g., formative, summative, alternate, norm-referenced, criterion-referenced) is well founded in pedagogy and is necessary if students' progress is to be measured. Assessments not only help the students demonstrate achievement, but can also help demonstrate mastery of subject matter as well. Assessments for learning improve teaching by showing teachers each student's developing abilities in relation to standards, key concepts, and fundamental skills (Earl, 2003). McNamee and Chen also state "the philosophy behind assessment for learning is that assessment and teaching should be integrated into a whole . . . It comes from recognizing how much learning is taking place in the common tasks of the school day—and how much insight into student learning teachers can mine from this material" (p. 76).

The impact of NCLB will continue to be felt for years to come. Spelling (2006) reports that the intent of the 2002 legislation is that we, as a nation, have a responsibility to ensure every student can read and do math on grade level by 2014. Spelling admits that we still have a lot of work to do, but "we're on the right path because what gets measured gets done" (p. 11).

Standards-Based Assessment

At the broadest level, standards serve as guideposts for instruction. To gauge student progress toward the achievement of objectives, various assessments are an integral part of solid pedagogy. Goos and Moni (2001) state that "school-based assessment is continuous or progressive: setting tasks at various times over the course of study improves the reliability of summative judgments and enhances the validity of tasks by ensuring a better match with learning objectives" (p. 74).

In the current era of educational accountability, one would be hard-pressed to argue against the inclusion of standards-based assessments in education. To avoid becoming burdened with standardized assessments and to make the content of lessons more meaningful to students, other types of assessment can be used as well. Well-constructed self-assessment and peer-assessment exercises have the potential to provide valuable learning experiences and life-long learning (Goos & Moni, 2001). A rubric or scoring guide is one tool that helps to organize and clarify scoring criteria and provide students with standards and expectations that can be used to evaluate their performance while completing the assessment.

It is important to consider the various standards that impact education. Since 1985, the NBEA standards have provided business educators with a tool to develop curriculum that could be integrated into other subject areas. State and national standards are critical to the mainstay of education reform and must be utilized by all programs. Mapping instructional practices provides educators with the mechanism to verify the use of standards and to account for student success.

DESIGN OF ASSESSMENT TASKS WITH MULTIPLE PURPOSES

Engaging students in real-world problem solving as they acquire the skills and knowledge needed for success in academics, work, and life is consistent with the goals of business education. Helping students see the connections between school and life can be accomplished by an interdisciplinary curriculum rooted in real-world topics. Student learning can be further enhanced through an authentic assessment approach that allows students to practice and be assessed on important work and life skills.

Assessment is fundamental to any notion of a national standards system. Information derived from assessments can help determine the effectiveness of education and training. Process- and outcome-oriented assessment should measure actual performance that identifies areas for improvement. Effective assessment plans are those that provide for multiple ways to measure success. An integration of business and academic standards and a variety of assessment techniques is necessary to prepare students for a career and continuing education.

Process and Outcome-Oriented Assessment

Process assessment is the bond that connects the students to the outcomes necessary for success. Gone is the day when a teacher had the responsibility for providing the instruction for one subject, utilizing one teaching technique that hopefully fit all students' learning styles in the classroom. Today, teachers have the responsibility to work with each other to provide students with a more integrated approach to learning.

Process- and outcome-oriented assessment provides students with instruction that is thematically focused around big issues and real-world problems. It is imperative in the educational process that students are challenged to develop critical-thinking skills and social awareness. Students have been trained to learn specific information about a certain subject; they tend to focus on learning facts rather than how to problem-solve and think critically. In many instances, teaching material used does not reference real life. An example of this would be a computer applications class where the primary learning taking place is from a textbook on how to use the software with applications that are not relevant to anything but learning the software. When an integrative approach is used, activities are created with a theme that takes into account multiple disciplines and real-life references. For instance, while introducing the lesson content, make the content meaningful for the students by using examples that will appeal to the learners (e.g., digital media).

There are many models that are used in the integration of student learning, two include High Schools That Work (HSTW) and Integrating Technology into the Classroom (NTeQ).

High Schools That Work (HSTW). High Schools That Work is a framework of the Southern Regional Education Board (SREB) State Vocational Education Consortium that began in 1987, and offers a systematic approach that allows teachers to be creative in revising curriculum to prepare students for the workplace and further study. This program blends traditional college preparatory content with technical/vocational studies. HSTW promotes an environment with 10 key practices: (1) high expectations (2) challenging vocational studies (3) increasing access to academic studies (4) a program of study that includes four years of English, three years of math, and three years of science (5) work-based learning (6) collaboration among academic and vocational teachers (7) students actively engaged (8) an individualized advising system (9) extra help and (10) keeping data to foster continued improvement.

The EHOVE (Erie, Huron, and Ottawa Vocational Education) Career Center (Southern Regional Education Board, 2004), adopted the HSTW framework for improving student achievement. The EHOVE staff signed a pledge to support the implementation of HSTW and focused on nine strategies: (1) get students to complete a strong academic core (2) revise the school schedule (3) raise expectations (4) engage students in completing challenging assignments (5) upgrade career/technical programs (6) use literacy as a strategy across the curriculum (7) improve guidance and advisement and involve parents in the process (8) provide extra help and (9) provide leadership for continuous school improvement (SREB, 2004).

The integration of HSTW plan provided the tool to successfully improve student achievement and the career preparation of its students. This was implemented by connecting the process with the outcomes (state and business standards) to develop techniques for assessing students through authentic forms, raising expectations, establishing an effective advisement program, adopting block scheduling, and gaining full involvement of local businesses, colleges, and the community.

Integrating Computer Technology into the Classroom (NTeQ). Well-structured lesson plans address what students will be learning (specify objectives), how the objectives are related to standards (state and/or national), how the students will let the teacher know what has been learned (results presentation), how the teacher will evaluate achievement (assessment), and a description of the activities (supporting activities). The Integrating Computer Technology into the Classroom (NTeQ) model (Morrision & Lowther, 2002) is a ten-step lesson plan that provides the template for integrating technology into the subject matter. The strength of the model is its insistence that computer use make sense in terms of the lesson objectives, student tasks, and an overall understanding of expectations by the students. Three of the ten steps to prepare the NTeQ lesson plan are specifically related to assessment practices: (1) results presentation (2) assessment and (3) activities after computer use (Morrison & Lothers, 2002).

Brubaker (2005) provides an excellent example of using the NTeQ lesson plan model to illustrate the use of academic and business standards, technology integration, and the inclusion of soft skills throughout the lesson. This specific lesson cites standards from the Communication and Entrepreneurship areas of the NBEA *Standards* (National Standards for Business Education, 2001), and the Reading, Writing, and Listening Standards of the Pennsylvania Academic Standards (Pennsylvania Department of Education, 2006). The following lesson shows how assessment can be integrated using several standards.

Entrepreneurship: Personnel (Hiring Employees)
Subject Area: Business and Technology
Grade Level: 10

Lesson Summary

Students will assume the managerial role of an entrepreneur. In this lesson, the student will use research to determine staffing requirements for a needed position, write a job description for this position, and prepare a job announcement for this position. In addition, given three fictitious resumes, the student will identify the best candidate to hire for this position. The student will then draft an offer letter to this candidate.

NBEA Standards

Communication/Foundations of Communication: Achievement Standard: Communicate in a clear, courteous, concise, and correct manner on personal and professional levels. Level IV (Employment Communication) Achievement Standard: Integrate all forms of communication in the successful pursuit of employment.

Entrepreneurship/Management: Achievement Standard: Develop a management plan for an entrepreneurial venture. Level 3 Performance Expectations: Design hiring procedures for a specific job, ranging from the initial advertisement to the final interview; Develop job descriptions for positions in a planned business.

Pennsylvania Reading, Writing and Listening Standards

RWL 1—Use and understand a variety of media and evaluate the quality of material produced.

- Select appropriate electronic media for research and evaluate the quality of the information received.
- Use, design, and develop a media project to demonstrate understanding.

RWL 2—Write with a sharp, distinct focus.

- Identify topic, task, and audience.
- Establish and maintain a single point of view.

RWL 3—Write using well-developed content appropriate for the topic.

- Gather, determine validity and reliability of, analyze, and organize information.
- Employ the most effective format for purpose and audience.
- Write fully developed paragraphs that have details and information specific to the topic and relevant to the focus.

Pennsylvania Science and Technology Standards

3.7.12 E—Assess the effectiveness of computer communications systems.

- Analyze the effectiveness of online information resources to meet the needs of research.

Learning Objectives and Results Presentation

1. After selecting and describing an entrepreneurial business venture, the student will determine a position needed in the business and will identify at least five key characteristics of a quality employee for this particular position.

   A. The student will select an avenue he or she would like to pursue as an entrepreneur and will then write a brief description of what this business venture would entail.

   B. The student will research his or her chosen business industry and determine positions that will be needed to run this company.

   C. The student will select one of these positions and will identify five key characteristics that a quality employee would have in order to successfully fulfill his or her position's job requirements.

2. Using the identified key characteristics, the student will compose a job description for this chosen position.

3. Using the previously developed job description, the student will write a job announcement for his or her chosen position.

4. Given three fictitious resumes and using the previously developed job description and job announcement, the student will select the most qualified candidate for his or her chosen position and compose a job offer.

Computer Functions

1. The student will use the computer to conduct research via the Internet for an industry-specific entrepreneurial venture. (The research will be used to determine positions needed in the company.)

2. The student will use word processing software when composing a job description for the chosen position within the identified entrepreneurial company.

3. The student will use word processing software when composing a job announcement for the chosen position with the identified entrepreneurial company.

Assessment

A scoring guide will be used to assess the quality of the students' work. The overall goal of the three activities is to assess the student's performance level for each task. The scoring guide as shown in Table 1 should be presented to the students and discussed prior to the activity so there are no surprises in the assessment results.

Table 1. *Entrepreneurship—Managerial Role Project*

Scoring Guide			
Entrepreneurial Business Venture			
Requirement	**Pts.**	**Score**	**Description**
Avenue Selected	2		Student has evaluated his or her interests, and based upon these interests, has identified an entrepreneurial venture he or she is willing to pursue. (+2 for completing)
Avenue Researched	3		Student has conducted research on his or her chosen venture. (+1 for each site accessed; limit of three sites)
Avenue Described	5		Based upon research, student has written a description of the venture.(+5 for completing as multi -paragraph; +3 for completing as one to two paragraphs; +1 for completing as one paragraph
Positions Needed	10		Positions needed in order to run venture–five to be identified or justification for less is provided.(+5 for listing positions; +5 for providing rationale for each position)
Selected Position Analyzed	13		Identifies five key characteristics (knowledge, soft skills, or technical abilities) needed to fulfill job requirements. (+5 for listing characteristics; +5 for providing rationale for characteristics)(+3 for including at least one characteristic from each of the listed areas)
Total Points			
Job Description			
Requirement	**Pts.**	**Score**	**Description**
Key Characteristics	5		Identified key characteristics are found in description. (+1 for each characteristics mentioned)
Criteria	**Wt**	**Business Expanding(+3)**	**Business Maintaining Status Quo (+2)**	**Business Closing(+1)**
Format	1		Includes title, heading, & other items used to enhance reading	Paragraph only–easy to read, but must make assumptions	Sentences with no transitions or outline format used

continued on next page

Scoring Guide					
Job Description *(continued)*					
Criteria	**Wt**		**Business Expanding(+3)**	**Business Maintaining Status Quo (+2)**	**Business Closing(+1)**
Typos	1		None	Spacing errors–no spelling errors	Strewn with typographical errors
English	2		Standard English with no errors	Standard English with minor errors– can still understand message	Major English errors that prevent reader from under- standing
Total Points					

Job Announcement			
Requirement	**Pts.**	**Score**	**Description**
Key Characteristics	5		Identified key characteristics are found in job announcement. (+1 for each characteristics mentioned)

Criteria	**Wt**		**Business Expanding(+3)**	**Business Maintaining Status Quo (+2)**	**Business Closing(+1)**
Format	1		Includes title, heading, & other items used to enhance reading	Paragraph only–easy to read, but must make assumptions	Sentences with no transitions or outline format used
Typos	1		None	Spacing errors–no spelling errors	Strewn with typographical errors
English	2		Standard English with no errors	Standard English with minor errors– can still understand message	Major English errors that prevent reader from under- standing
Total Points					

Entrepreneurial Business Venture Point Total _____

Job Description Point Total _____

Job Announcement Point Total _____

Grand Total Points Earned _____

Integration of Multiple Business Standards and Academic Standards

As educators in all disciplines work to raise the standards of the American educational system, many are crossing the boundaries of disciplines and designing curricula that encourage and demand that students apply knowledge and skills learned in one class to another completely different discipline. The following projects with authentic assessments blend several business content areas as well as academic standards.

Project Title: Creating a Business

Description: Students will have the opportunity to explore occupational options while they continue to develop technological skills as they create their own business. The project will give the students the opportunity to analyze the various aspects of creating a business (employees, inventory, income, expenses, and promotions).

Cross-Disciplinary Subjects: Business, English, Math, Social Studies

NBEA Standards: Project 1:
- Information Technology; VIII. Database Management Systems (Achievement Standard: Use, plan, develop, and maintain database management systems)

Project 2:
- Marketing; IV. Marketing Mix (Achievement Standard: Analyze the elements of the marketing mix, their interrelationships, and how they are used in the marketing process)
- Entrepreneurship; II. Marketing (Achievement Standard: Analyze customer groups and develop a plan to identify, reach, and keep customers in a specific target market)

Project 3:
- Accounting; III. Financial Statements (Achievement Standard: Prepare, interpret, and analyze financial statements using manual and computerized systems, for service, merchandising, and manufacturing businesses)

Objectives: The sample behavioral/performance objectives cited correlate with the assessment rubric:

Project 1:
1. Using relational database software, create a multiple table database that shares the following fields: Employee name, Hire date, Contact information. Note: number of tables sharing information could be adjusted to fit the needs of the

instructor. As a guide, a minimal relational database could contain three tables—one for employee names, one for compensation, and one for job description/assignment.

2. Using relational database software, create a three-table database that shares inventory information for the chosen good, product, service, or idea.

Project 2:

3. Upon the completion of a demographic analysis for a fictitious location (provided by instructor), students will choose the appropriate target market, method of advertising, good/product/service/idea to be advertised, and create the advertisement.

4. Upon completion of a demographic analysis for the city/town of the student, students will choose the appropriate target market, method of advertising, good/product/service/idea to be advertised, and create the advertisement.

Project 3:

5. Using sample data supplied by the teacher, students will create an income statement using spreadsheet software. Spreadsheet must utilize formulas for all calculations.

6. Using projected data for their company, students will create an income statement using spreadsheet software. Spreadsheets must utilize formulas for all calculations.

Resources for Learning:	Computer, Word Processing, Database, Spreadsheet, Desktop Publishing software, Internet access, Activity handouts
Assessment Strategies:	Utilize "real-world" examples to illustrate to students the rationale for completing the assessment activities related to creating a business. Provide students with Rubrics (see Tables 2, 3, and 4) to show necessary criteria to meet the specified standards.
Assignments:	The project will include three activities—

1. Set up two databases— employees and inventory. (business, math)
2. Determine where to advertise based on demographics of target population and create the promotions. (social studies, business/technology)
3. Create a spreadsheet for income and expenses. (math, business/technology)

Table 2. *Assessment Rubric*

Multiple Table Database	4 Advanced	3 Competent	2 Developing	1 Beginning
Business Standard: Use, plan, develop, and maintain database systems.				
Field Entries	All appropriate fields are included in the database with the appropriate details included for all fields.	All appropriate fields are included in the database but some field types are incorrect, i.e., date, currency, etc.	Not all database fields are included.	Database fields are not created properly.
Content	All data (100%) has been entered and is accurate.	Data is complete, but there are some inaccuracies.	Not all data has been entered.	No data has been entered.
Tables	All three tables (employee names, compensation, and job description/ assignment are included.	Two of the three tables are included.	One of the three tables is included.	Tables were completed incorrectly.

Table 3. *Assessment Rubric*

Advertisement	4 Advanced	3 Competent	2 Developing	Beginning
Business Standard: Analyze the elements of the marketing mix, their interrelationships, and how they are used in the marketing.				
Advertising Theme	Theme is specific and supportive of the target market.	Theme shows a general understanding of the needs of the general market.	Theme is loosely constructed around the product/service and does not take into account the market.	Theme shows no understanding of the product/ service or the target market.
Target Market	Advertisement shows a clear target audience through the chosen theme of the product/service.	Advertisement shows a clear but more general target audience.	Target audience is not clear from theme of the advertisement OR the audience is clear, but is not the most logical choice for the product/ service.	Advertisement shows no attempt made at reaching a target audience.
Text	Text provides at least three creative and specific examples of the product/service.	Text is supportive of the theme. It provides 2-3 specific and appropriate examples of the product/service.	Text provides examples of the theme (1-2) but does not show much creativity.	Text does not show a theme or specific examples to support it.

Table 4. *Assessment Rubric*				
Income Statement/ Electronic Spreadsheet	**4** Advanced	**3** Competent	**2** Developing	**1** Beginning
Business Standard: Prepare, interpret, and analyze financial statements using manual and computerized systems, for service, merchandising, and manufacturing.				
Income Statement Organization	Data is organized, revenues and expenses are grouped correctly, types of expenses and subcategory of expenses are identified, and proper formatting is used.	Some organization, revenues and expenses are grouped correctly, subcategory of expenses is identified, and some formatting is present.	Some organization, revenues and expenses are grouped correctly, subcategory of expenses is not identified, and some formatting is present.	Data is not organized, revenues and expenses are not identified, no formatting.
Accuracy of Data	All information is correct.	Data is entered correctly and both revenues and expenses are correct but the net income is incorrect.	Data is entered correctly and only one category (revenue or expense) is correct, the other is incorrect.	Data is not entered correctly, revenue and expense totals are incorrect.
Formula Usage	Functions used are all calculations, and correct formulas are used.	Simple formulas are used, but functions are not present.	No formulas present, but calculations done outside of spreadsheet.	No calculations present, no totals for revenues or expenses are present.

Real-world problem solving is an excellent device to assess student readiness for the workplace. Students want to know why they are learning the material and how it can be used in multiple settings. An assessment that is both process- and outcome-oriented will provide students with the necessary knowledge and skills to be successful. Technology integration allows the educator to create real-world problem-solving activities, so students can think critically and realize the importance of the individual components in the problem-solving process.

SUMMARY
All states have standards for core subject areas, but not all have specific standards for business education. The result is that business education standards must be integrated with other curriculum areas to provide opportunities for student assessment that integrates multiple standards.

The process of mapping instructional practices demonstrates a way for educators to reflect on past practices as well as encourage techniques for integration. It is important for educators to work together in designing assessment tasks with multiple purposes and break the barriers between subjects. There are many models and tools available in building integrated learning assessments including High Schools That Work (HSTW) and curriculum integration (NTeQ) models. Each technique can be used in building-integrated learning activities with a primary goal of providing students with a streamline model of how disciplines fit together in reaching goals for workplace readiness and academic success.

Helping students to become successful lifelong learners and productive members of society should be part of every educator's personal standards. Integration has become a major component in the teaching and learning arena. The Integrating Computer Technology in the Classroom (NTeQ) model provides a flexible framework in creating lessons that are problem-based with technology integrated as a component for meeting standards. No matter what the vehicle, the infusion of standards and integration helps to motivate students to learn by establishing relevancy. And, by making the lesson content meaningful through authentic assessment techniques, students can begin to see a purpose for what we do every day in our classrooms.

REFERENCES

Bernauer, J. (1999). Emerging standards: Empowerment with purpose. *Kappa Delta Phi Record, 35*(2), 68-70.

Brandt, R. (2003). Will the real standards-based education please stand up? *Leadership, 32*(3), 17, 19, 21.

Brubaker, M. (2005). *Entrepreneurship: Hiring employees.* Retrieved February 20, 2006, from http://www.eberly.iup.edu/moore/wayne/LESSON%20-NTeQ%20 Entrepreneurship.pdf.

Cochrane, D. J. (2001). Setting the standard for success. *Business Education Forum, 56(1), 6.*

Davila-Medrano, D. (2003). Standards-based curriculum development. *THE Journal, 30*(10), 40, 42-43.

Earl, L. M. (2003). *Assessment as learning: Using classroom assessment to maximize student learning.* Thousand Oaks, CA: Corwin Press.

Glenn, J. M. L. (2001). Serving all students: NBEA releases revised National Standards for Business Education. *Business Education Forum, 56*(1), 8-12.

Goos, M., & Moni, K. (2001). Modeling professional practice: A collaborative approach to developing criteria and standards-based assessment in pre-service teacher education courses. *Assessment & Evaluation in Higher Education, (26)*1, 73-88.

Jacobsen, C., Heth, K., Prigge, L., & Braathen, S. (2003). A model for the development of business education curriculum frameworks. *Journal of Applied Research for Business Instruction, 1*(2), 1-4.

Leckrone, M. J., & Griffith, B. G. (2006). Retention realities and educational standards. *Children & Schools, (28)*1, 53-58.

Lee, J. O. (2003). Implementing high standards in urban schools: Problems and solutions. *Phi Delta Kappan, 84*(6), 449-55.

McNamee, G. D., & Chen, J. Q. (2005). Dissolving the line between assessment and teaching. *Educational Leadership, 63*(3), 72-76.

Morrison, G., & Lowther, D. B. (2005). *Integrating computer technology into the classroom.* (p. 66). Upper Saddle River, NJ: Pearson Prentice Hall.

National Business Education Association. (1985). *Standards for excellence in business education.* Reston, VA: Author.

National Business Education Association. (2001). *National standards for business education.* Reston, VA: Author.

National Commission on Excellence in Education. (1983). *A nation at risk.* Retrieved February 4, 2006, from http://www.ed.gov/pubs/NatAtRisk/risk.html.

Ogawa, R., Sandholtz, J., & Martinez-Flores, M. (2003). The substantive and symbolic consequences of a district's standard-based curriculum. *American Educational Research Journal, 401*(1), 147-76.

Parker, B. S., & Forde, C. M. (2000). Business educators' awareness, implementation, and value of the National Standards for Business Education. *Business Education Forum, 54*(4), 14-18.

Pennsylvania Department of Education. (2006). Academic standards. *The Pennsylvania Code.* Retrieved February 6, 2006, from http://www.pacode.com/secure/data/022/chapter4/s4.83.html.

Rader, M. H. (2005). A comparison of state and national standards for business education. *NABTE Review, 32,* 10-15.

Saxe, D. W. (2003). On the alleged demise of social studies: The eclectic curriculum in times of standardization—A historical sketch. *International Journal of Social Education, 18*(2), 93-105.

Spelling, M. (2006). Five questions for Margaret Spellings. *American School Board Journal, 193*(3), 11, 59.

Sweeney, B. (1999). Content standards: Gate or bridge? *Kappa Delta Pi Record, 35*(2), 64-67.

Southern Regional Educational Board (SREB). (2004). Case studies. *High Schools That Work.* Retrieved February 2, 2006, from http://www.sreb.org/programs/hstw/publications/case_studies/EHOVE.asp.

Ten great reasons to support the National Standards for Business Education. (2002). *Business Education Forum, 57*(2), 72.

Selecting Appropriate Assessment Methods

Sandra R. Williams
University of Montana
Missoula, Montana

Donald K. Wattam
University of Idaho, Coeur d'Alene
Coeur d'Alene, Idaho

Roberta D. Evans
University of Montana
Missoula, Montana

Amid the pressure for high-stakes testing in schools across America, it is easy to lose sight of the wide array of assessment practices intended for instructional use. In truth, all teachers must develop a broad-based repertoire of assessment skills as they seek crucial insight into their students' levels of content mastery. Aggregate data from classrooms is informative, as curricula are articulated across grade levels and educators determine whole-school progress toward meeting standards. However, it is in the classroom where this information enables a teacher to accomplish three important goals: to determine whether his or her instruction is successfully conveying material to the class in general; to assess the knowledge level of each individual student; and to formulate a plan to enhance student learning.

This chapter is devoted exclusively to specific assessment strategies needed to achieve the three goals listed above. First, enhancing student achievement through the use of Bloom's Taxonomy and the Dynamic Instructional Design Model will be examined. Next, two of the main categories of assessment—authentic and alternative—will be reviewed. Then, a brief description of various assessment tools will be provided.

ENHANCING STUDENT ACHIEVEMENT THROUGH ASSESSMENT

For years, we have seen compelling evidence that when teachers employ overt, clear assessment strategies, two events occur. First, students develop an uncanny ability to self-assess and thereby feel empowered to gauge their own learning. Second, teachers articulate instructional goals more clearly and tend to give more thought to the methods they choose to use to enable students to meet the selected instructional goal.

Writing for *Essays in Education,* Amy Wyotek (2005) observed,

> Informing students of detailed expectations and specific learning objectives from the beginning of a unit or lesson creates clear, focused goals for students to pursue and jumpstarts them on their way to success. (¶4) …One method teachers can instigate this positive motivation-success cycle is to involve students in the process of assessment … By involving students in the assessment process, teachers encourage students to create a sense of internal responsibility for their achievement. (¶7)

To a significant degree, students' ability to self assess is contingent upon their teachers' goals for instruction in the first place. One way for teachers to examine their instructional goals is to apply Bloom's Taxonomy to their teaching. A companion to that examination is the clear articulation of instructional goals or looking at instructional systems, and the Dynamic Instructional Design (DID) model is one of those systems.

Bloom's Taxonomy

The foundational underpinning of all assessment lies in Bloom's Taxonomy, long trusted as the analytical framework for knowledge acquisition. Bloom coauthor David Krathwohl (2002) characterized the taxonomy as "a scheme to classify educational goals, objectives, and, most recently, standards" (p. 218). Krathwohl revised the original six major categories in the cognitive domain (Knowledge, Comprehension, Application, Analysis, Synthesis, and Evaluation) to more user-friendly terms: Remember, Understand, Apply, Analyze, Evaluate, and Create. Hoy and Hoy (2003) characterized the revision in this way.

> The taxonomy revisers have retained the six basic levels, but they have changed the names of three to indicate the cognitive processes involved and altered the order slightly. The six cognitive processes of the revised taxonomy are *remembering* (knowledge), *understanding* (comprehension), *applying, analyzing, evaluating,* and *creating* (synthesizing). In addition, the revisers have added a new dimension to the taxonomy to recognize that cognitive processes must process something—you have to remember or understand or apply some form of knowledge (p. 160).

Figure 1 provides a visual comparison of the two taxonomies.

75

Figure 1—Comparison of Original and Updated Bloom's Taxonomy

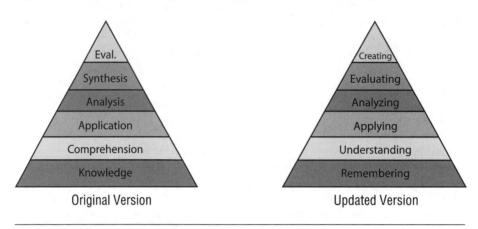

From Lynn Schultz, Old Dominion University, Norfolk, VA, and Richard Overbaugh (n.d.). See http://www.odu.edu/educ/llschult/blooms_taxonomy.htm. Used with permission.

Understanding the principles of the taxonomy enables educators to classify what exactly is being assessed. More importantly, the taxonomy reinforces the developmental shift that occurs regularly in the best business classrooms in America: moving students from merely memorizing facts through stages, culminating in their ability to integrate principles as they apply and actually expand current knowledge. The taxonomy enables the teacher to match his or her content objectives to student assessment approaches and is a perfect foundation for considering assessment options.

Dynamic Instructional Design (DID) Model

Instructional planning systems provide a framework for teachers to use when planning, creating, evaluating, and revising student learning opportunities. The foundation of the systems approach to curriculum development, generally credited to Robert Gagne (1965), is the instructional design model which serves as a template to identify learning goals and, ultimately, the steps to follow in reaching the goals. One such model, the Dynamic Instructional Design (DID) model, is especially responsive to the continual changes present in business and technology education.

Developed by Judy Lever-Duffy, Jean McDonald, and Al Mizell (2005), the DID model follows a six-step process for designing instruction that includes formative and summative feedback questions at each step. Formative feedback allows teachers to make adjustments at each step of the process, even as instruction occurs; and summative feedback "serves as a final check once all of the steps are complete" (p. 39). This emphasis on flexibility and the incorporation of continuous improvement in the teaching-learning process are hallmarks of the DID model (Lever-Duffy, McDonald, & Mizell, 2005). Table 1 provides an outline of the DID model.

Table 1. *Dynamic Instructional Design Model*		
DID Step	Formative Feedback Questions	Summative Feedback Questions
	Questions to Ask During the Process	**Questions to Ask at the End of the Design Process**
1. KNOW THE LEARNERS	• Am I responding to all learning styles? • Am I accurately depicting the students' developmental stages? • Am I correctly assessing student skill levels?	Did the design successfully meet the needs of the learners?
2. STATE YOUR OBJECTIVES	• Are my objectives targeting the performances I intended? • Are my objectives stated in a format that makes it possible to accurately measure performance? • Do my objectives include multiple levels of Bloom's taxonomy?	Did my objectives accurately capture, in performance terms, the essence of the content the students needed to learn?
3. ESTABLISH THE LEARNING ENVIRONMENT	• Does the physical space I am planning offer sufficient diversity to meet learner needs? • Is the environment nurturing and secure for all students? • Does the class management system promote positive and productive interaction? • Am I planning student and teacher exchanges that support and enhance learning?	Was the learning environment that I established effective in promoting learning?
4. IDENTIFY TEACHING AND LEARNING STRATEGIES	• Am I addressing all of the steps of the pedagogical cycle? • Does each step make sense in terms of the cycle and the student learning it is intended to promote? • Am I including sufficiently varied teaching strategies and learning activities to meet the needs of my diverse students?	Are the teaching and learning strategies sufficient for and effective in meeting the objectives I identified?
5. IDENTIFY AND SELECT TECHNOLOGIES	• Are the technologies I have selected appropriate to the content and pedagogy? • Am I selecting a variety of technologies that will meet the diversity of learning styles? • Are the technologies and support materials readily available?	Were the technologies I selected successful in supporting the targeted teaching and learning?
6. PERFORM A SUMMATIVE EVALUATION	• Am I identifying a method of assessment that will measure achievement of objectives? • Is the data to be gathered from the assessment useful to determine necessary revisions? • Are the evaluation techniques valid and reliable with references to the device?	Does the summative evaluation provide the data I need to determine whether the objectives were achieved? Was the data sufficient for effective revision?

Bloom's Taxonomy and the Dynamic Instructional Design Model provide the framework by which educators may evaluate the effectiveness of both their lessons and their students' learning. Ultimately, student achievement of instructional objectives is the most significant factor in assessment.

CONNECTING THEORY TO PRACTICE

Because assessment systems have been developed across a wide array of curricular areas over time, many theorists and researchers have attempted to formulate advice for teachers. Whether arguing that assessment approaches should be based upon theories of child development (Elkind, 2001), sociological context (Corbett & Wilson, 2002), or the content itself (Cogan & Schmidt, 2002), the advice converges when it comes to the "best practices" recommended. Specifically, experts tend to agree that assessment approaches should be authentic, involve various alternative practices, and be aligned with objectives, goals, and criteria.

Authentic Assessment

Authentic assessment practices came into play during the 1990's as Grant Wiggins and Rick Stiggins, working on different coasts of the country, simultaneously began identifying specific tools for teachers that would probe more deeply into determining levels of student learning. Separating these types of assessment from paper and pencil tests, these new practices were akin to clinical education, which has long required students to demonstrate competency by performing specific tasks. These demonstrations or performances could be classified and judged; hence, descriptors of the varying levels of success with regard to performance became essential.

One of the most important practices to emerge from authentic assessment was the notion of *rubrics*. These are scaled descriptors of performance through which teachers could describe students' level of mastery. When linked to curriculum standards or instructional goals, rubrics can provide teachers and students alike with specific information regarding where more instruction is needed and where content mastery has already occurred.

The philosophical underpinnings of authentic assessment echo pragmatism and Dewey-like ideals. University of Arizona's Anthony Nitko's classic and evolving work, *Educational Assessment of Students* (2004), clearly explains in its fourth edition the practices exemplifying these philosophical underpinnings.

> ...authentic assessment usually means presenting students with tasks that are directly meaningful to their education instead of indirectly meaningful. For example, reading several long works and using them to compare and contrast different social viewpoints is directly meaningful because it is the kind of thoughtful reading educated citizens do. Reading short paragraphs and answering questions about the "main idea" or about what the characters in the passage did, on the other hand, is indirectly meaningful because it is only

one fragment or component of the ultimate learning target of realistic reading. "Realistic" and "meaningful" are terms educators writing about authentic assessment often use...[and] these terms beg further questions, such as 'Realistic in which context?' and 'Meaningful for whom?' (p. 148).

Teachers familiar with the traditional high school business curriculum will recall a time when assessment of accounting, for example, was indirectly meaningful insofar as it was fragmented typically into vocabulary terms, recitation of principles, and short worksheets to test students' knowledge of increasingly complex bookkeeping formats. Conversely, many teachers today work with students to create on-campus businesses (selling such things as cappuccinos and school spirit attire), wherein knowledge of the same content is learned and ultimately demonstrated in a real-world context. Such demonstration or performance provides countless opportunities for directly meaningful assessment.

Alternative Assessment

Generally speaking, the "alternative" in alternative assessment refers to any type of assessment that does not include the classic objective formats of multiple-choice, true/false, fill-in-the-blank, and matching, continuing all the way to standardized achievement tests. Alternative assessment systems often provide both formative and summative data for teachers and students. Formative assessment is designed to give an ongoing picture of content mastery in such a way that students often revise and rework their assignments with ongoing teacher input. Along the way, the documentation focuses upon the students' progress and change. Ultimately, these indices lead to more summative or final assessment, resulting most often in a class grade as recorded on a transcript.

Alternative assessment systems include such things as the Dynamic Instructional Design Model and cumulative portfolios of students' work, where the teacher input is both ongoing and formative. Because the DID and related systems foster specific praise and increase communication, they are popular among students. Indeed, in the words of Catherine Taylor and Susan Bobbitt Nolen (2005),

> Students will be prepared to engage in...assessments—especially when the expectations for the quality and characteristics of the work (performance criteria) are known and practiced. This leads to the most important key to successful performances and performance assessment: clear expectations and directions to students (p. 83).

Alignment of Objectives, Goals, and Criteria

Linking assessment to the instructional plan is essential, as W. Edwards Deming noted early in his Total Quality Management theory by asserting that we evaluate what we value. Developing lesson plans and viewing assessment as an essential component of instruction has become part of the teacher's task list. Interestingly, a commitment to authentic assessment and alternative assessment systems often means, in addition, that students help establish their teachers' instructional objectives and goals, as well as the criteria by which these will be assessed. Perhaps Katie Wood Ray (2006) says it best in observing, "Expert teaching invites students to act with initiative and intention in shaping what happens to them throughout the day" (p. 60).

One of the best ways instructional objectives (the reason for teaching specific content) and goals (the content to be mastered) are presented to students is to be overt in describing them at the outset of instruction. Similarly, the best way to ensure follow-through of process and outcome is to establish the assessment criteria and present these early. In this way, there exists a perfect feedback loop related to what is planned for instruction and what is measured at the conclusion of the instruction. The teachers then are able to effectively, "begin with the end in mind," as Stephen Covey (1989) so eloquently stated in his book, *The 7 Habits of Highly Effective People*.

ASSESSMENT OPTIONS

Assessment can take many forms. The choice of the appropriate assessment is dependent upon the desired student learning outcome. The information in Table 2 provides questions teachers may ask themselves when selecting an instrument from their toolkit of techniques for assessing student performance.

Table 2. *Instructional Questions Guiding Assessment Choices*
What is the purpose of the assessment?
How does it relate to the objectives of the learning?
What collective and individual data emerge from it?
How complicated or simple should it be?
What investment in time and materials is needed to implement it?

Determining the answers to questions posed in Table 2 helps the teacher to better match assessment to instructional purpose. Descriptions of several types of assessment options will enable teachers to see where these tools might best suit their needs. The assessment options include quick-check vehicles, checklists, role plays, written evaluations, and rubrics.

Quick-Check Assessment Vehicles

Listed below are four assessment tools useful for quickly taking stock of a student's performance. Teachers will find these four activities nearly effortless to create, yet students' responses yield powerful information related to the next steps in classroom instruction, particularly where results indicate the content had not been adequately or incorrectly learned.

Three-Minute Write. The one-to-three minute write paper may be utilized to assess a student's learning after a lecture, presentation, video, or teaching of a concept. Students are given one to three minutes to respond to a teacher prompt, such as, "What is the most important concept I learned today?" or further prompting the students to respond to, "What question or questions from today's class remain unanswered?" These questions focus on the big picture—what is being learned.

Muddiest Point. The muddiest point, used in the middle or at the conclusion of a lesson, may be used to assess each student individually regarding what they find least clear or most confusing about a particular lesson or topic. This method provides the student perspective on the lesson at hand (Angelo & Cross, 1993).

Know-Want-Learn. The Know-Want-Learn (KWL) method is used at the beginning and ending of a lesson or unit. At the beginning of the lesson, a student is asked to respond to the teacher prompts of "What do I know?" and "What do I want to know?" about a topic or lesson. The information gleaned from the "What do I know?" section provides a teacher with a starting instruction point. Lesson plans are then created to assist students in discovering the answers to the "What do I want to know?" section. At the completion of the lesson or unit, the student responds to the "What did I learn?" question.

Think-Pair-Share. Think-Pair-Share is a cooperative learning technique used for students to test their knowledge with another student. Students are asked to think about a question (e.g., what was surprising in today's class?). The teacher divides the class into groups of two and then the students take turns stating their thoughts to one another. The next step is for the pair to report the discussion to others; this discussion summary may be given to another pair or to the entire class (Maier & Panitz, 1996).

Checklists

Checklists are useful when tasks may be separated into parts and each one checked for its presence or absence. Data collected provides limited feedback; however, it assists the teacher in recording and reporting student progress (Orlich, et al., 2004). Checklists are particularly useful for assessing rough drafts and preliminary planning completed by students.

Role Plays

Role plays may be used in most of the business education curricular areas and are an evaluation tool limited only by the teacher's and student's imaginations. Examples of role plays can range from a simple "How do I answer a telephone call?" scenario to a more complex or involved situation such as a mock interview or financial briefing. Role plays provide an opportunity for peer evaluation wherein classmate observers may provide written or oral feedback to the performers. This feedback may take the form of a statement or a question. For example, during a financial briefing, one student may act as the company accountant sharing financial information/documents with shareholders (played by other students). The shareholders may then ask the accountant questions for clarification or for further explanation of the financial information/documents.

Written Evaluations

In the words of Zessoules & Gardner (1991), "When students and teachers make use of reflection as a tool for learning and assessment, they are creating an opening that allows them to enter into a student's work, making sense of their endeavors and accomplishments, and learning how they judge their success" (p. 58). Indeed, Chaminade University of Honolulu's Amy Wyotek (2005) concurred: "Keeping learning logs or receiving frequent updates from the teacher can raise student awareness of progress" (¶ 8). Described below are three types of written evaluations: learning logs, journals, and reflections.

Learning logs. Learning logs consist of bits of information usually found in a table format. For instance, in a business reading log the column headings could be the date (that the article, chapter, or book was read), title, author, topic, and abstract. The abstract length could range from a few sentences to one or more paragraphs, covering the main focus of the material read. The log keeps track of the amount and variety of reading that a student does to supplement his or her learning. The brief abstract provides insight as to what the student believed was one or more major points the author was trying to make.

Journals. Journals are more in-depth than a log as each required entry could be several paragraphs long. The journal could be topic-specific or broad in nature. An example of a topic- specific journal could be a journal on teams. In this journal, the student could identify the one or more roles that he or she played during the team activity and describe events that occurred while working within the team environment. The journal would be kept throughout the entire team unit. Submission of the journal at the end of the unit should provide evidence of the student's growth in understanding the workings of a team and how the student can best enhance the team experience for not only him or herself, but also other team members.

A free-write journal is one that a student completes periodically to detail the learning that has taken place since the last journal entry was made. The student can describe specific topics of instruction that were interesting and explain why, or the teacher can tell the student what type of learning the student was to discuss in the journal entry. The number of entries for either type of journal will vary, depending upon the time available for both students to write and the teachers to grade, and on the duration of the journal activity itself; i.e., more entries will be written if the journal is to last all semester rather than just a few days or weeks. Journals and learning logs require a significant investment of time for both the teacher and student; nevertheless, many teachers assert these tools also provide immense insight into a student's mastery of content.

Reflections. Reflections are generally written at the end of a learning unit, although sometimes instructors will break an exceptionally long unit into two sections, placing a reflection at the midpoint. As the student writes, he or she focuses on the process undertaken to learn the material presented. Reflections tend to be summative and may include hints as to changes the student would make if given a second chance with the learning opportunity.

Rubrics

Rubrics, considered one of the most effective assessment measures for authentic constructivists projects, guide students to desired outcomes. Joette Stefl-Mabry (2004) believed a good rubric to be a promise between the teacher and student and that the elements listed were valued and would be assessed, ultimately, with the purpose of improving student performance.

When designing a rubric, consider learner outcomes and how to recognize the learners' achievement of the outcomes. Rubrics may be created by the teacher or by the teacher and the student together. Time spent creating rubrics provides a common focus for student and teacher while maintaining clear understanding of the expectations of how and what will be assessed. Thus, making the feedback process to the point while also decreasing the time spent by both student and teacher (Stanford & Reeves, 2005). Table 3 chronicles the steps necessary for designing a rubric.

Table 3. *Steps for Creating a Rubric*
1. Decide on elements of performance or product
2. Review student work to ensure all elements included
3. Refine and consolidate elements
4. Define each element
5. Develop a scale to describe the range of performance/products on each of the elements
6. Evaluate the rubric
7. Pilot test rubric using student work
8. Revise rubric
9. Ask colleague to test rubric with their students
10. Share rubric with students and parents
Adapted with permission from Chicago Public Schools, 2000.

Rubrics are best applied to specific aspects of instruction. Many educators find them particularly suitable for portfolios, projects, presentations, and writing assignments. Additionally, they can be useful for holistic group scores involving many students, where students assess one another's participation in the group utilizing the rubric.

Portfolios

A relatively new assessment tool is the portfolio. Portfolios are used in a wide array of educational settings, including preschool, K-12 schools, and universities. This is undoubtedly due to their malleable nature; they can be made applicable to every subject area and every assessment purpose where the target is the individual student. Hoy and Hoy (2003) garnered a list of possible entries from the related literature and concluded that "written work or artistic pieces are common contents of portfolios, but students might also include graphs, diagrams, snapshots of displays, peer comments, audio- or videotapes, laboratory reports, computer programs—anything that demonstrates learning in the area being taught and assessed" (p. 259-260).

Teachers and students may communicate with each other through the portfolio. Milson and Brantley (1999) found portfolios to be useful in capturing a complex web of communication, where the assessment process focused on the recurring dialogue between students, self, student to student, and student to teacher.

Portfolios are popular due to their broad utility. They have been focused upon for both short- and long-term learning, content and affective classroom goals, metacognition and self-reflection, and public and private discourse. Moreover, they are beneficial to developing a student's organizational skills. For example, just in the area of self-reflection alone, Chappuis (2005) noted, "Student portfolios can also promote a student's self-reflection. In collecting their work and insights in portfolios, students have the opportunity to reflect on their learning, develop an internal feedback loop and understand themselves better as learners" (p. 42-43). All of these artifacts are often kept together in one bound volume, thereby enabling students and teachers alike to chart growth and progress in their work. When used in this ongoing communication manner, assessing the portfolio occurs over multiple dates and times.

The following table provides a succinct overview of the assessment options discussed, including the purpose of the tool, how the tool ties to a lesson's learning objective, the data produced by the tool, the level of complex thinking undertaken by the student, and the investment of time in terms of both the student and the teacher.

SUMMARY

This chapter was designed to afford a glimpse into the selection of assessment tools. Amid a myriad of instructional and organizational needs, schools rely on teachers to apply their professional knowledge and creativity to bring "best practices" to life. Despite a national testing agenda, national and state curriculum reforms, and district-wide attention to curriculum, it is the daily activities within individual classrooms that most impact student learning.

Our very definitions of "knowledge" have changed. Thanks to Bloom et. al., we expect to advance student proficiency well beyond rote memorization of content to include the highest-level thinking skills, analyzing, evaluating, and creating. New

Table 4. *Forms of Assessment Decision-Making Matrix*

Assessment Tool	Assessment Purpose	Learning Objectives	Data Produced	Simple/ Complicated	Time Investment
Quick Check Vehicles	Formative	Tied directly to learning objective—usually one point at a time	Student learning needs	Simple—tends to focus on remembering or understanding level	Minimal— prep, review, completion
Checklists	Formative	Process-oriented in nature	Gaps or redundancies	Simple—tends to focus on remembering or understanding level; final items might be applying	Minimal— prep, review, completion
Role Plays	Formative	One or more objectives may be viewed	Addresses how a student would act in a given situation	Complicated— applying, analyzing, evaluating, and creating	Time Consuming— prep, review, completion
Logs	Formative, Summative, Formal when rubric is used for reflection	To encourage learning in a certain area	Shows student commitment to, interest in learning, and ability to write summary	Complicated— will range from remembering to creating levels	Time consuming to read, write; easy to grade w/checklist or rubric
Journals	Formative, Summative, and Formal when a rubric is used	Several learning objectives — separately or together	Extent and depth of learning is described	Complicated— will range from understanding to creating levels	Time consuming to prepare, review, and write
Reflections	Formative, Summative, or Formal when rubric is used	One or more learning objectives	Written evidence of the depth and breadth of a student's knowledge	Complicated— will range from understanding to creating levels	Time consuming to read, review, write; easy to grade w/ checklist or rubric
Rubrics	Formative, Summative	Analytical— One learning objective; Holistic, multiple learning objectives	Identifies level of expertise gained	Complicated— applying, analyzing, evaluating, and creating	Time consuming to prepare, review; completion time minimal
Portfolios	Formative, Summative, or Formal when rubric is used	Tied to several learning objectives	Demonstrates the student's depth and breadth in one or more specific areas	Complicated— will range from understanding to creating levels	Time consuming to read/assemble; easy to grade w/checklist or rubric

definitions of our expectations for learning must be fulfilled through changes to curriculum and ultimately to assessment practices.

Growth and change are inherent in the work of business teachers. As technological, economic, and entrepreneurial forces impact the workplace, teachers must adapt their curricula to meet the needs of the twenty-first century. The result is a desire to design and implement change—perhaps more intense among business teachers than in any other educators responsible for the high school curriculum. Knowledge of assessment is crucial, as teachers must be adept at developing various assessments designed to provide immediate information about their students' levels of achievement.

REFERENCES

Angelo, T. A., & Cross, K. P. (1993). *Classroom assessment techniques: A handbook for college students.* (2nd ed.). San Francisco, CA: Jossey Bass.

Chappuis, J. (2005). Helping students understand assessment. *Educational Leadership, 63*(3), 39-43.

Chicago Public Schools. (2000). *How to create a rubric from scratch.* Retrieved February 20, 2006, from http://intranet.cps.k12.il.us/Assessments/Ideas_and_Rubrics/Create_Rubric/create_rubric.html

Cogan, L. S., & Schmidt, W. H. (2002). Culture shock—eighth grade mathematics from an international perspective. *Education Research and Evaluation, 8*(1), 13-39.

Corbett, D., & Wilson, B. (2002). What urban students say about good teaching. *Educational Leadership, 60*(1), 18-22.

Covey, S. (1989). *The seven habits of highly effective people.* New York: Simon & Schuster.

Elkind, D. (2001). *The hurried child: Growing up too fast too soon.* (3rd ed.). Cambridge, MA: Perseus Publishers.

Gagne, R. M. (1965). *The conditions of learning.* Austin, Texas: Holt, Rinehart, and Winston.

Heafner, T. (2004). Assessment as a magnification of internal, parallel, and external reflection. *Action in Teacher Education, 25*(4) 14-19.

Hoy, A. W., & Hoy, W. K. (2003). *Instructional leadership: A learning-centered guide.* Boston, MA: Allyn & Bacon.

Krathwohl, D. R. (2002). A revision of Bloom's taxonomy: An overview. *Theory into Practice, 41*(4), 212-218.

Lever-Duffy, J., McDonald, J. B., & Mizell, A. P. (2005). *Teaching and learning with technology.* (2nd ed.). Boston, MA: Pearson Allyn & Bacon.

Maier, M. H., Panitz, T. (1996). End on a high note: Better endings for classes and courses. *College Teaching, 44*, 145-148.

Milson, A. J., & Brantley, S. M. (1999). Theme-based portfolio assessments in social studies teacher education. *Social Education, 63*(6), 374-377.

Nitko, A. J. (2004). *Educational assessment of students* (4th Ed.). Upper Saddle River, NJ: Pearson/Merrill, Prentice Hall.

Orlich, D. C., Harder, R. J., Callahan, R. C., Gibson, H. W. *Teaching strategies: A guide to better instruction.* (6th ed.). (2001). Boston, MA: Houghton Mifflin Company.

Ray, K. W. (2006). What are you thinking? *Educational Leadership, 64(2)*, 58-62.

Schultz, L. (n.d.). *Bloom's Taxonomy.* Retrieved September 27, 2006 from http://web. odu.edu/educ/llschult/blooms_taxonomy.htm. (n.b. Web site currently inaccessible.)

Stanford, P., Reeves, S. (2005). Assessment that drives instruction. *Teaching Exceptional Children, 37(4).* 18-22.

Stefl-Mabry, J. (2004). Building rubrics into powerful learning assessment tools. *Knowledge Quest, 32(5),* 21-5.

Taylor, C. S., & Nolen, S. B. (2005). *Classroom assessment: Supporting teaching and learning in real classrooms.* Upper Saddle River, NJ: Pearson Prentice Hall.

Woytek, A. (2005). Utilizing assessment to improve student motivation and success. [Electronic version]. *Essays in Education, 14,* 1-6. Retrieved from http:// www.usca.edu/essays/vol142005/woytek.pdf on February 17, 2006.

Zessoules, R., & Gradner, H. (1991). Authentic assessment: Beyond the buzzword and into the classroom. In V. Peronne (Ed.), *Expanding student assessment.* Alexandria, VA: Association of Supervision and Curriculum Development.

Technology Tools and the Assessment Process

Kelly L. Wilkinson
Indiana State University
Terre Haute, Indiana

Assessment is an important key to a successful learning experience. Whether the assessment is informal or formal, it becomes the road map for success in the classroom. The results guide the educator in the right direction to insure productive student learning.

Technology can be the ideal vehicle for obtaining these assessment results. The ability to blend various technology tools within assessment activities allows the educator to match a student's learning style with the appropriate assessment tool. This matching of assessment tool to learning style ensures that the instructor will connect with the student to obtain desired results. Meanwhile, the student will feel comfortable and confident in completing the assessment.

This chapter discusses the topic of student-centered assessment within the context of a technological environment. First, a connection between technology and learning will be established. Next, specific technology tools available for the new "traditional" business education classroom will be discussed. Finally, online assessment issues will be addressed.

CONNECTING TECHNOLOGY AND LEARNING

Assessment is the heart of every educational endeavor and it is important to remember that the student should be the center of all assessment—not teacher or the content being presented, and certainly not the technology used to obtain the assessment information. In this section, the need for student-centered assessment will be established, as well as the practical use of technology in administrating the assessment.

Learner-Centered Assessment

A student-centered assessment philosophy helps educators focus on students' becoming self-directed in learning plans and activities. A self-directed learner is defined as a student who takes responsibility for his or her learning. They then build their own learning process based on their previous knowledge, skills, and/or experiences. The use of constructivist theory or student-centered learning changes the traditional view of teaching and learning. "The student-centered model of learning encourages teachers to view their students as academic partners who work together to produce relevant and meaningful learning experiences," (Muirhead, 2002, p. 2).

Huba and Freed (2000) identified eight key ideas that are the hallmark of learner-centered teaching:

- Learners are actively involved and receive feedback.

- Learners apply knowledge to enduring and emerging issues and problems.

- Learners integrate discipline-based knowledge and general skills.

- Learners understand the characteristics of excellent work.

- Learners become increasingly sophisticated learners and knowers.

- Educators coach and facilitate, intertwining teaching and assessing.

- Educators reveal they are learners too.

- Learning is interpersonal, and all learners—students and educators alike—are respected and valued (p. 33).

Pragmatic Use of Technology

A learner-centered approach makes the student an active participant in the learning process by allowing the learner to inquire and acquire new information and skills in a variety of ways. Learners must seek learning in their own way and be able to discuss what they "discovered" in their own way. Student-centered learning requires the use of a variety of informal and formal assessments to guide both the educator and the student toward educational goals. Technology provides educators with tools to develop alternative, and in some cases, individualized informal and formal assessments that provide needed feedback for students and educators. Online assessment can be the tool to provide prompt, varied, holistic responses to inform both the educator and the learner about the quality of the learning experiences (Muirhead, 2002).

It is important, however, to realize that technology must be used with a purpose. "Simply adding technology to instruction/assessment does not guarantee improved . . . learning," (The University of Texas at Austin, 2003, p. 1). The use of technology for technology's sake is a poor reason for using technology; it can overshadow the reason for the assessment. Russel T. Hurlburt, a professor at University of Nevada, Las Vegas, (UNLV) and an early adopter of technology stated, "If you can't make technology do something better or more convenient than you can do without technology, then you shouldn't do it" (Hurlburt, as cited in Cloud, 1999, p. 20). It is extremely important that educators make a significant connection between technology use, teaching, and student learning. Using technology does not guarantee student learning (The University of Texas at Austin, 2003).

Making the connection between technology use and learning is important. The following guidelines should be considered when adding technology to the assessment process.

- Assessment should be driven by instructional purposes, not by the "razzle-dazzle" of available technology.

- Assessment should reflect a comprehensive concept of learning—technology may only be one component of the learning.

- Assessment should focus on the learning processes as well as the learning outcomes—not all students will benefit from the use of technology.

- Assessment should be an ongoing process—using technology for assessment in informal and formal ways. (The University of Texas at Austin, 2003, p. 3).

Technology can be the bridge that connects students with learning in a student-centered environment. Technology provides the vehicle for students to have a variety of learning opportunities. However, technology usage for assessment must not be the focus. It is important to remember that student learning is the focus for the use of technology.

THE NEW "TRADITIONAL" CLASSROOM

When a student walked into a business classroom twenty years ago, the appearance was not much different than that of a regular classroom. Typewriters were arranged in rows with a book holder on one side, and stacks of paper and containers of "correct-type" sat next to each typewriter. The accounting area was just a row of desks with calculators. Charts with accounting information and those identifying the home row keys were hung around the room. Students sat quietly typing and trying not to make mistakes in their accounting workbooks. Learning was done only by direction of the teacher.

The new "traditional" classroom looks vastly different. A variety of computers sit on tables throughout the room. A large projection screen covers the front of the room. On some tables, several devices that look like remote controls allow students to answer questions that are projected on the large screen. Some students are working together to answer the questions posted on the Smartboard, while others are working on accounting software learning about debits and credits. Still other students are using Web cameras and conferencing software via the Internet to discuss entrepreneurship questions with an expert. In the new traditional classroom, students choose their method of learning by using available technology, whether it be a Smartboard classroom, laptop cart classroom, hybrid classroom, or laboratory classroom.

Classroom with Smartboard

One way a business classroom might look different from the business classroom of 10 years ago is that it contains a Smartboard. One of the more popular tools in the new traditional classroom, a Smartboard allows a large screen to act as a touch-sensitive computer monitor so students can see what the educator is doing while using the computer software. If the educator were entering journal entries into a computerized ledger, the students would see how it is done and also see how account codes and other information are utilized within the software. The educator has the ability to stop during the demonstration and explain the purpose of each action, as the Smartboard shows each step taken.

Classroom with Laptop Cart

The conversion of the traditional classroom into a computer laboratory can be done easily by a laptop cart, which can hold 25 to 30 laptop computers. Each computer can be placed on the cart for recharging. A laptop cart can change any classroom to a lab. This transformation allows students to begin drafting and revising documents during class time, rather than waiting until the student has time to use computers in the library or use the computer at home. This eliminates the concern many educators have regarding student access to computers.

The laptop cart allows an educator to give an online assessment with all students in one location. This can ease educator's concern regarding who is actually completing the assessment.

Hybrid Classroom

Many college courses use a hybrid classroom. This type of classroom is defined as a face-to-face classroom that blends online tools into class content and assessment (Zeliff, 2006). Most of these hybrid classrooms use Blackboard, WebCT, Angel, or other course management software to facilitate discussion, house content, and administer examinations. The benefit of the hybrid course is the use of technology to encourage continued learning beyond the classroom. Students can measure their learning by engaging in informal assessments typically set up as quizzes; by reviewing lectures notes posted as a Word or PowerPoint document; or by engaging in online discussions scheduled at a set time and day regarding course content. Students have the ability to access the content at their convenience.

Laboratory Classroom

Traditional classrooms can be transformed into technology classrooms by adding laptops or by accessing a generic computer laboratory in the school. If the classroom is not available, most schools have labs that can be reserved at specific times for specific uses such as assessment. Utilizing the generic computer lab can provide students with technology interaction by using Web quests (an inquiry based learning activity that uses the Internet as a resource) and other types of activities found on the World Wide Web.

In the new traditional classroom, there are a variety of technology-enhanced learning environments available to allow educators to provide a vast array of assessments used to ascertain student learning. The goal is to match the environment with the desired assessment tool.

INFORMAL ASSESSMENT TOOLS

Informal assessment is one way of measuring student learning and is an important piece in the learning puzzle for educators. These assessments can be used as diagnostic tools to evaluate students' knowledge or skill level about specific content. Using informal assessments during the course of the learning process provides educators with information regarding students' retention of content. This assessment process allows educators to make adjustments during the course. Both uses of informal assessment help educators individualize delivery and content to students who need more help. Online assessment can provide educators efficient ways to perform informal assessments typically used throughout the learning process to gage knowledge or skill retention. Technology in the traditional classroom can help facilitate informal assessment. Common technology tools used for informal assessment are Smartboards, student response systems, Breeze Presenter, simulations, and reinforcement software.

Smartboards

Smartboards can be used to demonstrate a simple skill such as good handwriting or to facilitate a brainstorming or recalling session. One useful application of the Smartboard is to reinforce content in job hunting. An important aspect of job hunting is using good handwriting techniques when completing a job application. Many work places scan job applications into a database for electronic storage. It is imperative that students understand they must have good handwriting to complete a successfully converted application. To evaluate student handwriting, a student should go to the Smartboard and print his or her name. Then, the student draws a box around the name and touches the text conversion button in the box around the name. When the name converts successfully to computer text, the handwriting is appropriate for a job application. If the student does not have a successful conversion of text, the educator may want to have the student practice preparing job applications to improve handwriting before running the Smartboard test again.

Another way of using a Smartboard as an informal assessment tool is to use a wireless keyboard for student input. An educator can place questions in Word, project the question on the board, and then have the students pass the keyboard around the room, inputting an answer when it is his or her turn. Students are put into groups, and a topic is chosen for groups to consider. When one group decides on an answer, the teacher passes the keyboard to the students for them to input their answer. The information the student keys shows up on the Smartboard screen. Each group inputs information as the keyboard is passed from group to group. Students can also correct sentences by using the wireless keyboard. With the combination of both the Smartboard and the wireless keyboard, students can be involved in a class from where they sit, even if no computer is found on the desk.

Student Response Systems

The ability to measure students' understanding of a subject and how comfortable students are in their decisions is not easy to do. Usually an educator has to guess if students are confident in their answers. Student response systems can give educators valuable affective domain feedback. To use this system, students are given what looks like a remote control. On the student response pad are several buttons numbered and labeled with letters. A student's input is captured by a transceiver connected to a computer. Questions used by educators to assess content knowledge are embedded in a PowerPoint presentation used for lecture or in an informal quiz created to see what knowledge was attained and what needs to be readdressed. Students then input their answers, along with feedback on how confident they feel about the answer. The answers are collected and shown on the slide. Results can be saved and reviewed by the educator. If the educator wants to add more questions to the assessment, another slide is created. It is really as easy as creating PowerPoint slides utilizing the embedded plug-in.

Student response systems are usually portable systems. They are easy to use and can be transported from room to room. For college courses, student response system pads can be packaged with textbooks. The student response system works well with large lecture halls. For college professors, a student response system can help with attendance and with informal assessment. The student response system provides the lecture hall professor a way to assess the knowledge and views of a large group of students while allowing the student to see the response of the class as a whole.

One other use of the student response system in large student classes is to assess attendance. When a student purchases his or her own student response pad, the student's name can be imported into the system. Professors who teach in large lecture halls can check for attendance by having all students log in at the beginning of the class. The professor can check the log later for attendance. If students have someone log in for them, the professor can also review the class participation log for the number of responses made by each student. More than likely, the student actually in class will respond to each posed question. The absence of a response log will indicate the student had someone else log them in.

Breeze Presenter

A multi-point software product called Breeze is available. Michael Fitzpatrick, senior product manager for Breeze, explained that with students using Breeze and a computer ". . . an instructor can speak to a class, . . . direct them to fill in answers on a quiz through their desktop browsers, and demonstrate to the students their understanding of learning by showing them their scores or other forms of feedback assessment" (Fitzpatrick, as cited in Babcock, 2005).

Breeze can be used in both informal and formal assessment situations. The use of Breeze in formal assessment will be discussed later in the chapter. The Breeze Presenter option is the part of Breeze that works well as an informal assessment tool.

Breeze Presenter is a plug-in within PowerPoint. An educator can create PowerPoint slides that students can watch any time. The educator creates the slide show by inserting questions. The student answers the question and then receives feedback regarding the answer. If the answer is correct, the student can move through the rest of the slides; if the answer is wrong, more questions can be given to the student to further drill this specific content area. The slides are created when the original Breeze presentation is created. The creator can program the Breeze presentation to generate the extra questions when a gap occurs in correct answers. When the presentation is created, it is published and assigned a URL. The educator provides the URL for the students to use while in the classroom lab or for when the student has access to a laptop.

Simulations

Simulations in education are assessment materials with elements of the real world (Joyce, Weil, & Calhoun, 2000). Typically, simulations are used in assessment to measure a student's baseline ability, to assess knowledge attainment, or to reinforce new content. Computer software makes a simulation an effective tool for educators to use. SAM, an educational testing tool, is used to assess student performance in a variety of computer software. The software creates short "real world" scenarios for students to perform specific tasks using a particular piece of software.

Other types of software can be important informal assessment tools for critical thinking, problem solving, or teamwork. SimCity is software that allows students to create a civilization. It is a tool educators use to observe students' decision-making skills and their ability to articulate their reasons for certain decisions. Students can work individually or in teams. Teamwork within the group can be evaluated by educators who use this software for group work.

Reinforcement Software

Reinforcement software allows students to self-assess and practice their knowledge and skills. This type of software can help a student develop an understanding of his or her current level of topic mastery and provide a foundation from which further learning can be built. Students can develop confidence in their ability to apply their knowledge in a low-stakes atmosphere, where the emphasis is on learning, and not on assessing. Because students are not penalized for their current level of knowledge and will have ample opportunities to expand this knowledge base, this type of technology tool provides a student with motivation to continue learning right up to the actual recorded assessment. Motivation and confidence-building will occur in the student if the instructor keeps these types of software assignments at the low stakes assessment level. If the instructor feels the need to write a grade for the time spent using the software, a defined effort grade using a checklist or rubric may be used, or something as simple as awarding 10 out of 10 points for participating. The following types of software are examples of reinforcement tools.

Drill and practice software. Software applications that accompany textbooks have become an important component for reinforcement of content. Many of these applications can be loaded on a server or accessed from a publisher Web site. Software for specific skills or knowledge reinforcement can include virtual flashcards that teach terms and concepts to be learned, or can be used for drill and practice to improve memorization. The game Hangman strengthens word spellings. For keyboarding, Word Drop or similar software helps teach concepts through repetition or reinforces those already-learned. Word Drop also allows students to focus on specific problems in keyboarding, such as working with numbers or working with letters using the fifth finger. In addition, it can improve hand-eye coordination by providing dexterity games that focus on specific keyboarding skills.

Tutorials. Tutorials are available as stand-alone software and as companion software with textbooks. This type of software can be an important informal assessment tool. At the end of a chapter or unit, a student can work through a tutorial and then take an online assessment to inform the teacher what information the student retained and what information must be revisited.

Some educators use tutorials in the opposite way. These educators use the tutorial as a pretest, gaining insight into what knowledge the student already possesses. This knowledge can allow the instructor to "jump ahead" in teaching the unit if all students already possess a working knowledge of the topic. If just one or two students are missing key concepts or each student is missing a different concept, specific tutorials can be assigned to help develop this knowledge or skill before the final assessment is given. Many of these tutorials are computer generated and automatically grade themselves as they are practiced, leaving time for the instructor to float around the room and provide specific help or encouragement as needed.

Games. Software games can be a creative way to informally assess student learning. Games created specifically for certain content areas can be entertaining and educational. One example of this type of game is Jeopardy for Business. This game can be developed using PowerPoint or can be found on the Internet. Students choose topics and then choose the answer that they think is correct. The game will give them feedback regarding the correctness of their answers.

Another game available both online and in content-specific books is The Stock Market Game. This software game is an effective tool for informal assessment of knowledge of the stock market as well as the measurement of problem-solving and critical-thinking skills. One online site with numerous assessment resources for teaching this topic is *StockQuest* at ttp://investsmart.coe.uga.edu/C001759/.

Informal assessment tools allow learners to demonstrate what they learned in less rigorous settings. These tools allow the educator to make adjustments in the learning environment to suit each student.

FORMAL ASSESSMENT TOOLS
Performing formal assessments online includes more than just the assessment tool; it includes tools that affect grading. Not only does technology provide easier ways of evaluating students, it can provide better and richer feedback to students. The costs of using technology for formal assessment can range from free to very expensive, depending on the commitment of the institution and the educator. Exam generators, application software, screen capture software,

Web-based tools, course management tools, and online conferencing tools are all examples of formal assessment technology.

Exam Generators
Most textbooks for college and secondary courses provide exam generators. These materials can be either electronic test banks that can be "dropped" into a word processing file to create a paper exam, or assessment activities that can be placed into course management tools that will be discussed later in the chapter. Exam generators are software that can create an online exam without having to access the Internet or use a course management tool. These generators can be loaded onto stand-alone computers for students to access a needed exam.

Application Software
Educators can use the Microsoft Word comment function as an assessment tool to provide student feedback. Tracking changes through Word can be a powerful tool to assess student homework, which can be submitted to the instructor electronically for downloading. The educator can highlight areas that need to be changed, as well as insert comments that show as balloons next to the Word document. Comment balloons allow educators to emphasize specific errors that need work and to compliment students on areas of improvement or excellence. The tracking feature allows an educator to follow the revision process of students. Each correction made to a document can be identified by the different color of the type. This is far more effective than the red pen (Gray, 2002). This assessment tool is effective for students in any classroom setting.

Screen Capture Software

Screen capture software can offer comprehensive utilities by recording cursor movements (Larson, 2005). Examples of screen capture software packages are Captivate, Camtasia, Snagit, and Impatica. These programs allow educators to create effective assessments by incorporating auditory and visual feedback. These software packages are relatively inexpensive and easy to use (Hill, 2005).

One practical use for screen capture software is to grade Web sites in a Web design course. Upon loading the Web site, the educator would "turn on" Captivate or Camtasia and then begin "talking" to the student about his or her Web site. While the educator discusses positive and negative aspects of the Web site, the software records the instructor's voice. If the student has a great flash file embedded in his or her Website, the educator can capture the action of the embedded file and the initial reaction of the educator regarding the student's Web site. If the educator finds a Web link that does not work, the software will capture the comments and the action of the educator clicking on the inactive link. Not only do the students hear the comment, they can see the result of the action by the educator. The captured video, along with a rubric, serves as feedback for the students (Wilkinson, Crews, & Hemby, 2005). The feedback given to the student is richer, since the student receives not only the rubric, but also a flash file of the captured actions and comments.

Course Management Tools

Several tools on the Internet can aid in assessment for both K-12 educators and higher education professionals. These tools range from course management tools such as Web-based assessments sold without curriculum content to Web-based assessments aligned with curriculum, to WebCT and Blackboard (Doe, 2004).

An example of a Web-based assessment sold without curriculum is Questionmark. The company produces software that creates a variety of assessment activities, including quizzes, surveys, and tests. These tools can be used for both informal and formal assessments and are prevalent in both higher education and K-12 because, "as connections and speed improve, the Internet's flexibility, accessibility, potential capacity for paper reduction, potential for superior data collection, analysis, reporting capacities, and potential reductions in cost makes [Web-based tools] very attractive" (Doe, 2004, p. 1). With state and federal agencies clamoring for solid data for accountability, Web-based tools become a vehicle to meet data requirements. These tools can provide multiple assessment activities and will collect the data over time as well as produce the results in report format. Examples of course management tools that are Web-based include examination engines, discussion boards, online journals, and informal online assessment.

Examination engines. Course management tools allow educators to do a variety of assessments using one software package. Primarily used by higher education institutions, course management tools such as WebCT and Blackboard have examination engines that allow educators to develop an exam with multiple choice, true/false, short answer, or essay questions. Educators can set the perimeters of the exam by programming a set time the exam is available, setting a password for exam access, limiting the completion time, scrambling questions and answers, and setting IP addresses. Setting the IP address for the exam will allow the exam to be taken at specific computers. If the IP address of the computer does not match the IP address programmed for the exam, access is blocked. The exam can be programmed to grade itself so students receive immediate feedback and teachers find an automatically posted score in the gradebook. Although course management exams can be taken at any computer, most educators administer them in a proctored setting. Web management exams can be given in a computer lab classroom or by using laptops in a traditional classroom.

Discussion boards. Discussion boards within course management tools can be used in both informal and formal assessments. Although students are in a classroom setting, using the discussion board may make some students more comfortable when expressing their opinions and asking questions. This technique can aid in assessing all students' knowledge. Parameters must be established as to what constitutes an appropriate posting on a discussion board, so educators must have some guidelines on how students should respond. An example would be the requirement that discussion postings must be in complete sentences, and that using phrases such as "I agree" and "that is right" don't constitute a complete posting.

Online journals. One new module that is a part of Blackboard is a journaling feature. Educators can use this module for formal assessment by asking students to discuss specific questions from a course or their opinions and feelings about subject matter, including problems with instruction or lack of understanding about content (Meyen, Aust, and Issacson, 2002). Students can reflect on what was covered in class and educators can read those reflections to gauge curriculum adjustments. Educators may want to use blogs as a way to encourage students to write. Blogs can be done without the need for specific software and would function in the same manner as online journals.

Other online assessments. Many K-12 educators do not have course management tools to use, but there are products that can provide some of the same assessment tools as WebCT and Blackboard. Web-based assessment products that are not closely aligned tend to have a narrow focus. They provide an online environment that allows educators to develop online activities with teacher-provided content. Sites such as Digital Teacher and Quiz Web allow instructors to create assessment activities such as puzzles, games, flash cards, and online exams. Neither product supplies content, but both provide templates for different assessment tools (Doe, 2005).

Most textbook publishers provide Web-based assessment tools as a complement to their textbooks. These tools usually include examination generators with questions tied to content already embedded in the generator.

Online Conferencing Tools

Online conferencing tools such as Centra or Breeze have transformed online education by creating an interactive bridge between students and the instructor, and among students themselves (Wilkinson, Crews, & Hemby, 2005). These tools can also be used in the traditional classroom to develop unique assessment activities.

Breeze Meeting is a part of the Breeze software package that allows multiple participants to interact. Using a Web camera and a headset with a microphone, students can see, talk, and listen to each other. Breeze also allows document sharing, white board utilization, and participant polling to ensure everyone understands the content. Another feature that makes Breeze attractive is that any session can be recorded and published to a URL for further review. These packages provide interaction and conversation in synchronous and asynchronous formats (Wilkinson, Crews, & Hemby, 2005). Synchronous interaction is communication in real time while asynchronous interaction is communication at various times convenient for the student/educator.

One interesting assessment project is the mock interview. Students submit their resumes to a person posing as a prospective employee, and then schedule an interview with the employer. The interview is conducted through Breeze Meeting and is recorded. After the interview, the student and the interviewer use Breeze to view the recorded interview together and discuss what was done well and what needs improvement. Students will be able to evaluate their own performances and compare their assessments with the interviewer's assessment.

Breeze Meeting is also an effective tool to use for student journaling. Students can create a video diary to discuss issues regarding a course or a subject. The student can load a paper into Breeze Meeting and discuss the paper. One practical application of this tool would be its use during internships, where journaling is often a requirement. Interns could be required to keep a video diary throughout the internship. Students would get questions regarding the internship workplace to address in an entry each week. When a student returned to campus, the internship coordinator and the student could review the diary and debrief about the experience. This activity can be an important assessment tool for internships and a conduit between work and academics.

Technical formal assessment tools run the gamut from simple exam generators to complex Web-based tools. Depending upon the time, space, and money available to the instructor, any number of these technical assessment tools could be used in a course.

ISSUES WITH ONLINE ASSESSMENT

Issues can arise with online assessment that must be considered. "Technological difficulty" is an occurrence that always seems to arise even with the best planning. Computers crash, connections become slow, and software fails; contingency plans must be in place for such emergencies. A byproduct of these difficulties can be the lack of confidence in students who may not be computer savvy. Be aware of these students and understand that their anxiety has foundations (Olt, 2002).

Another issue for online assessment is the time for planning and implementation. Using online assessment takes time. For the traditional classroom this may include planning for use of technology, as well as for planning for the process and for the implementation. Questions such as: "Are there available labs?" and "Is the laptop cart available for that day?" have to be addressed ahead of time.

Yet another interesting issue is the lack of respect among some educators for having traditional coursework conveyed online. Those educators, administrators, students, and other stakeholders who have some distrust of technology can create a negative perception of online assessment (Rowe, 2004). Others view the use of computer evaluation as busywork more than true assessment. Consequently, students might think of the assessment as a game and not take the assessment as seriously as they would a traditional assessment.

SUMMARY

Technology can be an ideal vehicle to provide informal and formal assessments within the student-centered environment. The new "traditional" classroom setting can be a model setting for utilizing technology for the benefit of students. Educators must strive to create a meaningful individual and collaborative environment of learning regardless of the type of classroom setting. Online assessment requires creativity and planning by the educator. There are a variety of technology tools available from software applications to Web sites that generate activities. Some tools are used by the student for assessment of learning, and other tools are used by the educators to provide better feedback to students. The adaptability of technology allows educators to use technology for the benefit of students in a variety of environments

Using technology tools can be a way to provide students with "real world" experiences within an assessment situation. These technology tools also provide educators an opportunity to assess soft skills such as problem solving and critical thinking that are sometimes hard to evaluate or overlooked in the evaluation processing when using traditional assessment methods. Continued exploration of the use of technology for assessment purposes will benefit students and educators.

REFERENCES

Abbott, L., Siskovic, H., Hogues, V., & Williams, J.G. (2000). *Learner assessment in multimedia instruction: Considerations for the instructional designer* (ERIC Document Reproduction Service No. ED444516)

Babcock, C. (2005). Macromedia says coordinating voice and visual presentations online is a breeze. *Information Week*. Retrieved September 18, 2005, from http://www.informationweek.com/shared/printale.ArticleSrc.jhtml?articleID=1621004842.html

Cloud, B. (1999). Entering the virtual classroom. *UNLV Magazine.* 7(9) Retrieved on November 8, 2005 from http://magazine .unlv.edu/Issues/Spring99/Virtual.html.

Doe, C. (2004). A Look at . . . Web-based assessment. *InfoToday,* 11(2) Retrieved on November 10, 2005 from http://www.infotoday.com/MMSchools/mar04/doe.shtml.

Doe, C. (2005). A Look at . . . Web-based assessments *MultiMedia & Internet@Schools,* 12(3), 10-14.

Gray, R. (2002). Assessing students' written projects. *New Directions for Teaching and Learning,* 91, 37-42.

Hill, J. (2005, Mar). Screen-capture to go. *Presentations,* 19(3) 36-40.

Huba, M.E., & Freed, J.E. (2000). *Learner-centered assessment on college campuses: Shifting the focus from teaching to learning.* Boston, MA: Allyn & Bacon.

Joyce, B., Weil, M., & Calhoun, E. (2000). *Models of teaching.* Boston, MA: Allyn & Bacon.

Larson, H. (2005). Captivate me. *T + D,* 59(6). 74.

Meyen, E.L., Aust, R.J., Issacson, R. (2002). Assessing and monitoring student progress in e-learning personnel preparation environment. *Teacher Education and Special Education.* 25(2) 187-198.

Muirhead, B. (2002). Relevant assessment strategies for online colleges & universities. *USDLA Journal 16*(2). [Online] Retrieved on January 30, 2006 from http://www. usdla.org/html/journal/feb02_issue/article04.html.

Olt, M.R. (2002). Ethics and Distance Education: Strategies for minimizing academic dishonesty in online assessment. [Electronic version]. *Online Journal of Distance Learning Administration,* 5(3). Retrieved on November 10, 2005 from http://www. westga.edu/%7Edistance/ojdla/fall53/olt53.html.

Rowe, N.C. (2004). Cheating in online student assessment: Beyond plagiarism. [Electronic version]. *Online Journal of Distance Learning Administration,* 7(2). Retrieved on November 10, 2005 from http://www.westga.edu/%7Edistance/ojdla/ summer72/rowe72.html.

The University of Texas at Austin, Division of Instructional Innovation and Assessment (2003). . *The University of Texas at Austin,* Retrieved January 30, 2006 from http://www.utexas.edu/academic/diia/assessment/iar/resources/best_practices/ index.php.

Wilkinson, K.L., Crews, T.B. & Hemby, K.V. (2005). Assessment tools for e-instructors, *Journal of Applied Research for Business Instruction,* 3(2), 1-4.

Zeliff, N.D. (2006). Business education methods – a splendid blended course. *Business Education Forum,* 60(3), 54-56.

Online Learning and Assessment Solutions

Dale W. Maeder

University of California Extension, Los Angeles

Los Angeles, California

Web-based instruction is here; in fact, it is everywhere. And from every indication, distance learning assessment appears to be on the cutting edge of online education. Educators are beginning to address in earnest the reliability, validity, appropriateness, and authenticity of rating student learning, measuring program effectiveness, and evaluating technology performance in the Web-based learning environment. This chapter will emphasize the emerging role of assessment in the delivery of instruction from remote locations, specifically addressing distance learning assessment issues, online assessment tools, aspects of security and authentication of test takers, alternative online assessment strategies, and evaluation of online student participation.

DISTANCE LEARNING ASSESSMENT ISSUES

All measurement is imprecise, partly because it is difficult to accurately measure an intended outcome and partly because assessment involves measuring people who are, to a large degree, also imprecise. Moreover, an evaluation that confers an online graduate degree or certificate obviously has much more at stake than an informal self-check in the middle of an online lecture. The purpose of the assessment is closely tied to expected learning outcomes and reliability, i.e., how consistently the online assessment measures what students are expected to know or do. The stakes of subsequent decisions involve validity, i.e., how well inferences based on online assessment results reflect past performances and predict future ones. Table 1 (Maeder, 2004) lists 14 distance learning assessment issues, four of which can be addressed more thoroughly by online instructional designers than by their face-to-face counterparts.

Table 1. *Distance Learning Assessment Issues*
What exactly is the purpose of the particular assessment in question?
What are the stakes of the decisions made as the result of the assessment?
Specifically, what will the students be expected to know or do?
How well will they be expected to know course content or perform skills?
Will students be compared to each other (or past groups) or held to a predetermined standard?
How flexible is the evaluation standard, i.e., will students help set the evaluation standard?
Will the assessment be a learning event, i.e., will students learn new concepts/skills during the assessment?
Does the assessment occur transparently or are students aware that formal measurement is taking place?
Which assessment formats are best suited for the students and the subject matter?
From where will sample assessment items be drawn, e.g., past exams, content experts, students?
How is the assessment type selected appropriate to the media of the online course?
What evidence will be collected to demonstrate authentic authorship during assessment?
What evidence will be collected concerning the assessment's reliability in measuring student learning, program effectiveness, and technological performance?
What evidence will be collected concerning the validity of inferences drawn as a result of the assessment?

First, conducting a formal assessment transparently, i.e., without student awareness that evaluative data is being collected, is a tricky arrangement in the traditional classroom. The on-campus instructor can collect informal data concerning student performance; but when reliable, formal assessments are conducted, the assessment is usually done overtly with full student awareness. The tools available to the online instructor provide more options with respect to assessment transparency, e.g., the instructor can check the Web-based course statistics function to ascertain how many students read a lecture, completed a self-check, or visited related links.

Second, an online assessment's format can more closely match the subject matter to the students' learning preferences. Online assessments can be proctored or not proctored, timed or not timed, taken once only or set up for retesting, automatically scored, and designed for any assessment format from forced-choice to open-ended items. Based on the purpose of the assessment and stakes of the decisions, the online instructor can create a Web-based assessment that most closely approximates the authentic nature of the skill or knowledge being measured. For example, in an Introduction to e-Trading course, in which each student is given a mock portfolio of stocks and bonds, students can be assessed by how well they conduct online transactions with a hypothetical broker using actual marketplace data.

Third, since online assessments can be delivered as text, audio, graphics, or video, the online instructor can design the most appropriate assessment that matches the online course media. An International Marketing online course is not relegated to a final exam containing textbook multiple-choice items and dated or fictitious case studies. With Web access, current assessment items of any media type that match student interests can be selected and easily updated or verified.

Fourth, the issue of authentic authorship in an online assessment, practically meaningless in an ungraded self-check, is critical in a Master's thesis or qualifying exam. Security measures to ensure that online assessments are password protected and free of plagiarism will be discussed in more detail in the third section of this chapter.

Although some assessment issues are addressed differently when teaching from a distance, namely, transparency, matching students' learning preferences and course media, and authentic authorship, all online measurement efforts are still guided by the purpose of the assessment and the stakes of the decisions made as a result.

ONLINE ASSESSMENT TOOLS

Most Web-based courses are conducted in a course management system (CMS), a Web-based application program that functions as a complete online course environment (e.g., Blackboard, AngelLearning, GradeSource, Moodle, LearningLynx). Within the CMS, students take timed exams, complete surveys, and submit assignments without leaving the course Web site. With the basic test-related functionality handled automatically by the CMS, exams are time-released, password-secure, copy-protected, shut down, scored, and analyzed.

Using stand-alone assessment packages may make sense if the costs and complexity of complete course management systems are not needed, or if specific features of the assessment package lie outside of what the CMS can provide. Furthermore, recent research in the field of latent semantic analysis suggests that text-analysis software can be an effective tool to grade student writing. Nevertheless, all assessment software should be carefully evaluated before deciding which assessment tool is best suited for the online classroom.

Stand-Alone Assessment Software

Stand-alone assessment packages serve three purposes. They reduce the time and cost in developing and maintaining Web-based assessment tools. Second, they exist for institutions that want to augment traditional on-campus courses or in-house training programs with this kind of functionality. Third, an assessment package can be added to distance learning courses that primarily function through e-mail discussion complemented by news groups or mailing lists.

Stand-alone assessment packages can be used to turn any Web server into a survey, test, tutorial, or assessment server. Examples include TestPilot, QuestionMark, ExamView, Respondus, QuizMaker, Web@ssessor, QuizCenter, MicroTest III, and Tutorial Gateway. Most are downloadable for a fee but require no knowledge of programming language. Assessment styles include true/false, yes/no questions, check all that apply, matching, rearrangement, multiple choice, jumbled-sentence, crossword, fill-in-the-blank, and essay. Assessment options include automatic scoring, downloadable scores, survey questions with automatic statistical analysis, seamless integration with course management systems, selectable point awards for each user response, mathematical formula handling with random variables, customizable item feedback, score-based branching to remedial or advanced material, random question selection, and use of image, audio, video, streaming Internet media, and MIDI music. Free versions offer short-term availability or significantly reduced functionality.

Software applications to create, deploy, and analyze online surveys are valuable tools when measuring program effectiveness or evaluating technology performance, e.g., Zoomerang and FreeOnlineSurveys. In addition, most course management systems put in place a pre-course survey (e.g., "Is Online Learning For Me?") to alert potential students to study skills required in Web-based education or training. Finally, VARK – Video-Audio-Read/Write-Kinesthetic – (Fleming & Mills, 1992; Fleming, 2003) is an example of a questionnaire that provides free learning preference profiles to match potential participants with distance learning environments.

Text-Analysis Software

Considerable progress has been made in *latent semantic analysis* (LSA) research (Landauer, Foltz, & Laham, 1998; Foltz, Gilliam, & Kendall, 2000; Wolfe & Goldman, 2003). Software that analyzes and grades student writing is partly based on text-recognition, i.e., the algorithm checks for expected terms and phrases from domain-representative text input by the instructor. Such software also grades the syntax in the essay by looking for sentences that incorporate more complex sequences of thought, e.g., transition words, prepositional and adverbial phrases, use of analogies and metaphors.

LSA computer-determined essay grades are based on content rather than style and have been found to correlate as well with grades assigned by human experts as the expert scores correlate with one another (Landauer et al., 1998; Laham, 2003; Wolfe &

Goldman, 2003), suggesting a combination of the two for reliability and validity purposes. Two automated essay scoring systems are the Intelligent Essay Assessor and BETSY, (Bayesian Essay Test Scoring sYstem).

Evaluating Online Assessment Software

Regardless of whether the online assessment software is stand-alone or supported by an entire classroom management system, software evaluation should be conducted across eight dimensions (Maeder, 2005) as listed in Table 2.

Table 2. *Evaluation Criteria*	
Dimension	**Evaluation Criteria**
Versatility	Is the online assessment software best suited for rating student learning, measuring program effectiveness, evaluating technology performance, or all three?
Adaptability	How well can the resource be adapted to fit various academic disciplines and types of assessment styles?
Scope	How comprehensive is the software at collecting and evaluating survey data concerning student performance, course content, course instructor, course grading system, logon success, technical support, software ease of use, orientation, etc.?
Responsiveness	What types of test analysis is provided, (scoring, grading, statistics, or performance tracking data), and what type of feedback is provided during and after the assessment?
Flexibility	What types of multimedia can this assessment tool accommodate?
Security	What types of security controls does it employ?
Availability	What is the cost or prerequisite training for using this resource?
Suitability	What types of online courses or training situations are most likely to benefit from this particular assessment resource?

Consider two stand-alone assessment software packages previously mentioned: QuestionMark and Zoomerang. The former is designed to rate student learning and gets high scores across the adaptability, responsiveness, flexibility, security, and suitability dimensions. The latter is limited to survey data collection, scoring high marks in scope, responsiveness, and security. In a review of more than 30 different Web-based assessment tools, Zhang, Khan, Gibbons, and Ni (2001) note that (a) every assessment package has some, but not all, of the aforementioned styles and options, (b) Web-based testing systems always have to face the difficulty of authentication, and (c) tools for the development of performance-based assessments still lag behind tools for the development of objective item-type assessments.

Prerequisites for Selecting Online Assessment Tasks

Effective assessment in distance learning occurs when the online task is necessary, fair, authentic, and matched to intended student learning outcomes. Based on the knowledge, skills, and dispositions identified when the course was designed, the distance learning instructor selects the appropriate online assessment tasks after consulting with past tests, textbooks, other instructors, national standards, databases, etc. Table 3 (Maeder, 2004) lists six issues to consider when choosing an online assessment task.

Table 3. *Selecting the Online Assessment Task*
Does the task match a specific intended student outcome, i.e., is the task *necessary*?
Does the task adequately represent the content or skill, i.e., is the task *sufficient*?
Does the task allow students to demonstrate their progress and capabilities, i.e., is the task *fair*?
Does the task involve real-world situations, i.e., is the task *authentic*?
Does the task measure several types of cognitive, metacognitive, affective, or social goals, i.e., is the task *multidimensional*?
Does the task lend itself to other curriculum domains, i.e., is the task *interdisciplinary*?

Ideally, every assessment, from a quick self-check within an online lecture to a term paper or final exam, should satisfy these six conditions. For example, in a Real Estate Marketing Analysis online course that is part of a real estate certificate program, participants' term papers, 10,000-word analyses of the recent real estate boom in the Coachella Valley, are ranked and scored. This assessment authentically and fairly reflects the competitive nature of the real estate business world: success in one environment will hopefully transfer to success in the other. The course's follow-up assignment, revising the paper following instructor and peer critiques to create a frequently-asked-questions (FAQ) Web site for potential real estate clients, addresses the remaining issues of sufficiency, multidimensionality, and interdisciplinary domains.

With respect to an entire online course's assessment plan, consider an Introduction to Online Entrepreneurship course in which participants contract for their grades based on the following system: *C* grade – participants complete all the class activities, visit all of the links from the course outline, and maintain a weekly journal exploring resources available to small businesses; *B* grade – participants complete all the work for the *C* grade and also compare and contrast the business plans and marketing strategies of two Web-based businesses in their field of interest; *A* grade – participants complete all of the work for the *B* grade and also produce a preliminary business and marketing plan specific to their field of interest. *C* grade assessments are necessary, but not sufficient; *B* grade assessments add more authentic and multidimensional aspects; and *A* grade assessments come closest to addressing all six issues.

While course management systems often contain sufficient assessment tools for most online courses, stand-alone assessment software programs also fill an important need: some uniquely augment CMS assessment options (e.g., text-analysis software, online surveys), while others efficiently and economically meet assessment needs in courses that are not part of a course management system. An online assessment package should therefore be evaluated according to its versatility, adaptability, scope, responsiveness, flexibility, security, availability, and suitability. An online assessment task should be selected based upon whether it is necessary, fair, and authentic.

ASPECTS OF SECURITY AND AUTHENTICATION OF TEST TAKERS

Reliability in distance learning assessment refers to at least two types of consistency: *within the assessment* – checking to see if the test taker responds similarly to items measuring the same construct; and *from assessment to assessment* – checking to see if the test taker performs similarly on multiple assessments over time, measuring the same set of constructs. Since validity refers to how well inferences based on assessment results reflect past performances and predict future ones, increased reliability represents evidence of increased validity. In online courses, more so than in on-campus courses, verifying authorship, detecting plagiarism, and minimizing cheating play large roles in collecting evidence of reliability.

Verifying Online Authorship

Determining online authorship of an individual assessment or even an entire body of coursework may not be relevant if the stakes of the decisions are low or if student motivation to learn is high. Many of the online authorship issues are quite similar to those in on-campus courses. Nevertheless, the growing field of biometrics offers a number of ways to check students' cyber-IDs at the virtual classroom door.

Optical fingerprint recognition software, e.g., SecuGen's EyeD Mouse II and Digital Persona.com, enables a fingerprint scanner embedded into a mouse or via a separate USB-port device. Voice authentication systems, e.g., Nuance Verifier, provide secure access to sensitive information over the telephone. Multibiometric security technology companies, e.g., Identix, offer fingerprint and facial technologies for large-scale ID-management programs. Online signature systems, e.g., Cyber-SIGN, securely authenticate online identity by evaluating the shape, speed, stroke, pressure, and timing information to create a trusted electronic signature.

Biometric system applications (e.g., BNX Systems) provide a software solution: a centrally managed authentication server supporting both Windows and Web-based environments where any type of biometric device (fingerprint, voice, face, iris, signature, USB token, and password authentication) can be recognized. The software provides detailed reports (e.g., successful and failed logon attempts), making it a valuable security resource for high-stakes Web-based assessment (e.g., timed final exams). While no system is foolproof, recognition systems, available in the $50-200 per user price range, are advisable.

Detecting Online Plagiarism and Cheating

Issues of academic integrity take many forms, the most publicized of which is plagiarism. There are Web-based resources that will check and compare writing styles to previous essays and to classmates' essays such as Turnitin.com, Plagiarism.org, Essay Verification Engine (EVE), and IntegriGuard. These programs take a single document or an entire class of term papers, scan the Internet, cross reference the entire set for any signs of intellectual thievery, and provide originality reports detailing the findings of the search.

Although there are many software detection services available to detect plagiarism, the systematic and scientific detection of cheating on online multiple-choice tests has received less attention. Assessment Systems Corporation's Integrity is a secure online application designed to look for patterns in answers to forced-choice tests, provide detailed information regarding the performance of multiple-choice test items, and conduct advanced collusion detection analyses.

Minimizing Online Cheating

Hudspeth (1997), Olt (2002), and McMurtry (2001) suggest a number of strategies, as compiled in Table 4, so that the temptation to cheat in Web-based courses can be minimized.

Table 4. *Minimizing Online Cheating*
Identify the disadvantages of academic dishonesty.
Design effective assessments with specific goals and instructions.
Rotate the curriculum to include original assessment.
Institute and thoroughly review an academic integrity/dishonesty policy.
Know what's available online before assigning a paper.
Give students enough time to do an assignment.
Design the course with clearly stated outcomes perceived by the learner as useful and desirable.
Make sure that the assignments are judged by the learner as relevant, and that the assignment resources are available and current.
Make sure that help is available.
Test everything in advance.
Give learners some control over what and how they learn, e.g., examples, non-examples, nice-to-know material, support.
Provide some type of feedback or acknowledgement within 24 hours.
Provide progress indicators so that learners know how far they've come and where they're headed.

The array of assessments in a Web-based course should be diverse, addressing cognitive, affective, and (perhaps) motor skills, and include open-ended items. Hudspeth (1997) also notes that the conventional notion of a learner contract, held between the facilitator and the participant, may prove to be a useful mechanism for making the transition from face-to-face courses to distance learning. The contract proposes what the facilitator and participant agree to do, such as required assignments, optional coursework, special activities or projects, and any grading system requirements. Su (2005) suggests that all distance learning programs should educate participants about what constitutes plagiarism and require completion of a short plagiarism detection training module. Finally, it makes sense to collect evidence more than once when assessing an important concept or skill, since multiple measures bring more data; more data brings increased reliability.

To collect evidence of reliability in online assessment – and therefore to collect evidence of valid assessment decisions – Web-based instructors now have many tools and strategies to verify online authorship and to detect and minimize online plagiarism and cheating.

ALTERNATIVE ONLINE ASSESSMENT STRATEGIES

Assessment items are often categorized by the complexity of the problem-solving skill underlying them; true/false items require simple recognition, for example, while case-based analyses require extensive problem solving. Fortunately, the distance learning instructor has additional assessment options to address the issue of answer construction. An alternative way to schematize the various types of test items available to online instructors is to organize them into four categories – standardized, simple completion, complex completion, and presentation – according to the constraint exerted on the nature and extent of the student's response (Snow, 1993).

Scratch-Off Test: An Alternative to Standardized Assessment Items

Category A, *standardized*, contains test items in which only one solution is correct. As discussed in this chapter's second section, Web-based assessment software can quickly create, administer, score, and provide feedback for forced-choice items to efficiently collect evidence of mastery in low-stakes assessment situations (e.g., self-checks, quizzes). Note too that a standardized item's high degree of constraint does not preclude answer construction, nor does it eliminate complex problem solving, which may be required by many multiple-choice tasks.

A new development in multiple-choice testing now allows for partial credit and instant feedback. Epstein's (2003) Immediate Feedback Assessment Technique, or IF-AT Scratch-Off Test, (motto: "IF-AT first you don't succeed, try, try again"), provides immediate corrective or affirming feedback to students for each answer and permits the allocation of partial credit for a student's second or later selection when the first selection is incorrect. The computer records which answer choice is selected first, second, third, etc., until the correct response is selected. An optional extension is a

Web-based version of Davis' (1993) *test insurance page*, where test takers can purchase a clue to a problem and have points deducted from their score. A simpler variation to scratch-off testing is the *multiple-choice justification exam* (Maeder, 2005). Test takers receive half-credit for selecting the desired response and an additional half-credit for correctly justifying their answer choice. Test takers might have the right reasoning but the wrong choice (due to carelessness) or the right answer without a satisfactory justification (due to guessing).

Test-Correction Tactic: An Alternative to Simple Completion Assessment Items

In Category B, *simple completion*, a one-word or one-number solution is generated by the student. Web-based assessment software can easily be programmed to accept various acceptable versions of a forced-choice item. Examples include substitution, simple completion, and simple problem solving.

If the results of an online assessment do not meet expectations, students can be asked to correct their tests back up to 100%. Three scoring options are (a) allow the test score to be raised no higher than 89% (or the equivalent of a B+ grade); (b) average the student's original test score with the corrected one; and (c) count it as extra credit. The *test-correction tactic* can also be conducted collaboratively by pairing lower test scorers with higher ones. Transcripts of online chats and e-mails can be submitted to the instructor to provide additional evidence of authenticity of each student's contributions. The incentive for online students to complete this activity is real, and the class does not move on until sufficient mastery has been demonstrated by all concerned.

Bid Tests and Vignettes: Alternatives to Complex Completion Assessment Items

Category C, *complex completion*, involves the construction of a total unit by the student. More open-ended than the first two categories, complex completion requires answer construction by the test taker, rather than answer recognition. Traditional examples include short-answer essays and complex problem solving.

An addition to the complex completion category is the *bid test* as a way to assess student performance over a large body of course content. Students download a packet of problems (usually 25) to be solved on their own during a one- or two-week period, after which they submit a document numbered 1-25, indicating the problem numbers that they wish to remove from consideration. The number of problems that remain when divided by 25 constitutes their *bid* score for the test, e.g., a student who chooses to remove problems #3, 12, and 21 bids 22/25, or 88%.

When the bid test is administered, each student is given a unique selection of five problems chosen from each student's amended list of problems, (in the above example, the five problems selected could not include #3, 12, or 21). Each student's set of five problems is graded very carefully. The test score is the product of the percentage the student receives on the five problems and the bid, e.g., if all five problems are solved correctly, 100% • 88 = 88%; if four out of five problems are solved correctly, 80% • 88 = 70%. Bid tests promote process over product, collect evidence of students' sense of self-efficacy, and cover a significant amount of content.

A recently researched type of short-answer essay is the *vignette assessment task.* Vignettes are defined as "incomplete short stories that are written to reflect, in a less complex way, real-life situations in order to encourage discussions and potential solutions to problems where multiple solutions are possible" (Jeffries & Maeder, 2004, p. 20). The five criteria in the vignette definition are (a) it is a story; (b) it is under 200 words; (c) it simplifies a real-life situation in which no participant is likely to have expertise; (d) its set of tasks are directly connected to a scoring rubric; and (e) it is purposely incomplete, either requiring problem solving when the plot line stops at a critical juncture or analysis when the story's details are omitted so that multiple interpretations can be defended (Jeffries & Maeder, 2006).

Vignettes can be used as effective online instructional tasks to promote discussion as well as reliable online assessment tasks to rate student learning (Jeffries & Maeder, 2004; 2006). While standardized assessments primarily collect evidence of recognition and simple completion items essentially collect evidence of recall, vignette assessment tasks reliably collect evidence of recognition, recall, and transfer (Jeffries & Maeder, 2006). Coupled with a well-defined scoring guide, online vignette assessment tasks are not only highly correlated with more traditional forms of online assessment, but the open-ended nature of the assignment and the emphasis on justification and defense using course content produce unique responses and make online authenticity much easier to verify.

Web-Based Portfolio: An Alternative to Presentation Assessment Items

Category D, *presentation*, represents the highest degree of student construction of assessment response in the online environment. Also classified as *authentic* or *performance-based assessment*, these tasks are intended to replicate the challenges and standards of performance that typically face members of a professional discipline. Therefore, the tasks are highly contextualized, often require collaboration, presuppose an audience (e.g., a panel of judges), and require human judgment during evaluation. When the student performance is delivered under real or simulated conditions, e.g., teach-back procedure, demonstration, or term project, the manner of performance is just as much a part of the assessment as the final product.

A *Web-based portfolio*, also known as a *webfolio*, *e-portfolio*, or *process-portfolio*, is a Web-based collection over time of a selected class of constructed responses most closely associated with assessing a particular construct or set of constructs (Barrett, 2005). While portfolios have been widely recognized as authentic assessment, webfolios add an additional component in that they integrate technology into the curriculum. Webfolios not only provide students and faculty with access to the most current resources available through the Web, but also foster collaborative efforts among students, faculty, and practitioners as they share ideas and resources during the process of portfolio development, when students need them, rather than at the end of portfolio completion (Kim, 1999).

Webfolios have four purposes: *review* – to indicate content mastery; *growth* – to indicate progressive development; *showcasing* – to present evidence of quality work; and *presentation* – to deliver items to a specific audience. Consider an Ethics for Human Resource Professionals online course in which the final assessment task is a webfolio collection of sample coursework drawn from vignette-based quizzes, case studies, reflective responses to peer critiques, an ethics code handbook (group project), and a term paper. Each student creates a portfolio cover sheet describing the purpose of the collection and the criteria for the selection of samples, as well as a scoring rubric and a final reflective essay concerning the webfolio assignment. In this example, the student selects the samples to be included in the webfolio and assigns weights to the individual components in the scoring guide, perhaps subject to mini-mum requirements set by the online instructor. In effect, the student and the instruc-tor share the responsibility of evaluation.

Web-based assessment options include all those from traditional education as well as unique variations tailor-made for the digital learning environment, e.g., scratch-off tests, test-correction tactic, bid tests, and vignettes. Web-based portfolios shift the target of assessment so that instructors *and* students rate student performances, providing an opportunity for students to experience the synergy of collaboration rather than the competitiveness experienced during examinations or the isolation often felt in distance learning classes.

EVALUATION OF ONLINE STUDENT PARTICIPATION

Evaluation of student participation is a critical consideration in online assessment that is both formative (ongoing) and summative (end of unit or course). Fortunately, most online course platforms have some sort of history function that allows the facilitator to determine how often the student took part in the course. A point-system for calculating the discussion component of the course grade is easy to implement and justify: one point for brief comments; two points for more detailed responses; and three points for well-developed responses that indicated serious thinking by consider-ing other perspectives or raising new issues. Students typically receive a minimum number of participation points for completing coursework and a graduated point scale is used to rank students' participation credit. Evaluating online student participation may also involve student reflection and peer feedback as well as strategies to incorpo-rate a participation component as part of the grading for an online course.

Student Reflection and Peer Feedback

Although evaluating student work in a well-designed, learner-centered course is less likely to involve the problem of online student cheating (Palloff & Pratt, 1999), online students should still be asked to reflect on course objectives. It is important to reassure online students that their responses to formative and summative evaluations are collected and interpreted only as a group by sending them to a neutral site to preserve anonymity, for example. If an assignment is completed collaboratively, individuals can reflect on the group's performance as well as individual performances of assigned tasks, which may assist the instructor in assigning group and individual grades for online small-group work.

Incorporating a Participation Component

Consider an Introduction to Accounting online course with six 20-point assignments, six 25-point quizzes, a 100-point midterm, and a 100-point final exam. Table 5 illustrates five course grading systems, each one with an additional participation component.

Table 5. *Grading Systems with a Participation Component*

Assessment	Plan A		Plan B		Plan C		Plan D		Plan E	
	Pts	%	Pts	%	Pts	%	Pts	%	Pts	%
Assignments (6)	120	24%	600	40%	50	~13%	120	12%	120	20%
Quizzes (6)	150	30%	600	40%	50	~13%	150	15%	150	25%
Midterm	100	20%	100	~7%	100	25%	250	25%	120	20%
Final Exam	100	20%	100	~7%	100	25%	350	35%	150	25%
Participation	30	6%	100	~7%	100	25%	130	13%	60	10%
Total	500	100%	1500	100%	400	100%	1000	100%	600	100%

Note in Plan A that the weight of each assessment is unchanged from its original value; each assignment counts as 4% and each quiz counts as 5% of the total grade, reducing potential student anxiety, yet the assignments and quizzes still combine to more than half of the course grade. In this system, the participation component is only worth 6%; the accounting instructor may feel that this is a quantitative, product-based, content-heavy course where discussions are less likely to occur and collaborative (small-group) work is unnecessary. The midterm and final exams, which are cumulative in nature, warrant the higher individual weight (20% each).

The remaining four plans represent variations on each previous plan in which relative weights are changed to suit the instructor's teaching style and the students' preferred learning styles. In Plan B, every assessment weighs the same, a system well-suited to a process-based course. Plan C presents a balanced approach with a high participation component. Plans D and E present lowered participation variations on Plan C. All five schemes are supportable, yet they will result in different grading decisions.

Incorporating the evaluation of student participation into the course grading system effectively quantifies aspects of student performance not measured by course assignments. Functions of the course platform record time and frequency of participation and simple point systems efficiently keep track of discussion participation. Students' reflective comments concerning personal performance, peer feedback, and course objectives provide additional data when assigning weighted participation grades.

SUMMARY

The impact of distance learning on assessment amplifies issues not always sufficiently addressed in the face-to-face classroom. The degree of transparency, type of assessment items, appropriateness to the course media, and authentic authorship are key factors when rating online student learning, measuring online program effectiveness, and evaluating online technology performance. The lack of visual cues in the virtual classroom and the potential disconnect among online classmates implies a required participation component in every online course grading system. When online assessment tools and alternative assessment strategies are used, online students employ higher order critical-thinking skills.

Distance learning assessment is never a product, but a never-ending process. As the risk of breached test security is reduced, a much broader and more thorough set of snapshots of students' performances is captured. As a result, the assessment's reliability is strengthened, providing additional evidence of valid inferences when course grades are determined. The Web-based learning environment's flexibility with respect to location, time, pace, and access creates contexts for new and exciting assessment strategies that produce a more robust and dynamic collection of student performance.

REFERENCES

Barrett, H. (2005). Alternative assessments and electronic portfolios. Retrieved November 4, 2005, from http://electronicportfolios.org/portfolios/bookmarks.html

Davis, B. G. (1993). *Tools for teaching*. San Francisco: Jossey-Bass.

Epstein, M. (2003). *New multiple choice test allows partial credit and instant feedback*. Retrieved October 21, 2005, from Rider University Web site: http://www.rider.edu/news/newswire/newswireweb/IfAt.htm

Fleming, N. D., & Mills, C. (1992). Not another inventory, rather a catalyst for reflection. *To Improve the Academy, 11*, 137-155. Retrieved April 3, 2006, from http://www.vark-learn.com/english/page.asp?p=sitemap

Fleming, N. D. (2003). *VARK: A training resource*. Christchurch, NZ: Vark-learn.com.

Foltz, P. W., Gilliam, S., & Kendall, S. (2000). Supporting content-based feedback in online writing evaluation with LSA. *Interactive Learning Environments, 8*, 111-129.

Hudspeth, D. (1997). Testing learner outcomes in web-based instruction. In B. H. Khan (Ed.), *Web-based instruction* (pp. 353-356). Englewood Cliffs, NJ: Educational Technology Publications.

Jeffries, C., & Maeder, D. W. (2004). Using vignettes to build and assess teacher understanding of instructional strategies. *The Professional Educator, 26*(1 & 2), 17-28.

Jeffries, C., & Maeder, D. W. (2006). *Using instructional and assessment vignettes to promote recall, recognition, and transfer in educational psychology courses.* Manuscript submitted for publication.

Kim, L. (1999). *About webfolios.* Retrieved October 21, 2005, from California State University Los Angeles Web site: http://www.calstatela.edu/academic/webfolio/web1.htm

Laham, D. (2003). *Latent semantic analysis at CU Boulder.* Retrieved November 8, 2005, from Colorado University at Boulder Web site: http://lsa.colorado.edu/

Landauer, T. K., Foltz, P. W., & Laham, D. (1998). An introduction to latent semantic analysis. *Discourse Processes, 25,* 259-284.

Maeder, D. W. (2004). *Evaluating your students.* Unpublished manuscript, Education Extension, University of California, Los Angeles.

Maeder, D. W. (2005) *Distance learning assessment theory.* Unpublished manuscript, Education Extension, University of California, Los Angeles.

McMurtry, K. (2001, November). e-cheating: Combating a 21st Century Challenge. *The Journal, 29*(4). Retrieved October 21, 2005, from http://www.thejournal.com/magazine/vault/A3724.cfm

Olt, M. (2002). Ethics and distance education: Strategies for minimizing academic dishonesty in online assessment. *Online Journal of Distance Learning Administration, 5*(3). Retrieved October 21, 2005, from http://www.westga.edu/%7Edistance/ojdla/fall53/olt53.html

Palloff, R. M., & Pratt, K. (1999). *Building learning communities in cyberspace: Effective strategies for the online classroom.* Jossey–Bass: San Francisco.

Snow, R. E. (1993). Construct validity and constructed-response tests. In R. E. Bennett & W. C. Ward (Eds.), *Construction versus choice in cognitive measurement: Issues in constructed response, performance testing, and portfolio assessment* (pp. 45-60). Hillsdale, NJ: Erlbaum.

Su, B. (2005). *How to recognize plagiarism.* Retrieved November 5, 2005, from Indiana University Web site: http://www.indiana.edu/~istd/overview.html

Wolfe, M. B. W., & Goldman, S. R. (2003). Use of latent semantic analysis for predicting psychological phenomena: Two issues and proposed solutions. *Behaviour Research Methods, 35,* 22-31.

Zhang, J., Khan, B. H., Gibbons, A. S., & Ni, Y. (2001). Review of web-based assessment tools. In B. H. Khan (Ed.), *Web-based training* (pp. 287-295). Englewood Cliffs, NJ: Educational Technology Publications.

Data-Driven Instruction

Raholanda White
Middle Tennessee State University
Murfreesboro, Tennessee

The populace of the twenty-first century expects educators at all levels of instruction to be accountable. One way for business educators to demonstrate accountability to students, parents, alumni, and the community is through the analysis of data that drives instructional decisions. This chapter defines sources of data and identifies how to analyze the data to make curricular decisions. In addition, several examples of how schools and districts are working to use data more effectively are presented.

SOURCES OF DATA

Businesses have long used data from sales, marketing, demographics, and production costs to drive business decisions and to make future projections. Hopkins (2004) suggests that while businesses have always seen this approach to decision making as necessary, school districts and educational leaders have only recently begun using numerical data to evaluate and change curriculum for the purpose of turning out an improved end-product—students prepared to lead our world in the twenty-first century.

For teachers and administrators in the elementary, secondary, and postsecondary schools in this country, four sets of data—student learning data, demographic data, program data, and perception data—can be examined to create a clear picture of what schools must do to meet the needs of all their students, whether present or future. Teachers and administrators must understand what each of these four sources involves before implementing any processes for collecting and analyzing the data.

Student Learning Data

Student learning data can be derived from sources such as standardized tests, criterion-referenced tests, teacher observations of student abilities, and authentic assessments.

Standardized testing is able to provide assessments that are psychometrically valid and reliable, with results that are generalizable and replicable. Aggregation of data derived from a well-designed standardized test provides an assessment of an individual's mastery of a domain of knowledge or skill. This aggregation will provide useful information for an individual as well as for a group (Wikipedia, 2006).

The Educational Testing Service (ETS) has developed the Major Field Test (MFT), a test of achievement that measures the mastery of the comprehension, principles, and information within the student's major field of study, in this case, business (Black and Duhon, 2003). The MFT examines a student's performance in accounting, economics, management, quantitative business analysis and information systems, finance, and legal and social environment. At many institutions of higher education, students majoring in business education, entrepreneurship, and office management, as well as in other business-related programs, are required to take the MFT as an exit exami-nation for graduation. The information derived from the MFT is useful in providing both individual student data and department data.

Criterion-referenced tests (CRTs) are intended to measure how well a person has learned a specific body of knowledge and skills. CRTs are a standards-based assess-ment that is developed on the egalitarian belief that all students can succeed regardless of ability or economic background (Wikipedia, 2006). In business education, CRTs usually are designed to determine whether a student has learned the material taught in a specific course (Fair Test: The National Center for Fair & Open Testing, 2006). A business communication teacher would develop a CRT that included questions based only upon appropriate material taught that is related to the standards or the criterion for the course.

For example, a teacher introducing a chapter on intercultural communication would cover material that would include technological advancements, globalization of mar-kets, and intercultural workforces. The class would have discussed the roles these factors play in enhancing intercultural communication. A relevant example includes a video clip on diversity within a department store: the clip includes activities about prejudging, scenario cards, and the fact that the store celebrated one week of Christmas, Kwanza, and Hanukkah because of its diverse employees and customers. Another week brought a celebration of ethnic foods with employees preparing and sharing a variety of dishes from their countries. At the end of this unit, and after showing the video clip and analyzing it thoroughly with students, the teacher would design a test to cover all material discussed in class about intercultural communication and diversity in the department store. This is one example on ethnic diversity. In general, however, faculty members, either individually or collaboratively, would be responsible for developing a relevant CRT for topics included in the course or courses they teach.

Teacher observation of students' abilities provides another method for how student learning data is derived. When educators carefully note how students are responding to material being taught, the immediate student reactions usually give the teacher a good basis for judging how well the students comprehend concepts they are expected to master. The close contact teachers have with their students in the classroom allows the teachers to assess achievement continuously and gather data in a variety of ways.

Authentic assessments are those that incorporate real-world situations. For example, teachers might assign students to teams and give them a scenario or problem that would incorporate use of higher level thinking skills. One such scenario might be to have teams think about the many uses of databases for everyday living. Teams would have to create an original database in Access and develop a basic structure for it.

The instructor might also consider forming a partnership with a local business and have students create a database using Access 2003 after spending some time at that business. This real-world experience would give students the opportunity to use many features of Access while forming a working relationship with a company that relies on Access to help organize their business in a practical way. The students would be able to see the practical applications of Access in a real-life situation, which would reinforce the theoretical aspects of databases they had studied in the classroom. Authentic assessments designed to incorporate meaningful contextual experiences are another source of student learning data.

Demographic Data

Demographic data include enrollment, attendance, ethnicity, and gender figures, grade levels, dropout rates, and socio-economic information. The underlying premise for collecting demographic data is to have a clearer picture of a district's students— who they are, what trends are seen in the student population, and what factors outside of school may assist administrators and teachers to better understand students.

Demographic data is an important component of assessment data. Because of the No Child Left Behind (NCLB) legislation and the increasing acceptance of school choice, administrators and teachers must come to know their communities. Without knowing the school population, school district personnel are hard pressed to clarify problems and/or needs. The data that should be collected would provide the following information:

- Demographic information on students in the school district and on their parents as well

- Student transportation needs

- Neighborhood characteristics

- Parental involvement

- Mobility patterns in and out of grades and/or schools

- Behavior and social problems of students

- Rate of enrollment in special programs such as ESL, special education, or after school (Guide to Using Data in School Improvement Efforts, 2004).

Student demographic data should be collected over a five-year period to account for trends and to make more effective predictions. Data from each five-year period should be arranged by year so as to facilitate comparison.

Program Data

According to Bernhardt (2003), program data, or school processes data, are a description of school programs, instructional and assessment strategies, and practices in the classroom. Guide to Using (2004) makes the point that collecting program data is seen as action research, which involves gathering data that will enlighten future decision making about programs and curricula. An assessment of educational programs includes collecting data that outline the enrollment in the school's programs and courses and that provide information about the performance of standards-based curricula.

The Business Communication and Entrepreneurship Department (BCEN) at Middle Tennessee State University in Murfreesboro, Tennessee, collected data from students in business communication classes, using written and oral scoring guides that accompany the business communication textbook currently in use. Data was collected on five types of communication: direct letters, indirect letters, application letters, resumes, and oral presentations. The data collected in the fall of 2006 will be compared to the pilot data that was previously gathered in the spring of 2006. The data will provide information for the continuing development of business communication assessments that will evaluate students on the established criteria that has been communicated to them. The scoring guides being used as a data source are shown in Table 1.

Perception Data

Perception data consist of individual views, beliefs, and values about systems in the workplace and in academic settings, and may be collected through questionnaires, interviews, and observations (Education Commission of the States, 2002). These data can be very enlightening for educators in helping them recognize and respond to the opinions and ideas of the wider school community. These community members include parents, community citizens, community businesses, and regional colleges and universities (Guide to Using, 2004). When gathering perception data, one should take care to ensure that the data collected provides an honest portrayal of the district and school climate. Creative methods for data collection, such as surveys, polls, and analyses of local newspaper editorials and letters can be helpful in determining school

Table 1. *Business Communication Scoring Guide*

Business Communication Scoring Guides

Written Communication

Description	Pts.	Score	Evaluation					
Content			Excellent = 5 Mailable as is with no revision	4*	Acceptable = 3 Needs some revision	2*	Unacceptable = 1 Not mailable: needs major revisions	
Format								
Composition								
Grammar								
Punctuation								
Spelling								
Vocabulary								
Total Points								
			*In-between points					
Overall Score								

Oral Communication

Components	Pts.	Score	Evaluation				
Eye Contact			Excellent = 5	4*	Acceptable = 3	2*	Unacceptable = 1
Format							
Composition							
Grammar							
Punctuation							
Spelling							
Vocabulary							
Total Points							
			*In-between points				
Overall Score			Total Points divided by 7				

Adapted from Guffey, M.E., & Seefer, C.M. (2006). *Business Communication Process & Product Instructor's Manual (5th ed.).* Mason, OH: Thomson South-Western.

climate and in identifying areas of concern that need addressing immediately or in the near future. For example, data collected from parents, community members, and business executives could be derived from surveys via the Internet (electronic surveys) to see what skills and knowledge are expected from students when they begin to work in the local job market. This survey could include a list of skills needed by today's managers, as well as courses taught and would give individuals a chance to see if specific courses are relevant and successful, or whether they should be re-evaluated and modified.

Since perception data is an area that is often overlooked and underevaluated, it is important that educators make an effort to collect and examine this information carefully, as a routine step in their analysis of the academic system as a totality. The data will provide a broader scope of information in planning for the future of the entire community.

These four types of data—student learning data, demographic data, program data, and perception data—are collected with the paramount goal of assisting school directors or superintendents, school board members, principals, and faculty in improving and updating the curriculum.

ANALYZING DATA

Data are useful when administrators, faculty, and staff thoughtfully analyze the information gathered to improve and facilitate student learning. Changing and improving the curriculum should be driven by the analysis of the data from the four sources identified.

Student Learning Data

Once student learning data have been collected from sources such as standardized tests, criterion-referenced tests, teacher observations, and authentic assessments, educators can organize the information for analysis.

The BCEN Department administers the MFT in business to graduating seniors during the fall and spring semesters. Students are tested in business education (the nonteaching segment), entrepreneurship, and office management. In addition, business education students who are preparing to become certified as teachers must take the Praxis Business Education Specialty Exam, a derivative of the National Teachers Exam (NTE.) Data are analyzed for the nonteaching segment, entrepreneurship, and office management by using descriptive statistics that show the number of students, mean, standard deviation, standard error, and range. The mean scores for each major are compared to the national mean/pass rate from one year to the next. For example, in business education the mean for spring 2005 was 146.60. This result was compared to the national mean of 151.60. Values were assigned in a plus or minus range and scored average, above average, or below average. The department then determined where it ranked on a national scale and made appropriate curricular adjustments. In addition, administrators and faculty were able to interpret the data for an individual student as well as for all students in the department. The information gathered was then used to drive decisions regarding curriculum change or modification.

Data for the Praxis Business Education Specialty Exam is provided to the BCEN Department chairperson by the Educational Testing Service. After the department chairperson receives the data, the BCEN Assessment Committee reviews the data, reports the results, and makes recommendations for curriculum development as well as improvement.

Demographic Data

Demographic data are invaluable in responding to the needs of a community and its school district and in providing appropriate academic or vocational experiences in higher education. A school cannot be isolated from its surrounding environment.

Demographic data from the MFT for the BCEN Department are analyzed by breaking the demographic characteristics into the following categories:

- Number of Students

- Percentage of Males/Females

- Percentage of Caucasian Students

- Percentage of Transfer Students

- Percentage of Full-Time Students

- Percentage of Undergraduates with Grade Point Average 3.00+

- Percentage of Majors with Grade Point Average 3.00+

- Percentage of Students Planning to Pursue a Master's Degree or Higher

These demographic data are also compared to one another from semester to semester and from one year to another to see what the historical trends are for the department. For example, in spring 2005, 67% of students majoring in entrepreneurship achieved a grade point average of 3.00 or better, while in the fall of the same year the average was 86.7%.

Program Data

Business education programs have seen tremendous changes since the 1990s due to legislative initiatives, technological advances, workforce demands, special needs, teacher licensure trends and issues, and competitive needs of business and industry. After business educators analyze the program data, they must respond to and reflect these changes in the curriculum.

In the BCEN Department, program data are analyzed by looking at the pass/fail rate on comprehensive master's exams, comments and concerns from the advisory committee for the Jennings A. Jones College of Business, BCEN Department, results of survey data from current students, and survey data from alumni.

When alumni are surveyed, the department can obtain a better understanding of how many graduates are employed, how many have jobs related to their majors, what percentage of alumni were pleased with their degree program in the department, how satisfied they are with their positions, and how many are making a competitive salary. These data, when received and analyzed, give the department a thorough understanding regarding what subjects to continue teaching, how to improve instruction, and what programs will be most beneficial to the department and its graduates in the future. Program data from previous years should be continuously compared to updated results and used to improve and change curriculum.

Perception Data

Perception data are more subjective in nature; they consist of values and opinions held in the workplace and community. The information collected from polling, questionnaires, and analysis of editorials can shed light on the perception of school systems within the community. Perception data can be gathered and analyzed from questionnaires that have been sent to and completed by community leaders, business and industry higher-level managers. One example of collecting perception data would be for the department chair and faculty of a department to observe during a school open house the reaction of parents and community members to current technology that is installed in computer labs for students in business education. Administrators, faculty, and staff can usually sense if the business personnel and members of the community are pleased with the equipment and software. They can receive positive and negative feedback, as well as potentially helpful suggestions, and then modify or adapt as appropriate.

Yet another way to analyze perception data is through interviews with key individuals who will have a direct affect on the educational program. It is informative to interview politicians, parents, and bankers who may potentially provide access to funding and resources. These interviews could possibly be videotaped and shared later with other constituents. First-hand information from these individuals will provide immediate feedback useful in determining program and curriculum improvement. Quantitative data from these same sources outside the learning community can then be compared to those from within. Analysis can be made for points of variance, and then solutions sought for closing the gap. For example, if business and industry higher-level managers were surveyed, and the results revealed that better written and oral communication skills in graduates were needed, administrators and faculty could respond by ensuring that these skills were included within each course.

Another example is a wider study conducted by Chadd and Drage (2006) that looked at the perception of teachers and high school principals related to the benefits of Career and Technical Education (CTE) in helping high schools achieve the goals of NCLB. The results of the surveys are presented in Table 2.

Table 2. *Teacher and Principal Survey*

Questions	Teachers*	Principals
CTE courses help prepare students to take tests that assess English language arts.	78% strongly agreed 22% strongly disagreed or disagreed	74% strongly agreed 26% strongly disagreed or disagreed
CTE courses help prepare students to take standardized tests that assess math.	90% strongly agreed 10% strongly disagreed or disagreed	86% strongly agreed 14% strongly disagreed or disagreed
CTE courses incorporate developmental reading.	89% strongly agreed 11% strongly disagreed or disagreed	85% strongly agreed 15% strongly disagreed or disagreed

*44 percent were from business departments

Data from the surveys were analyzed using a chi-square test to determine if there was a difference between the perceptions of principals and teachers. Descriptive statistics were used for compiling and reporting the rest of the survey data. The research revealed that participants perceive that CTE has the ability to help schools meet high academic standards as well as to assist students in graduating from high school.

Business educators can analyze student learning data, demographic data, program data, and perception data to place students in appropriate courses, to monitor quality of instruction for student learning, and to develop working relationships within the community in order to enhance the business program.

USING DATA EFFECTIVELY

School leadership teams are currently stressing the importance of using data effectively. Data-driven analysis can be appropriate for an individual school or an entire district. Many school districts have already begun to move in this direction by working with leadership teams to understand data and how that data can be used to drive improvement in the curriculum.

The following three examples show how data can be collected, analyzed, and applied to make positive changes. In each of the three examples presented, a school portfolio has been used to collect, analyze, and use the data. Bernhardt (2002a) indicates that in order for teachers to use data effectively, they must understand the data tools that are an important component of the school portfolio. The data tools include the following:

- Student Information Systems—Databases that primarily house demographic data collected during the school day. These databases are networked and automate the repetitive collection of data such as class attendance, tardiness, discipline referrals, and enrollments.

- Data Warehouses—This tool allows school districts to analyze data across several databases such as student information systems, databases of test results and school programs, and databases containing information about students. In addition, data warehouses perform statistical procedures such as analyzing longitudinal data and disaggregating data. This is useful in following students' educational histories from present to past.

- Instructional Management Systems—These systems assist school personnel in analyzing student performance on ongoing assessments and reveal how closely student learning matches the content a teacher has presented in class. Additional features include standards-based lesson plans (Bernhardt, 2002b).

Example 1: A High School Case Study

Westerville South High School in Westerville (Ohio) School District is a suburban district with over 13,000 students and 20 schools. Each of the schools developed a school portfolio as a part of the Continuous Improvement Plan (CIP) that aligned with both the district's and the state's plan to reform school programs (Education for the Future, n.d.a.).

Westerville has updated their CIP by including specific targets to determine their goals. The district is committed to the Baldrige in Education Initiative as well as the Battelle for Kids. Both projects involve gathering and analyzing data. Since the major reason to gather and analyze data is to use the information provided to improve student learning, the school portfolio provides a superb storage framework for the data to be collected and analyzed. In this case, Westerville decided to use the Tetra-Data Corporation to provide the structure for the collection and analysis of their data.

Westerville is convinced that it is only through making decisions informed by data that significant changes can be implemented with a positive impact on the entire school.

Example 2: A School District Case Study

San Jose Unified School District (SJUSD) is among the thirty largest urban school districts in California with 41 schools and an enrollment of 32,000 students. The cultural diversity and socio-economic demographics of this district present significant education challenges. According to Marcy Lauck, Manager of Continuous Improvement Programs, "the pressure for accountability and improved school performance created a definite need for data solutions and for data-based decision making." (personal communication, February 22, 2007)

In the process of applying for grants, teachers in the district discovered Education for the Future's school portfolio process. Data is at the heart of this process. Once administrators and teachers in San Jose schools began to comprehend the importance of individual student, classroom, grade level, subject area, and school data, they restructured the student information and assessment system so that they would have full and timely access to critical student achievement data (Education for the Future, n.d.b). Teachers knew they needed access not only to digital cumulative files for every student, but also to an instrument that would let them easily manipulate the data. A data warehouse developed by TetraData Corporation, plus new technology called Data on Demand that refreshes core data every night, has led to significant changes in the way San Jose Unified School District schools can access and analyze data to meet individual student needs. According to Marcy Lauck, "Site data teams now can identify which standards students are struggling with, what support teachers need to help them meet students' needs, and which students need additional assistance." (personal communication, February 22, 2007).

At the school sites, key individuals make up data teams that develop expertise in accessing and formatting key performance data and facilitate staff and administrative analysis of that data. At the district level there is a data and systems resource teacher. Instructional coaches use the data to help teachers plan instructional strategies and determine how they will know when students are meeting the standards. The instructional coaches model lessons for teachers that feature effective instructional strategies to be used for teaching to identified standards.

A particular example of data analysis and changes at the classroom level occurred for a physics teacher at one of the high schools. The teacher asked the data team for information on how students performed on the physics test. Three standards were identified with which students were experiencing difficulty. The teacher restructured the class curriculum to emphasize those standards in a new way. As a result, in the first year 76% of his students scored "proficient" or "advanced" on the California Standards Test. In year two, 84% scored "proficient" or "advanced." This particular teacher now continually uses student performance data to structure the class curriculum and modify his pacing calendar (M. Lauck, personal communication, February 22, 2007).

Teachers in the district have indicated that "access to data has changed their conversations. It is no longer why students are failing, but rather how teachers are teaching with the use of a system that leads to student success." (M. Lauck, personal communication, February 22, 2007).

Example 3: A School District Case Study
Yet another example of using data effectively is found in the Greenville County Schools in South Carolina. Greenville County also uses the school portfolio process to improve student achievement.

During the summer of 2002, 760 teachers and other school staff were trained as part of leadership teams for their 83 schools. Professional development focused on quality planning and research as the foundation for establishing baselines in the seven portfolio continuums, which include information and analysis, student achievement, quality planning, professional development, leadership, partnership development, and continuous improvement and evaluation (Education for the Future, n.d.c).

School teams worked with other school staff to review existing values and beliefs and developed a mission and vision statement. Using the new district data warehouse, achievement gains and other data were analyzed, focusing on the intersection of demographics, parent and student perceptions, student achievement, and school process data. Due to a review of multiple data sources, root causes for gaps in achievement and programs were identified and long-range goals, objectives, and strategies were created. The action plans developed by each school will continue to be monitored and supported by the district administration.

The focus of the portfolio process has been on teacher discussions of academic standards, articulation, instructional delivery, group processes, and assessment practices. Due to the portfolio process, the culture of schools is changing through conversations among teachers, parents, and other stakeholders.

Since using the portfolio process, district representatives have observed that more staff members comprehend and use student achievement data to improve instruction. Student achievement information produced by new data warehousing solutions is linked to programs and individual student records and organized in understandable language, which is essential to teacher ownership in supporting systemic change. Since recommendations must be agreed upon, teamwork has become the standard, and stakeholders, including parents and community members, have collaborated in designing research-based strategies for focusing on disparities.

The applications presented here can be adapted to apply to business education as well as to other educational situations or needs.

SUMMARY

Collecting, analyzing, and understanding how to use data effectively is a continuing process. Demonstrating the desire to improve student achievement through professional development workshops is essential in the twenty-first century. This chapter has defined sources of data, presented some ways to analyze data, and provided examples of how to use the data to improve curriculum and make instructional changes. One important component of any school district's assessment program is to have a strong leadership team and provide the team with extensive training in data collection, analysis, and effective use of the data. Since today's students are our future leaders in business education and the world, it is imperative that they become high achievers. Vigilant attention by educators through data driven instruction will ensure that they succeed.

REFERENCES

Bernhardt, V.L. (2002a). The school portfolio toolkit: A planning, implementation, and evaluation guide for continuous school improvement. [Electronic version]. Larchmont, NY: *Eye on education.* Retrieved October 11, 2006, from http://www.eyeoneducation.com.

Bernhardt, V.L. (2002b). The school portfolio: A comprehensive framework for school improvement. *Education for the future.* Retrieved December 3, 2006, from http://eff.csuchico.edu/expert_development/school_portfolio.php.

Bernhardt, V.L. (2003). No schools left behind. *Educational Leadership, 60*(5), 26-30.

Black, H.T., & Duhon, D.L. (2003). Evaluating and improving student achievement in business programs: The effective use of standardized assessment tests. *Journal of Education for Business, 79*(2), 90-99.

Chadd, J., & Drage, K. (2006, November 16-18). *No Child Left Behind's impact on Career and Technical Education.* Paper presented at the National Delta Pi Epsilon Conference, Bloomington, MN.

Education Commission of the States. (2002*). No Child Left Behind issue brief: Data-driven decision making.* Retrieved November 29, 2005, from http://www.ecs.org/clearinghouse/35/52/3552/pdf.

Education for the Future. (n.d.a). *Case studies.* Retrieved December 3, 2006, from http://eff.csuchico.edu/case_studies/high_school.php?

Education for the Future. (n.d.b). *Case studies.* Retrieved December 3, 2006, from http://eff.csuchico.edu/case_studies/urban_district1.php

Education for the Future. (n.d.c). *Case studies.* Retrieved December 3, 2006, from http://eff.csuchico.edu/case_studies/urban_district2.php

FairTest: The National Center for Fair & Open Testing. (2006). *Criterion-and-standards reference tests.* Retrieved September 6, 2006, from http://www.fairTest.org/facts/csrtests.html.

Guffey, M.E., & Seefer, C.M. (2006). *Business communication process & product instructor's manual* (5th ed.). Mason, OH: Thomson South-Western.

Guide to using data in school improvement efforts: A compilation of knowledge from data retreats and data use at learning point associates. (2004, December). Naperville, IL: Learning Point Associates, sponsored under government contract number ED-01-CO-0011.

Hopkins, G. (2004). Data is making a difference in these schools. *Education World.* Retrieved November 29, 2005, from http://www.education-world.com/a_admin/admin/admin280.shtml.

Wikipedia. (2006). *Standardized test: Advantages.* Retrieved October 28, 2006, from http://en.wikipedia.org/wiki/Standardized_testing.

Proof of Student Achievement

Betty J. Brown and George A. Mundrake

Ball State University

Muncie, Indiana

Educational assessment produces information that must be used for accountability, for measurements of student progress, and for evaluation of teachers and programs. Teachers collect assessment data in each classroom; schools collect assessment data at the building, system, and district levels; and state and national assessment programs collect data for generalizations about American education. This chapter will address types of assessment data, assessments related to course content and standards-based assessment as sources to verify student achievement. In addition, guides for the use of assessment data as proof of student achievement and ways to recognize and celebrate student accomplishments will be presented.

TYPES OF ASSESSMENT DATA

Educators are increasingly accountable for documenting student achievement and reporting results at various levels. Students and their parents/guardians are the first level to which teachers report on student progress, but an increased emphasis on standards has extended that accountability to the district, state, regional, and national levels. Assessment data are used to validate course content, student knowledge and skills, and other expected learning outcomes. Assessment objectives must be matched to curriculum and course objectives. Those objectives are used as guides for various assessment tools developed and used by classroom teachers.

Matching Assessment Objectives to Curriculum and Course Objectives

To measure student performance meaningfully, performance standards must be translated into assessment and reporting methods that students, teachers, and other stakeholders understand and interpret appropriately. Objective tests have long been a staple in assessment because one correct answer can be clearly understood and can be used to create a "grade." When student-constructed responses must be interpreted, rubrics are a tool that describe and scale the levels of student achievement on tasks. Rubrics are not just a checklist of completed items; they are a guide to quality. Students may view graded sample work ranging from one end of the continuum to the other. Because these samples are graded, students should understand completely the rubric's criteria and description. Students may then compare their own work to these samples or to the rubric itself.

Rubrics also can be associated with more traditional numeric scores and grades. Solomon (2002) identified three types of rubrics that can be used to report student achievement: a *task-specific rubric*, which measures achievement on a single task; a *developmental rubric*, which assesses a progression of knowledge or skill acquisitions; and a *relative rubric*, which gives little feedback about specific expectations but is easier to design and grade.

A task-specific rubric evaluates a student's ability to perform a single task, such as formatting text into a block-style letter. A rubric for this task could evaluate work on three criteria: position on the page, placement of all parts of the letter, and correctness of content.

This rubric evaluates quality on each criterion by assigning points (1 for not meeting the criterion, through 4, for meeting the criterion at a high level, for example). Points represent a measure of the ability to perform the task to acceptable standards or students' ability to demonstrate mastery of the task.

A factor such as class participation could be evaluated by a developmental rubric that includes several factors. Five components of the rubric could be behavioral descriptives such as pays attention, responds reflectively to others, expresses complete thoughts, displays logic and insight, and relates ideas to previous comments. Students are evaluated on the extent to which they exhibit these behaviors in class projects such as brainstorming, problem-solving assignments, and case studies.

A relative rubric evaluates accomplishments over a period of time. A rubric on an ongoing project such as a multipart case study in business law may include criteria such as contributions to the project, focus on the task, ability to work with others, effective use of time, and ability to identify the central idea in the case. A teacher can assign points to assess a student on each criterion.

Some stakeholders who are accustomed to traditional grading systems may not be comfortable with the use of rubrics. They also may wrongly perceive rubrics as "too subjective" or "too qualitative." However, rubrics can assign a quantitative "score" to student achievement, or a certain number of grades can be assigned. Like more traditional assessments, rubrics can be used to show that individuals do not acquire knowledge to the same level, or learning is not an "all or nothing" process. Explicit criteria, stated in rubrics, provide a clear picture to students and teachers about expectations.

Well-written performance standards and articulate rubrics can clearly show what teachers want students to know and be able to do and can clearly delineate how progress is assessed. Rubrics can be used for formative evaluation to provide feedback about progress toward attaining course objectives. In turn, standards tell teachers what needs to be on a test; teachers can build follow-up tests on feedback from evaluation on rubrics. Tests that are well matched to course objectives and tools such as rubrics that have been used in formative evaluation provide good information to students, teachers, parents, and anyone else who examines student achievement. Comparing formative evaluation and summative results also helps to make both assessment types reliable and valid.

Teacher-Made Assessments

Teacher-made assessments are the most common kind of classroom assessment of student progress and achievement. Stitt-Gohdes (2002) commented that assessments help teachers to find answers to questions such as these: How do I know whether students are learning what I am trying to teach them? How do students find out how they are doing, and can they use that information to their benefit? Can students tell what I think is important for them to learn by looking at the assignments that "count" in the course?

Teachers use their assessment tools for several purposes. Probably the primary purpose is to determine grades. Assessment also can be used to group students, diagnose student strengths and weaknesses, motivate students to learn more, plan instructional content and pedagogy, communicate expectations to students, and evaluate instruction.

Bedwell (2004) contended that the best assessments are developed by teachers, rather than imposed from the outside. As a result of their assessments, teachers make decisions about students' progress, provide remediation or reinforcement, and communicate their expectations to students. They use a variety of assessment methods, such as pretest/posttest, quizzes, rubrics, individual and group project checklists, performance assessments, oral questioning, assignments, peer ratings, and self-ratings to assist in their decision-making.

Suitability of teacher-made assessments. A beginning point for teaching and learning in a course is to determine course objectives or goals. What does the teacher intend for students to learn? If students are to be able to identify and evaluate the uses of credit, for example, they must know what they must demonstrate to prove that they understand those concepts about credit. When students know the goals, and the teacher matches learning experiences to assessments (and vice versa), then students stay focused on what is important to learn. They are more likely to see the purpose of class activities, assignments, and assessments and take more responsibility for their own learning.

Popham (2001) identified reliability as one characteristic of a good test, focusing on the consistency with which a test measures what it purports to measure. In addition, content validity is essential for teacher-made assessments. A first step in constructing an assessment is to identify the objectives for the knowledge and skills to be assessed. Based on those objectives, a teacher prepares a table of specifications, a two-way chart that lists instructional objectives, lists course content, and matches objectives to content (Linn and Miller, 2005). A teacher also must consider the instructional strategies and activities and how to include assessment that matches those strategies and activities.

The table of specifications identifies a type of assessment for each objective and the number of assessment items for each content area. One objective may be measured best with a series of multiple-choice questions. Another may be measured best with an essay question. Still another may be measured best with a performance assessment. The table of specifications becomes the guide for selecting or writing suitable assessment questions or activities. For example, a quiz prepared for a business economics class could contain five test items on basic terms about the role of credit in the economy; two test items on application; and one analysis question. Therefore, 8 of the 35 test items will measure student knowledge and understanding of the role of credit in the economy. The other 6 objectives have test questions categorized in the same way: basic terms, performance, and interpretation. Through this process, an assessment instrument, the objectives for student learning, and learning activities are closely aligned, and the assessment tool has content validity. Table 1 shows a sample table of specifications for the business economics quiz.

Popham (2001) stressed that the most important factor in test use is the inference made about a student, based on the student's test performance, not just that the test is "valid or invalid." In Popham's words, "The more satisfactorily a test represents the body of knowledge, skills, and affect it is supposed to represent, the more valid will be any inference about a student's status with respect with what's been measured" (p. 30). Therefore, the inferences based on test scores that teachers and others make about a student or group of students is the important characteristic of any testing.

Teachers are responsible for making valid inferences about students based on classroom assessments. Teachers test to capture the kind of information they need to make better instructional decisions. Their tests sample the combination of knowledge,

Table 1. *Table of Specifications for 35-Item Quiz on Consumer Credit*

Cognitive Level of Objectives Question Content	Knowledge and Comprehension Basic Terms	Application Performance	Analysis Interpretation	Total Number	Percent of Items
Role of credit in the economy	5	2	1	8	23%
Advantages of credit	2	1		3	9%
Disadvantages of credit	2	1		3	9%
Sources of credit	2	3	3	8	23%
Types of credit	3	1		4	11%
Criteria for granting credit	1	1	3	5	14%
True cost of credit	1		3	4	11%
Total no. of test items	16	9	10	35	
Percent of test items	46%	26%	29%		100%

skills, and affective outcomes that are the reason for their instruction. Popham (2001) posited, "Based on students' responses to the assessment, a teacher infers the degree to which the student has mastered that larger body of content. Relying on such inferences, the teacher decides how best to teach the students" (pp. 28-29).

Alternative teacher-made assessments to measure higher-order thinking skills. More "traditional" assessment methods such as objective tests are sometimes criticized as "unable to measure higher-order thinking skills." However, well-designed tests measure all levels of achievement. Other assessment methods can measure a different set of skills or performances or can supplement information from tests.

Portfolios and projects provide ways for students to demonstrate knowledge and skill. Teachers have given increased attention to ways of using portfolios, projects, peer evaluation, rubrics, performances, and group activities to allow students opportunities to demonstrate progress in learning. With rubrics, checklists, and such tools for evaluation, teachers feel more comfortable evaluating student achievement on essays, case studies, reflections, logs, portfolios, and creative projects.

Data on student achievement originates at the classroom level. Within the class-room, teachers manage and assess student performance with the aid of technology, portfolios, and multiple assessment tools. "Traditional" assessment tools, such as multiple-choice, true-false, and other objective test questions, are excellent tools. In addition, teachers can use a variety of other tools to gather needed data and to demonstrate that students know and are able to do what is expected of them.

Zeliff (2000) cited a number of assessment strategies that would be appropriate in accurately assessing student program and achievement: essay questions, oral reports by small groups, portfolios of student work over time, teacher observations of students individually or in groups, peer evaluation, and videotaped performances of student work. She also identified three types of alternative assessment strategies. Evaluation of the process by which students complete their work includes anecdotal records, observation checklists, evaluation by peers or self, interviews, and demonstrations. Written evaluation included essays, case studies, reflections, and logs. Portfolios included student reflection of what was learned, what was experienced, and how the individual learned with the process.

How can students show what they know? Teacher-made assessments are a primary source of student evaluation. Tests and alternative assessments provide information to enable a teacher to give feedback for grading purposes. A variety of quality teacher-made assessment tools provides opportunity for teachers to acquire data that validates student achievement.

ASSESSMENTS RELATED TO COURSE CONTENT

The results of assessment should be thought of as information, not just data. A teacher who analyzes and properly interprets these results translates data into information for planning in-class experiences and/or remediation. There are both purposes and ways of reporting course-related assessments.

Purposes of Course-Related Assessments

All methods of reporting student achievement have advantages and disadvantages. For that reason, reporting results in more than one form will provide information for evaluation decisions and proof of student achievement. That proof can be demonstrated with pretest/posttest, on-demand, and over-time assessments.

Pretest and posttest measures. Teacher-constructed classroom tests are used for three purposes: to give students grades, to motivate students, and to help make instructional decisions. If teachers can use information from tests to determine whether to provide additional instruction on a particular topic or move to a new topic, Popham (2001) described that function of test information as "a tremendously positive development" (p. 33). Using some variation of pretest-posttest data gathering, teachers can get an idea of how well they have taught. A teacher can give a pretest over basic economic concepts to be included in a unit of introduction to business to determine what students know. A posttest measures student mastery of those concepts. If students do worse on a posttest than on the pretest, the teacher wonders how instruction could have been changed to be more effective between the two tests.

However, if students do better on the posttest, a teacher can have some assurance that instruction was appropriate.

On-demand measures. Many of the assessment measures used in the classroom are measures of student knowledge and performance over a relatively short period of time. These evaluations often are in the form of a quiz or test that takes a snapshot of student knowledge and performance at one point. Bedwell (2004) described multiple choice tests as fixed-choice assessments. Multiple-choice tests are a good example of on-demand assessment; the results are easy to obtain and are easy for students to understand. They can translate a score on a single test into an evaluation of their achievement. For example, a student may think, "I have a score of 90% on that test; I'm satisfied that I mastered most of the content."

On-demand assessments may be formative or summative. If a teacher wishes to assess students informally only for the purpose of determining the next steps in classroom activities, listening to student responses about recent learning activities provides feedback that can be used to adjust instruction. A quiz that is given for the purpose of checking student progress is a formative assessment.

On-demand assessments are often summative. If a teacher wants to know how well a student has mastered content and activities related to a topic of instruction, a "summary" test can be used to evaluate knowledge or performance. In a typical course, results on summative assessments signal whether or not students are ready for the next chapter, unit, or topic.

Computer-based testing programs provide on-demand assessments and excellent recordkeeping. Teachers design and prepare assessments (both formative and summative) that students can access on demand. As students complete the assessment activities, results are immediate. Business educators can use computer-based programs for frequent, relevant assessments on keyboard skill development, problem-solving with computer application packages, training sessions, and examinations over course content.

Over-time assessment. Teachers are required at some point in a course to report to students and their parents/guardians a "summary" of student achievement and performance, often in terms of a course grade. Data on various quizzes, tests, portfolios, projects, and other assessments are reported individually or are summarized into a composite measure. In arriving at a measure of student achievement over time, a teacher must analyze and weigh all assessment results and decide what the data involve, what they do not involve, and what criteria were met and to what degree. Portfolios, logs, journals, and projects are good measures over time. They enable students to collect, display, and reflect upon their learning and present this evidence in a comprehensive format.

Ways of Reporting Course-Related Assessments

Course-related assessments are reported to students regularly. Each time teachers return a project, test, or paper, students see how they are doing. As they progress through a class, students should be aware of the extent to which they are meeting course objectives and grading requirements. Teachers report student achievement to parents through report cards, online reports, or progress reports. Periodic reporting encourages students to take responsibility for their learning.

Communicating course objectives and evaluation methods is an important first step in reporting whether students are achieving. Are students fully apprised of course objectives? Do they know what types of classroom activities will "count" toward the course grade? Were these activities assigned in advance and in explicit terms? Were students given information about their grades and how grades will be determined? When performance assessments are used, teachers can give students written feedback with indicators of how well students have met the objectives.

Written assignments may be used for both formative and summative evaluation. If formative evaluations are not to be used for grades, students should know the assignments are for practice, not for grades. Summative assessments then provide evidence of how the practice assignments, required material, and other class activities were mastered.

Enough evidence should be gathered over time so that a teacher can accurately determine the amount of required material mastered by each student. "Fair" evaluation, in a student's opinion, involves enough opportunities to demonstrate achievement. Knowing what is expected, a student can assume responsibility for a grade.

For a given time period, students in business classes usually earn points, letter grades, or percentage scores on such assignments as homework, in-class assignments, projects, quizzes, tests, and portfolios. If students see the relationship of all of these assessment activities to the course objectives, they understand "how they are doing" relative to the objectives. In business classes with a substantial component of performance assessment, students can demonstrate their ability to complete performance assessments (homework, in-class assignments, projects, and performance tests) successfully. If they receive feedback beyond a letter or number grade on projects and portfolios objectives, they understand better how they have progressed toward meeting course objectives.

Assessments related to course content can be used to measure student progress, provide feedback on instruction, and report to students and parents/guardians about student progress. Pretest/posttest, on-demand, and over-time assessments provide information for those purposes.

STANDARDS-BASED ASSESSMENT DATA

Beyond the classroom, standards-based assessments provide data for validating curriculum and reporting to all stakeholders. As a result of expectations that schools must be accountable for what they do, educational standards have been developed and are used at all levels in our educational system. Standards and performance expectations spell out what is expected in each subject-matter area at each level in the educational process. Curriculum within the school addresses those standards and performance expectations. Hopefully, high-stakes assessments, such as statewide examination programs, are matched to those standards and performance expectations, also. Standards-based assessments are matched to standards imposed by various sources. Data from assessments can be used to validate the business education curriculum.

Purposes of Standards-Based Assessments

For a classroom teacher, use of student achievement data, even though often perceived as relatively "low-stakes," is a critical factor. Evaluation must be matched to the standards to which students are to be held for a course. In turn, the extent to which curriculum standards are met is influenced by classroom evaluation methods and use of achievement data.

Assessments must be aligned with standards. In other words, the test content and level of difficulty of test items must reflect what was communicated by the standards. Do the assessments and standards capture the same content knowledge or skills? As Hamilton et al. (2002) stated, "Standards that do not clearly convey what is expected . . . make it difficult for teachers, administrators, parents, and students to gear their efforts toward meeting those standards and increase the risk that educators will focus too intently on specific content of tests to ascertain what should be emphasized in instruction" (pp. 29-30).

Standards-Based Assessments Affecting Business Education

Popham (2001) commented that large-scale assessments, systemwide or statewide, may or may not be "high-stakes" assessment. Assessment is high-stakes if there are significant consequences linked to individual students' test performances and if students' test scores determine the "instructional success" of a school or district. Given that standards-based assessments currently are used to measure the success of most schools, everyone is affected by the interpretation of assessments.

Those who have power over schools and even educators themselves do not always share the same opinion about what should be measured. Business educators use content standards to describe what students should know and be able to do. For example, teachers want students to be able to demonstrate acceptable oral communication skills (content standard). They use performance standards as clear levels of acceptable performance. To demonstrate oral communication skills, students present a two-minute summary of a reading assignment and will be evaluated on use of appropriate wording and grammar, inclusion of major points of the reading, and use of visual aids suitable to the audience and topic (performance standard). Performance standards are a translation of content standards that provide an expectation level and indicate "how good is good enough."

Malone and Nelson (2006) commented that students need to be prepared for their future roles. With a standards-based curriculum, stakeholders must avoid the tendency to focus on minimum levels of acceptable performance. Malone and Nelson reported that, in some cases, student achievement increased by as much as 10% to 35% when content standards were clearly stated and reinforced (p.123).

Ways of Reporting Standards-Based Assessments to Validate Curriculum

Achievement test scores do not reveal all of the important outcomes of schooling, but they are widely used to evaluate schools. Teachers make their own decisions about which educational ends they want students to achieve; but, in today's environment, higher authorities stipulate what those ends ought to be (as evidenced by standardized assessments).

Assessment results can be used to clarify curricular aims. Popham (2003) advocated a process of teaching toward "test-represented targets," not toward tests. A test represents a sampling of the skill, knowledge, or affective outcomes that a school or state wants the curriculum to develop. Popham's point is that teachers can aim instruction toward what a test represents, not toward the test itself. If teachers analyze the assessments, they can then clarify their curriculum goals accordingly. They can develop their own understanding of their curriculum goals by considering all of the various ways that students' achievement of those goals can be assessed. Then they can be assured that their curriculum is validated by assessment results; their curriculum represents the outcomes that the assessment measured.

USE OF ASSESSMENT DATA AS PROOF OF STUDENT ACHIEVEMENT

Members of the audience for schools (including elected officials and the public) often are skeptical about the effectiveness of schools and their work with students. Therefore, evidence about student achievement and school effectiveness must be credible. How can teachers collect credible evidence to inform all about the quality of instruction they deliver? Many people consider cognitive growth to be the most significant contribution of education, but affective outcomes are also important. Assessment data is used for accountability within the school to demonstrate adherence to accreditation standards, to report to stakeholders, to provide evidence that curriculum standards are met, and as proof of student achievement.

Accountability within the School/School System

If cognitive growth is considered most important by the school community, much of the evidence about student achievement should report student gains in cognitive skills. How well does instruction help students achieve the outcomes identified as most important? Compelling and credible evaluative data is solid evidence that students have mastered cognitive skills and thus have demonstrated achievement of curriculum goals and content standards. The results on classroom tests are a powerful report of instructional effectiveness. Popham (2003) encouraged teachers to use pretest/posttest data gathering methods to provide evidence that students have gained or achieved.

Data from standardized state tests, results on PSAT, ACT, and SAT tests, performance on Advanced Placement exams, and subject area data that have been gathered within the school and system can be used to report student achievement. To analyze student achievement in one Indiana high school, teachers also use data from writing samples evaluated with rubrics. They also consider student, teacher, and parent survey data, in addition to test data (J. Law, personal communication, January 30, 2006).

Accreditation

Accreditation of educational programs, schools, and school districts has been standard for decades. Frank (2004) reported that six regional accrediting associations evaluate and accredit more than 70% of all primary and secondary schools in the United States and, at the high school level alone, more than 90%. Accreditation affects everything from community morale to property values. College officers use school accreditation as one criterion for admission. Parents may check school accreditation when choosing a neighborhood. Students who transfer among high schools may not receive credit for prior work completed at a nonaccredited school.

The National Study of School Evaluation (NSSE) (2004), a national organization for accrediting agencies, works with schools and school districts for school improvement. Three indicators of school quality identified by NSSE are students' achievement of schoolwide expectations of their learning; quality of work of the school; and the school's plans for improvement and for putting best practices to work. Each regional accrediting association, part of the Commission on Accreditation and School Improvement, provides extensive guidance to schools and districts. The North Central Association Commission on Accreditation and School Improvement, for example, accredits more than 9,000 public and private schools in 19 states, the Navajo Nation, and the Department of Defense Dependents' Schools worldwide. (North Central Association, 2006). Accreditation requires a commitment to rigorous standards and a process of continuous improvement.

A school district must document student performance results, reporting progress toward student performance goals, attendance, and retention rates. At the district level, a school district must implement a continuous improvement process at the district, building, and classroom levels. Follow-up studies of graduated or promoted students are reported to determine the degree to which students have made successful transitions. School districts are required to document the satisfaction levels of various groups, such as past graduates, promoted students, dropouts, teachers, parents, advisory boards, universities, and employers, to measure the success of students who have moved to the next level of learning or other transition. Accreditation ratings take place at the state, regional, and national levels. Schools and school districts must meet state standards or may receive warnings.

Reports to Stakeholders

Stakeholders in education include students; their parents/guardians; administrators; the general public in the school community; and local, state, and federal education agencies. These groups represent different levels to which student achievement data are reported. Reporting to students and their parents/guardians is the first level of reporting for teachers.

Electronic report cards make it possible to track a number of objectives and give feedback on all objectives, rather than just assigning a letter grade for the grading period. Software for reporting grades allows students to check progress and view assignments, due dates, and weights for those assignments. Students and parents can access the records with a login and password. Those records show not only progress reports but also course objectives and standards for the curriculum. Thus, stakeholders can see that students are accountable for those objectives and standards.

Teachers can use an electronic report card system for midterm reports, letting students know about their progress. An Indiana high school uses an electronic system that enables students and parents to check progress on class assignments, projects, and tests, as well as receive grade reports (J. Law, personal communication, January 30, 2006). Class, school, and system Web sites and e-mail systems can be good commu-nication tools, also. Reporting to the public, not just parents, is possible through Web sites. System and school assessment information can be posted so anyone in the school community may access the information.

Everyone is a stakeholder in education. People within the school, the public, and various groups locally and nationally have a keen interest in how "their" schools perform. Rose and Gallup (2005), in the 2005 Phi Delta Kappa/Gallup Poll of the public's attitudes toward public schools, found that the public believed that schools have the major responsibility for student achievement. Respondents believed that parents and students have more to do with whether students learn than do teachers, but they still assign responsibility for achievement in schools.

In accounting for student achievement, teachers and schools may have to counter public perceptions about how achievement is measured. In a thought-provoking essay, Ickes-Dunbar (2004) analyzed the role of report cards as indicators of much more than mastery of a subject. She characterized report cards as evidence of intellectual superiority, a validation of struggle or hard work, and currency to exchange for material goods, tangible rewards, or money for some students, but for other students, as a badge of shame and mortification. For teachers and students alike, a report card represents a fresh start. For the future, Ickes-Dunbar anticipates a time when students and teachers can grapple less with the challenge of grades and more with the challenge of ideas.

Aggregate data on student achievement must come from schools and school systems to stakeholders beyond students and parents/guardians. Such data must demonstrate a match with curriculum standards.

Evidence That Curriculum Standards Are Met

How can schools articulate clearly to stakeholders how students' performance matches the standards on which the curriculum is built? At the school or district level, classroom assessment data can be compiled into aggregate data about student achievement. Popham (2003) advocated that administrators build a powerful case to demonstrate that instruction is meeting curriculum standards by collecting as much pertinent and credible evidence as possible. A single source of data for important educational decisions is not wise. Both test and nontest evidence can be used. Affective evidence, for example, can show that students have confidence in their ability with significant cognitive skills. If students have positive attitudes toward learning and subject-matter content, their attitudes are powerful evidence for instructional success.

The use of student achievement data can range from "low-stakes" to "high-stakes." The consequences of low achievement on a single evaluation measure in the classroom may have a very small impact on a student's progress through a course. Data on standardized achievement tests, such as the assessments most states administer to students each year in all schools, however, can mean that students cannot progress and the school may be penalized.

Evidence of Student Achievement Success

In the classroom, teachers must have adequate time to develop evaluation plans, prepare assessments, analyze and interpret data from assessments, and plan how to report findings to students, their parents, and other stakeholders. Teachers have used paper-and-pencil tests, oral reports, laboratory assignments, collaborative learning, text-based questions and tests, and project and product assessments for decades. These types of evaluation tools are still useful, and they yield data that can provide the types of information that teachers, students, and parents want. Whatever information is provided by assessment methods, the inferences drawn from the information must be valid and reliable.

If those inferences are to be valid, assessment methods must be linked to the intended uses of evaluation. Students must have opportunity to demonstrate the knowledge, skills, attitudes or behaviors to be evaluated. The Joint Committee on Standards for Educational Evaluation (2003) offered guidelines to teachers for all types of evaluations, from low-stakes situations, where students receive a grade but are not prohibited from progressing, to high-stakes situations, which may deny progression to the next unit or grade or even graduation. Any student evaluation which does not fit the content to be evaluated can affect a student adversely.

Among recommendations from the Joint Committee are these procedures to assure that evaluations are appropriately handled:

- Ensure that assessment methods are representative of the knowledge, skills, attitudes, or behaviors identified for use of the evaluation.

- Use more than one assessment method to ensure that comprehensive and consistent indications of student performance are collected.

- Before assessment, prepare a scoring procedure to use when judging a performance or product.

- Adjust scoring procedures in light of unanticipated but appropriate responses.

Proof of student achievement goes beyond the school and the school system. Accreditation and stakeholders outside the school system demand evidence that students have achieved at levels that meet accreditation and curriculum standards.

CELEBRATING STUDENT ACCOMPLISHMENTS: RECOGNITION

When students meet standards and performance expectations, they appreciate recognition of their achievements. Grades are a reward in themselves, but teachers seek other ways of recognizing student accomplishments. They can recognize student accomplishments with membership in honor groups; recognition within the classroom or school of a "student of the week" or a "student of the month;" public recognition by posting photos or information in a display case; and news items in local papers highlighting student achievements.

One Indiana high school celebrates student accomplishments by giving a class award every six weeks. The award can be based on student improvement in one of several areas, such as good work on a project, top score on a test, or overall progress in meeting course objectives. At an award session each student (with parents in attendance) is recognized with a certificate, a class award key chain, and ice cream. Students attend a school board meeting to be recognized, their accomplishments are publicized on the school and system Web sites, and they are recognized in school announcements and on the school TV station. The top 25 students in each of four grades are recognized at the end of the school year at a formal banquet for students and their parents (J. Law, personal communication, January 30, 2006).

All students who earn a place on the honor roll each trimester in a second school receive a certificate for pizza at a local restaurant, and their names are published in the local newspaper. A "student of the week" in the business co-operative program is recognized in the local newspaper; and at the end of the year, a student in that program is recognized at a banquet as "student of the year." The student receives a plaque for the honor (E. Hanna, personal communication, June 29, 2006).

Another school has a competition called "Flying Aces." Anyone in a class who earned an "A" grade for the trimester is given paper to make a paper airplane. Students assemble in the gymnasium to "fly their airplanes." A large bin in the center of the floor is the "destination." All students who manage to fly their planes into the bin receive a gift certificate for a local shopping mall. Teachers describe this activity as a fun activity for students, as well as recognition for good work in the classroom (E. Ramey, personal communication, June 29, 2006).

Teachers in the business department at a fourth school choose a "student of the semester" for each business class. All of those students are invited to a pizza lunch at the school, catered by a local restaurant. Pictures of all the honorees are posted on the school Web site and in the school. This school's Ninth Grade Center organizes all ninth-graders into seven teams. Each nine weeks, each team selects 25 students who have performed well in the classroom. Those students receive ice cream as a reward and receive free passes to athletic events and dances. "Students of the month" receive pins for their lanyards and a certificate of achievement and are listed in a newsletter that is sent home to parents (R. Lazzer and M. Bankert, personal communication, June 29, 2006).

SUMMARY

Business educators recognize that there are many types of assessment data. Assessments related to course content can provide valid information about student achievement. Standards-based assessment provides a common language and reportable data to be shared by all stakeholders. Assessment methods must assure that all stakeholders receive needed information about student performance and achievement so that they see "proof" and can "celebrate" the fact that students are achieving.

REFERENCES

Bedwell, L. (2004). *Data-driven instruction*. Bloomington, IN: Phi Delta Kappa Educational Foundation.

Frank, T. (2004). Making the grade keeps getting harder. *Christian Science Monitor*. Retrieved January 17, 2006, from http://www.csmonitor.com/2004/0113/p11s01-legn.htm.

Hamilton, L., Stecher, B.,& Klein, S., (Eds.). (2002). *Making sense of test-based accountability in education*. Santa Monica, CA: RAND Education.

Ickes-Dunbar, A. (2004). Beyond the dunce cap: "What's my grade?" *Phi Kappa Phi Forum, 84*(4), 3.

Joint Committee on Standards for Educational Evaluation (2003). A. Gullickson, Chair. Thousand Oaks, CA: Corwin Press, Inc.

Linn, R., & Miller, M. (2005). *Measurement and assessment in teaching, 9th edition.* Englewood Cliffs, NJ: Prentice-Hall, Inc.

Malone, B., & Nelson, J. (2006). Standards-based reform: panacea for the twenty-first century? *Educational Horizons, 84*(2), 121-128.

National Study of School Evaluation (2004). *Technical guide to school and district factors impacting student learning.* Retrieved January 25, 2006, from http://www.nsse.org/resources_tools/

North Central Association (2006). *About the NCA Commission on Accreditation and School Improvement.* Retrieved January 17, 2006, from http:www.ncacasi.org/

Popham, W. J. (2001). *The truth about testing: An educator's call to action.* Alexandria, VA: Association for Supervision and Curriculum Development.

Popham, W. J. (2003). *Test better, teach better:Tthe instructional role of assessment.* Alexandria, VA: Association for Supervision and Curriculum Development.

Rose, L., & Gallup, A. (2005). The 37th annual Phi Delta Kappa/Gallup poll of the public's attitudes toward the public schools. *Phi Delta Kappan, 87*(1), 41-57.

Solomon, P. (2002). *The assessment bridge: Positive ways to link tests to learning, standards, and curriculum improvement.* Thousand Oaks, CA: Corwin Press, Inc.

Stitt-Gohdes, W. (2002). *The business education profession: Principles and practices.* Little Rock, AR: Delta Pi Epsilon.

Zeliff, Nancy (2000). Alternative assessment. In J. Rucker (Ed.), *Assessment in business education* (Yearbook No. 38, pp. 91-102). Reston, VA: National Business Education Association.

Feedback for Professional Development

Martha E. Balachandran, Robert B. Blair, and Stephen Lewis
Middle Tennessee State University
Murfreesboro, Tennessee

Accountability demands brought about by various stakeholders have placed assessment "front and center" in the daily activities of teachers and school administrators. Teachers and administrators at all levels must examine their knowledge and ability to assess student learning. The growth and success of teachers is closely related to student learning, which means successful teachers must conduct effective assessments. Assessment offers fertile ground for teacher professional development across a range of activities because of the close integration of assessment, curriculum, teaching, and learning (National Research Council, 2001). This chapter focuses on the need for professional development, use of assessment to determine appropriate professional development, assessment of professional development, and methods of providing professional development.

NEED FOR PROFESSIONAL DEVELOPMENT

The Policies Commission for Business and Economic Education (PCBEE) (PCBEE, 1997, No. 60) defines professional development as "the process that improves the job-related knowledge, skills, and attitudes of business educators." The PCBEE contends that the goals of professional development are to advance students' learning and to improve the practice of teaching. Technological changes occurring almost daily require teachers to continually upgrade their skills and content knowledge. These changes require modifications (or sometimes sweeping changes) in assessment techniques. An excellent way to maintain current knowledge is through professional development activities.

"High-quality professional development can be an important catalyst for improving learning and teaching amid changes in delivery, subject-matter content, student needs, schools, society, and the workplace" (PCBEE, 1997, No. 60). The significance of obtaining industry certifications, becoming highly qualified, and being held accountable for student learning has influenced the need for assessment-driven professional development, which may require assessment reform. Even so, care must be taken that teachers do not become disenchanted with professional development opportunities offered to them. Educators who realize the relevance of professional development activities in meeting their needs are more likely to be interested in and encouraged by participating in those activities.

Industry Certification

Industry certification has become an important credential for educators, students, and educational programs. Educators and students benefit from industry certification by demonstrating technical abilities and meeting specific competencies set by experts in that particular field (Foster & Pritz, 2006). According to Wilcox (2006), "... the appeal of industry-based certifications emerges from a continuing need to prove relevance and impact" (p. 21). Schools must be able to show program relevancy—that a program is preparing students for the labor force—as well as to prove accountability and consistency. To prepare students for industry certification, teachers may need to become industry certified themselves. By achieving industry certification, they prove that they have the skill set required of their students, they improve their credibility, and they model professionalism. Therefore, professional development leading to industry certification should be provided.

No Child Left Behind—Being Highly Qualified

Programs at the federal level, such as No Child Left Behind (NCLB), have forced states to provide evidence that teachers are highly qualified to teach core academic subjects. To be highly qualified, teachers must hold a baccalaureate degree, obtain full state certification, and demonstrate subject-matter competency. Meeting the NCLB mandates varies slightly from state to state but may require teachers to complete additional coursework in a specific subject or to participate in a series of professional development activities. These activities may include in-service, noncredit courses, research, and/or administrative evaluations. Teachers who become highly qualified enhance their credibility and become more confident in their content knowledge and instructional delivery methods. Ultimately, becoming highly qualified should have a positive impact on student learning.

One goal of the NCLB initiative is for students to improve their performance on standardized tests. Opponents of the program argue that following the NCLB program may result in teachers "teaching the test," thereby diminishing the quality of children's education. Pros and cons of NCLB have appeared frequently in the literature. Perhaps students, teachers, and other stakeholders would be better served if the focus on assessment shifted to using the results to learn about students' skills and about the effectiveness of instruction—and then to use that learning as a guide for instructional improvements and professional development (Boudett, Murnane, City, & Moody, 2005).

NCLB and similar programs look primarily at summative assessments—assessments conducted at a particular point in time. Formative assessments—those completed over a period of time—are generally perceived as more authentic by most educators. Both are valuable tools for teachers. "Just as there is powerful evidence that formative assessment can improve students' learning and achievement, it is just as clear that sustained professional development for teachers is required if they are to improve this aspect of their teaching" (National Research Council, 2001).

Teacher and Program Accountability

With the current impetus on teacher and program accountability, there is reason to think that more focus would be placed on assessment training. However, Trevisan (2002) points out that, despite national recognition of the need for assessment-competent personnel, the assessment literacy of school staff members is still lacking. A possible explanation for this deficiency is that assessment leads to accountability, and accountability is not always perceived positively (Popper, 2005). "Building the capacity of teachers to design, use, and interpret student performance data becomes a focal point of reform efforts in today's high stakes accountability environment" (Whittaker, 2002). This capacity might best be accomplished through meaningful professional development activities.

Boston (2002) addresses the issues of time and support given teachers to learn and apply suitable assessment techniques. "Training and professional development in the area of classroom assessment are essential in order to provide individual teachers with the time and support necessary to make changes" (p. 4). Time is needed for teachers to reflect upon their own assessment practices, to consult other teachers about effective practices, and to make necessary changes.

Assessment Reform

Many individuals see meritorious intent in NCLB and other educational initiatives related to assessment; some, however, feel the programs need further modifications to achieve desired positive outcomes. In New Jersey, a collaborative effort of various school administrators and business people resulted in eleven major recommendations for assessment reform. One recommendation was that the state should emphasize and provide necessary support for high quality professional development of educators in the

- development and implementation of valid and reliable performance-based assessments,

- use of resultant diagnostic information to improve teaching and learning,

- use of effective strategies for addressing individual student needs,

- closing of the achievement gap, and

- implementation of best practices identified through a continuous educational improvement model (New Jersey Principals and Supervisors Association, 2002).

Operation Public Education (OPE), based at the University of Pennsylvania, suggests further assessment reforms that will complement NCLB. Some of the suggested reforms include (1) evaluating teachers based on student learning results and observation of teachers in the classroom; (2) rewarding good teachers with merit pay and more responsibility, giving higher salaries to teachers in hard-to-fill vacancies, and requiring poor teachers to participate in remediation activities; (3) having teachers evaluate other teachers; and (4) using an integrated student assessment approach, including both formative and summative assessments (Hershberg, 2005).

Another type of assessment reform is value-added assessment. Developed for the state of Tennessee, value-added assessment separates annual student growth into two parts: growth attributed to the student and growth attributed to the classroom and other factors. Assessment data is analyzed and used to project a student's future test score as well as determine the impact the teacher has on learning (Hershberg, 2005). These assessment reforms, as well as other changes in education, create a need for quality professional development.

Disenchantment with Existing Professional Development

Most public school systems require that their teachers complete professional development activities throughout their careers. Teachers and administrators alike recognize the need for staying current in course content and delivery techniques as well as assessment strategies. However, as undeserving as its reputation might be, professional development has been tainted by systems offering and requiring attendance at in-service activities that provide little if any useful information. Where professional development is concerned, Finch & Moore (1997) indicate that ". . . the focus [of professional development] is driven by needs and context as well as the content to be delivered and potential benefit to recipients" (p. 96).

Johnson (1999) found that teachers are often uncomfortable with assessment, and this discomfort affects their sense of competence, which in turn affects their ability to teach and assess. Teachers responding to this research study indicated a high interest in more professional development, particularly in the area of alternative assessments. Dynamic curricula continue to compel teachers to search for effective assessment procedures.

A statement often repeated is that "nothing is more central to student learning than the quality of the teacher" (Galluzzo, 2005, p. 142). It should be clear even to a novice educator that good assessment is critical for students as well as other stakeholders. Conversely, poor assessment will likely result in ineffectual programs that are unable to identify weaknesses and incorporate appropriate solutions for those weaknesses. Business education programs, as well as licensure programs in general, typically provide little instruction in assessment. Consequently, professional development, whether self-taught or gathered from other sources, will continue to provide the assessment knowledge needed by business educators.

During the past 25 years, political and corporate leaders have expressed concern about the U.S. educational system. Laws have been passed and programs implemented to ensure school, program, teacher, and student quality. As a result of initiatives such as industry certification, NCLB, assessment, accountability, and other reforms, teachers have become somewhat discouraged with professional development opportunities that are offered. Effective assessment should signify areas where professional development is needed.

USE OF ASSESSMENT TO DETERMINE APPROPRIATE PROFESSIONAL DEVELOPMENT

Determining appropriate professional development for a group of teachers can be a difficult task for system and school administrators. Where assessment knowledge is concerned, as is true with most topical areas, individual teacher abilities differ greatly; so planning professional development to meet the needs of multiple teachers in diverse disciplines can be futile. Some teachers may be quite knowledgeable; others will need basic information. This section addresses assessment as it relates to faculty development, student performance, and other types of assessment.

Assessment-Centered Professional Development

Faculty development should be ". . . a lifelong process directed towards catalyzing professional growth" (National Research Council, 2001). Assessment-centered professional development focuses not only on assessment, but is closely linked to curriculum, teaching, and learning. Therefore, it offers a range of activities that encompasses the teaching and learning processes.

Because of the complexity and serious nature of assessment, professional development activities designed to examine assessment should be of a continuous nature rather than the occasional one-day workshop or in-service training. Research indicates "a 'one-shot' teacher professional development experience is not effective in almost any significant attempt to improve teaching practice" (National Research Council, 2001).

Even though time consuming, assessment-centered faculty development can be of benefit to both teachers and students. It includes establishing goals for student learning, developing assessment instruments and rubrics, implementing the assessment plan, assessing student performance, and evaluating the assessment process.

During the process, teachers should reflect on and share their experiences with others. They may need to identify student misunderstanding and consider what causes the misunderstanding. One way to do this is to talk to students about the processes they use to determine an answer. Perhaps students' thought processes and perceptions are different from those of the teacher and those in the textbook. Students' feedback may seem quite logical when teachers listen, and that feedback may then lead teachers to rethink their understanding of the topic and the methodology they used to teach it. Feedback may ultimately result in improvements to teaching and learning.

Assessment Related to Student Performance

From local, state, and federal agencies to regional and national accrediting associations, educators are being forced to verify the effectiveness of their programs. Pressure to assess and continually improve educational programs is felt at elementary, secondary, and post-secondary levels. Individual courses, curricula, and entire programs must be examined frequently to ensure that students at each level are capable of progressing to the next phase, whether that is additional education or employment. Program effectiveness may be verified in several ways. National Standards, the Major Field Test, and the PRAXIS Series of examinations provide appropriate verification measures.

National Standards. Various national educational organizations have developed standards or guidelines for specific subject matter areas. The National Council on Economic Education (2006), for example, publishes the *Voluntary National Content Standards in Economics*. This resource contains economic education benchmarks indicating attainment levels for grades 4, 8, and 12. The National Business Education Association publishes the *National Standards for Business Education*. "This collection of national standards is a forward-looking synthesis of what students should know and be able to do in business" (National Business Education Association, 2006). Although national standards differ in content from one subject to another, their purposes are parallel: they provide excellent ranges of coverage with valid benchmarks for student achievement. These benchmarks, in turn, provide direction for teacher professional development. An assortment of national standards for several subject areas may be found online at http://www.education-world.com/standards/national/index.shtml.

Major Field Test. Business education assessment tools at the postsecondary level have a dual focus. As with most assessments, content knowledge is evaluated. Beyond content knowledge, however, is the need to assess general and subject-specific teaching skills and knowledge. Because business teacher educators need to know how their students compare with other students throughout the nation, assessment instruments offering national norms are typically used. For business students not seeking teacher licensure, a content-based test such as the Major Field Test (MFT) may be an adequate assessment tool. The MFT evaluates ". . . students' ability to analyze and solve problems, understand relationships, and interpret material" (Educational Testing Service, 2006a).

PRAXIS. Most states require successful completion of the PRAXIS Series of examinations for licensing new teachers. PRAXIS I measures basic skills in reading, writing, and mathematics. It is taken by students majoring in education prior to their being admitted to a teacher education program. PRAXIS II is taken by individuals entering the teaching field as a part of the initial teacher licensing process. It measures content knowledge in the specific area for which the prospective teacher has trained. Some states require PRAXIS III for beginning teachers. This test assesses the effectiveness of beginning teachers through direct classroom observation, reflective activities, and semi-structured interviews (Educational Testing Service, 2006b).

Other Types of Assessment

Major Field Tests and PRAXIS exams supply useful assessment data reflective of professional development requirements of beginning teachers. Experienced teachers may look for other types of assessment activities to meet their professional development needs. Business educators, in particular, might want to research various industry certifications or the National Board Certification as a means of professional development. Possibly the best, and certainly the least expensive professional development is done through self-assessment or through collaboration with fellow educators.

Industry expectations. Industry certifications are being used more extensively by employers to determine whether potential employees meet the technical competencies they require. Industry certifications aid employers in recruiting, selecting, and training employees; in setting benchmarks for evaluating and compensating employees; and in enhancing customer confidence in products or services offered. "For business educators, industry certification increases awareness of industry trends, sharpens focus on specific competencies . . . provides guidance in developing learning objectives for curriculum, and enhances respect for educators and business programs" (PCBEE, 2003, No. 72).

Teachers frequently find themselves in situations where they need to add a certification to their licensure or obtain industry certifications to meet the "highly qualified" designation required by No Child Left Behind. Adding a certification to a current license may involve no more than taking a course or two in the content area or a subject-specific methodology course and successful completion of the PRAXIS test for the subject. Studying for and completing Microsoft Office Specialist (MOS), Certified Computing Professional (CCP), Internet and Computing Core Certification (IC^3), or other similar industry assessments are forms of professional development teachers might consider for career enhancement.

National Board Certification. Perhaps the ultimate certification any teacher might seek is National Board Certification, administered by the National Board for Professional Teaching Standards (NBPTS). This is a nationally recognized indication of quality teaching with nationwide standards for evaluating teachers. Teachers seeking this certification must complete a portfolio consisting of work samples from their classroom experiences including exercises ". . . designed to tap the knowledge, skills, disposition and professional judgment that distinguish their practice" (NBPTS, 2006).

Self-assessment and collaboration. "Business educators recognize the need for ongoing professional development when they analyze their own teaching, observe others teaching, are observed, share and discuss ideas critically, challenge their own and others' assumptions, and examine beliefs and practices" (PCBEE, 1997, No. 60). Teachers are sometimes at a loss for exactly what they need, hence, the necessity for assessing teacher needs for determining appropriate faculty development. Finch and Moore (1997) suggest that teachers must differentiate between their needs and wants. Moreover, teachers may require assistance in understanding their needs. They must be acutely aware of what they are facing. "Some have argued that a lack of training opportunities in pre-service programs is the reason for poor quality of assessment practice in our schools" (Trevisan, 2002, p. 766).

Assessment that is beneficial in determining professional development needs may be obtained from numerous and diverse sources. The sources cited in this section are excellent starting places. Scores on a Major Field Test or PRAXIS exams provide feedback for beginning teachers. Veteran educators may find more useful information by researching industry standards or National Board Certification. Continual professional development opportunities are available for all teachers through self-assessment, collaboration with their peers, and assessment-centered activities.

ASSESSMENT OF PROFESSIONAL DEVELOPMENT

Teachers are sometimes uncomfortable with assessment, particularly assessment of their own performance. This is due, in part, to their perception that they are being evaluated based on the performance of their students; and to some degree, this may be the reality. Most assessment programs separate program assessment from teacher evaluations. However, teachers may find it necessary to change their delivery methods because course goals are not being met. For some, any change is difficult (Evans, 2002). Program administrators must first encourage "buy in" from teachers by showing them how appropriate assessment can benefit them personally; and secondly, they must provide teachers with meaningful professional development opportunities.

Ensuring "Buy In"

To ensure "buy in" from teachers, they must be shown how their professional development will be helpful to their students as well as to themselves. This can be accomplished by tying professional development to meaningful student outcomes. For example, administrative support staff in offices today might be expected to hold or obtain specific certifications, such as Microsoft Office Specialist (MOS) or Internet and Computing Core Certification (IC[3]). Obviously, if teachers are going to train students to acquire these certifications, the teachers need a thorough understanding of the skills and concepts necessary to master the examinations. Perhaps the best way for teachers to obtain this understanding would be through sitting for whichever examinations they intend to emphasize.

Acquiring Meaningful Professional Development

Teachers are universally concerned with seeing their students excel. They seek meaningful professional development activities, wherein they are trained in the implementation of appropriate assessment techniques and where they can be shown direct and immediate student benefits. "We believe that as business educators implement individualized, ongoing professional development plans, the results should lead to strengthened teacher roles and improved student learning" (PCBEE, 1997, No. 60). Specifically, teachers should pursue professional development activities that coincide with the curriculum they teach. By doing so, they will achieve the knowledge and confidence levels needed to develop students capable of coping with business and industry expectations.

Although teachers do not always perceive their performance assessments positively, their anxiety may be reduced if they can be shown how they and their students will benefit from the process. Relating personal assessment to student achievement makes the entire process more palatable. Meaningful professional development, that is, activities linked directly to curricular issues, is what teachers want and need.

METHODS OF PROVIDING PROFESSIONAL DEVELOPMENT

Professional development has taken on a new focus in contemporary educational practices. Today's educators see professional development as an ongoing process. "Delivery of professional development experiences is directly linked to teacher learning considerations: learning contexts, learning motivators, and learning types" (Finch & Moore, 1997, p. 110). Thus, diversity in delivery methods is needed. Professional development strategies assume many different forms, including both formal and informal methods: reflection and inquiry, formal instruction, professional organizations, and mentoring and peer collaboration.

Reflection and Inquiry

Faculty should have ample opportunity for reflection and inquiry. Inherent in successful professional growth strategies is the use of data from a teacher's own classroom and experience. Teachers examining their own teaching begin to notice incidents and patterns that they may otherwise overlook. Teachers should allow feedback from their own practice to influence their future practice, including their beliefs and understandings involved in teaching. The National Board for Professional Teaching Standards (NBPTS) presented a vision for "accomplished teaching" that included five core propositions. The fourth proposition asserts that teachers should "think systematically about their practice and learn from experience" (National Board for Professional Teaching Standards, 2006, www.nbpts.org). "Reflection and inquiry into teaching, and the local practical knowledge that results, is a start towards improved assessment in the classroom" (National Research Council, 2001, p. 80).

Professional development through inquiry may take multiple forms, including action research, collaboration, and portfolio development. Action research is conducted by teachers to improve their teaching. It is based on the principle that practical teachers are directed toward action in their classrooms. "By making changes in their own professional activities, teachers learn about themselves and the improvements they desire" (National Research Council, 2001, p. 81).

Other forms of inquiry into teaching might include collaboration with peers and portfolio-based performance assessment. Since teachers work in an ostensibly solitary environment, they can learn through their interactions with other teachers (National Research Council, 1999). They can also learn by utilizing the NBPTS teacher assessment system. For example, the NBPTS National Board Certification is a portfolio-based performance assessment system that looks at a teacher's content knowledge and pedagogical skills, the students' performance, and the teacher's reflections and explanations regarding effectiveness. Content knowledge is measured by having the teacher respond to six essay questions. Pedagogical skills are demonstrated using two videotapes of actual lessons. Samples of students' work provide information about student performance. Finally, the teacher's reflections about teaching and learning effectiveness are included (Galluzzo, 2005).

Formal Instruction

Business and technology education programs are dynamic, requiring business educators to continually update their skills and to learn new skills. In recent years, Web page design and computer programming courses have been added to the business technology curriculum. A variety of programs are being used to teach these courses (e.g., Dreamweaver, JavaScript, Visual Basic, C++, Captivate, etc.). Additionally, new and updated programs are constantly being released.

Formal instruction through college courses, workshops, seminars, and Web-based training provides an excellent way for business educators to enhance their teaching and to learn new technological skills. Continuing education credit is offered by many universities and professional organizations.

Professional Organizations

Business educators who actively participate in professional organizations benefit from the experience in a variety of ways. Organizations, such as the National Business Education Association (NBEA) and its regional and state affiliates, promote the "creation and distribution of knowledge, the sharing of best practices, [and] a framework for solving problems and obtaining advice . . ." (PCBEE, 2006, No. 79). They encourage professional growth through their conferences, publications, and workshops. These workshops provide professional development opportunities that assist educators in becoming highly qualified.

Mentoring and Peer Collaboration

Mentoring can have a significant impact on business teacher educators. Gailbraith (2003) defined mentoring as a mutual interaction, whereby both the "mentor and protégé experience personal, professional, and intellectual growth and development" (p. 2). PCBEE Policy Statement Number 68 (2001) suggests that business educators who have more experience should serve as mentors for and develop meaningful relationships with new teachers. Peer collaboration and peer coaching offer additional avenues for professional development. Taken together, collaboration and coaching allow teachers to realize the synergistic effects of working collectively and to benefit from coaching one another, which, in turn, result in providing an improved learning environment for their students.

Ultimately, assessment should point administrators and business educators to areas where improvement is needed; then, professional development can be provided in those areas. Teachers and administrators should keep in mind that the most successful faculty development activities extend over a period of time, require commitment and support, and encourage the development of teacher learning communities (National Research Council, 1999, p. 142). The types of activities mentioned in this section grow learning communities by allowing for collaboration and reflection.

SUMMARY

Added emphasis on accountability in assessment in education has forced teachers and administrators to reconsider their assessment strategies. Government agencies at multiple levels have increased their expectations for student achievement outcomes. Newer and better and sometimes more complex assessment techniques are required. These factors, in sum, have compelled educators to search for more effective professional development outlets. Thus, *feedback for professional development* has become a critical issue for administrators and teachers alike.

Professional development, at one time viewed as a one-day in-service activity, has taken on a new focus in contemporary education practices. Much like assessment, today's educators see professional development as a formative activity—that is, as an ongoing process. School administrators are recognizing the need for faculty members who are well versed in assessment and are providing the necessary support, financial and otherwise.

To ensure acceptance by teachers, they must be convinced that professional development activities will benefit them as well as their students; and because teachers have varying degrees of assessment knowledge, professional development activities must be selected carefully. Just as students' learning styles differ, so, too, do the learning styles of teachers. Thus, professional development strategies and delivery methods must take diverse forms.

Aside from the typical ways teachers seek professional development—formal instruction and participation in conferences—assessment knowledge can be gained through peer coaching, mentoring, and action research. Personal reflection and inquiry into their teaching practices may also provide an essential source of information. In the final analysis, teachers must choose strategies that suit their needs and that can be adapted to continuously evolving curriculum needs.

REFERENCES

Boston, C. (2002). The concept of formative assessment. *Practical Assessment, Research & Evaluation*. Retrieved March 28, 2006, from http://pareonline.net/getvn.asp?v=8&n=9

Boudett, K. P., Murnane, R. J., City, E., & Moody, L. (2005). Teaching educators how to use student assessment data to improve instruction. *Phi Delta Kappan, 86*(9), 700-706.

Educational Testing Service (ETS). (2006a). Major field test. Retrieved September 13, 2006, from http://www.ets.org/portal/site/ets/menuitem.1488512ecfd5b8849a77b13bc3921509/?vgnextoid=f119af5e44df4010VgnVCM10000022f95190RCRD&vgnextchannel=86f346f1674f4010VgnVCM10000022f95190RCRD

Educational Testing Service (ETS). (2006b). The PRAXIS series. Retrieved September 13, 2006, from http://www.ets.org/portal/site/ets/menuitem.fab2360b1645a1de9b3a0779f1751509/?vgnextoid=48c05ee3d74f4010VgnVCM10000022f95190RCRD

Evans, C. D. (2002). Understanding assessment. *Delta Pi Epsilon Journal, 44*(1), 3-12.

Finch, C. R., & Moore, M. (1997). Meeting business teachers' professional development needs in a school-to-work context. *Delta Pi Epsilon Journal, 39*(2), 95-111.

Foster, J. C., & Pritz, S. G. (2006). The certification advantage. *Techniques, 81*(1), 14-20.

Galbraith, M. W. (2003). Celebrating mentoring. *Adult Learning, 14*(1), 1-2.

Galluzzo, G. R. (2005). Performance assessment and renewing teacher education: The possibilities of the NBPTS standards. *The Clearing House, 78*(4), 142-145.

Hershberg, T. (2005). Value-added assessment and systemic reform: A response to the challenge of human capital development. *Phi Delta Kappan* (December). Retrieved October 2, 2006, from http://find.galegroup.com/itx/infomark.do?&contentSet=IAC-Documents&type=retrieve&tabID=T002&prodId=ITOF&docId=A139834743&source=gale&scrprod=ITOF&rserGroupName=tel_middleten&version=1.0

Johnson, S. T. (1999). Broadening the scope of assessment in the schools: Building teacher efficacy in student assessment. *Journal of Negro Education* (Summer). Retrieved March 29, 2006, from http://www.findarticles.com/p/articles/mi_qu3626/is_199907/ai_n8830291/print

National Board for Professional Teaching Standards. The five core propositions. Retrieved September 13, 2006, from http://www.nbpts.org/the_standards/the_five_core_propositio

National Business Education Association. (2006). Retrieved September 13, 2006, from http://www.nbea.org/curriculum/bes.html

National Council on Economic Education. (2006). Retrieved September 13, 2006, from http://www.ncee.net/ea/program.php?pid=19

National Research Council. (1999). *How people learn: Brain, experience and school*. J. R. Bransford, A. L. Brown, & R. R. Cocking (Eds.). Washington, D.C.: National Academy Press. Retrieved March 28, 2006, from http://www.nap.edu/catalog/9847.html

National Research Council. (2001). *Classroom assessment and the National Science Education Standards*. J. M. Atkin, P. Black, and J. Coffey (Eds.).. Washington, D.C.: National Academy Press. Retrieved March 28, 2006, from http://www.nap.edu/catalog/9847.html

New Jersey Principals and Supervisors Association. (2002). *A call to action for assessment reform*. Retrieved March 31, 2006, from http://www.njpsa.org/docs/asreformcall.htm

Policies Commission for Business and Economic Education (PCBEE) (1997). *This we believe about the professional development of business educators* (Policy statement No. 60). Retrieved March 17, 2006, from http://www.nbea.org/curriculum/no60.html

Policies Commission for Business and Economic Education (PCBEE) (2001). *This we believe about the emerging roles of the business educator*. (Policy statement No. 68). Retrieved September 15, 2006, from http://www.nbea.org/curfpolicy.html

Policies Commission for Business and Economic Education (PCBEE) (2003). *This we believe about industry certification*. (Policy statement No. 72). Retrieved September 10, 2006, from http://www.nbea.org/curfpolicy.html

Policies Commission for Business and Economic Education (PCBEE) (2006). *This we believe about the value of professional associations*. (Policy statement No. 79). Retrieved September 14, 2006, from http://www.nbea.org/curriculum/no79.html

Popper, E. T. L. (2005). Learning goals: The foundation of curriculum development & assessment. *Assessment of Student Learning in Business Schools: Best Practices Each Step of the Way, 1*(2), 1-23.

Trevisan, M. S. (2002). The states' role in ensuring assessment competence. *Phi Delta Kappan, 83*(10), 766-771.

Whittaker, A. (2002, Summer). Tensions in assessment design: Professional development under high-stakes accountability. *Teacher Education Quarterly*. Retrieved March 29, 2006, from http://www.findarticles.com/p/articles/mi_qa3960/is_200207/ai_n9097922/print

Wilcox, D. (2006). The role of industry-based certifications in career and technical education. *Techniques, 81*(1), 21-23.

Assessment of Research

James Calvert Scott
Vancouver, Washington

Carol Blaszczynski
California State University, Los Angeles
Los Angeles, California

Research assessment is critical to ensure the well being of business education, its practitioners, and their constituencies. The assessment of research is the quality control process that should determine which curricular and teaching practices are sound and subsequently implemented by business education professionals for the benefit of others. This chapter discusses understanding research and why research assessment is important, finding business education research, assessing business education research, and implementing business education research findings.

UNDERSTANDING THE IMPORTANCE OF RESEARCH AND RESEARCH ASSESSMENT

This section discusses why research, research assessment, and scientifically-based research matter to business educators.

Why Research Matters

Research as reflected in the literature serves as the foundation of the business education profession by offering information and guidance about many topics (Scott, 2003b). According to Lambrecht (2003), "Research and its dissemination are the foundation of a viable, thriving professional community" (p. 1). Among other things, research develops the knowledge base, enhances teaching, facilitates real-world application, and strengthens not only the discipline but also the researcher's perceived image (Scott, 2003a). Research gives shape and identity to a discipline. Without its own distinct body of research, that discipline does not exist independently and must be considered part of a larger disciplinary entity (Lambrecht, 2003). Historically speaking, business education has had a rich research legacy.

Why Research Assessment Matters

Research assessment matters because it seeks reliable and valid meanings (Davis, 2003). Research assessment is the critical evaluation of the strengths and weaknesses of research. Not all research is well conducted, and the challenge for business educators is to scrutinize all research, differentiating the good from the bad. Some research will be found lacking in critical areas and, consequently, must be discounted or discarded. Other research will be found to have been rigorously conducted and should be embraced, either tentatively or absolutely, depending on the strength of its merits. Only by pondering research can business educators find the reliable and valid meanings and best practices that lead to the well being of students, teachers, and other constituent communities (Hostetler, 2005).

Why Scientifically-Based Research Matters

Scientifically-based research is evidence-based practice (Beghetto, 2003). It is "the application of rigorous, systematic, and objective procedures to obtain reliable and valid knowledge relevant to education activities and programs" (Software & Information Industry Association, 2004, p. 1). Scientifically-based research is required for all federally funded programs under the No Child Left Behind Act of 2001. Scientifically-based research seeks to improve education and to develop a knowledge base about what actually works. At a minimum, public school employees receiving federal funding, including business educators, are required to choose both instructional programs and practices that are supported by scientifically-based research (Beghetto, 2003).

Thus, research, research assessment, and scientifically-based research do matter to all business educators, be they teachers, administrators, or researchers.

FINDING BUSINESS EDUCATION LITERATURE

This section discusses the *Business Education Index*, databases, fugitive literature, and the literature search process.

The *Business Education Index*

From 1940 through 2000, the *Business Education Index* was the way to find business education literature categorized by both subject and author (Blaszczynski & Scott, 2003a). It is an invaluable research tool when following research about a topic over a number of years.

Databases

For more than a decade business educators have used databases to retrieve literature. Among the more useful databases for retrieving business education-related literature are ABI/INFORM Global, Business Source Premier, Inspec, Factiva Select, Education Full-Text, ERIC, Computer Science Index, Academic Search Premier, ISI Web of Science, Business Periodicals Index (Wilson), and Current Contents, depending on the specific topic being researched (B. Fagerheim, personal communication, April 17, 2006). If business education researchers use a number of databases, they will find more of the existing relevant literature. However, it is a myth that databases alone provide adequate access to existing business education literature (Blaszczynski & Scott, 2003b).

Fugitive Literature

Fugitive literature, which is literature that is challenging to secure, is a problem for business educators, since many of their periodicals are not indexed in print or electronic form and can be found only if one personally knows about them and where they can be located (B. Fagerheim, personal communication, November 3, 2005). Some highly regarded business education publications, such as *NABTE Review*; some more recent business education publications, such as the *Journal for Global Business Education*; many conference-related publications, such as most of the books of readings for the Delta Pi Epsilon national conferences; and virtually all regional, state, and provincial business education publications, such as the *Ohio Business Technology Educator*, vanish upon publication as pieces of fugitive literature, never to be known or retrieved by most business educators. Officials of organizations that create fugitive publications need to make every effort to get them indexed and stored somewhere so that they can be accessible and useful to the profession at large.

Literature Search Process

Wilhelm and Kaunelis (2005) provided business educators with a methodical literature search process based upon an analytical thought process. They advocated that business educators (a) identify the search descriptors, (b) organize the literature search process, (c) conduct the literature search, (d) assess the relevant citations, (e) organize the resulting data, and (f) evaluate the acquired information. They also offered implementation tips for various aspects of the process, including extracting search terms and phrases from inquiry questions; searching library catalogs, databases, and the Internet; using a ten-step plan to ensure the best possible outcomes from the search; using abstracts to screen out irrelevant publications; developing a color-coding system to mark information related to major search descriptors to help organize uncovered information; and asking 12 questions to help evaluate the relative strengths and weaknesses of the uncovered literature (Wilhelm & Kaunelis, 2005).

Thus, relevant business education literature can be found using the *Business Education Index*, databases, fugitive literature, and a methodical search process.

ASSESSING BUSINESS EDUCATION RESEARCH

This section discusses understanding assessment procedures commonality, evaluating research outlets, understanding the research cycle, and evaluating study components.

Understanding Assessment Procedures Commonality

Regardless of the role, be it classroom teacher, college professor, administrator, researcher, or author, all business educators share commonality when it comes to research assessment procedures. In other words, all types of business educators should implement the same process and methods when they critically evaluate business education research. The fundamentals of research assessment procedures remain constant regardless of who does it. What may differ among assessors are such things as the purposes for scrutinizing research, the sophistication that is employed in the assessment process, and the type of research information that is sought.

Evaluating Research Outlets

One common method of assessing research is to consider the ranking of the periodical where the research is disseminated. The underlying assumption is that high quality publication outlets tend to publish high quality research. Nevertheless, perceptions of quality, and consequently, related rankings, are subjective and mean various things to different people in varied settings (Clyde, 2005). For example, while DuFrene, Shane-Joyce, and Zimmer (1990) found that business education and office systems department heads ranked the top five business education publications as (1) *The Delta Pi Epsilon Journal,* (2) *NABTE Review,* (3) *Business Education Forum,* (4) *Journal of Business Communication,* and (5) *Journal of Education for Business,* Blair and Balachandran (2002) found that NABTE institution representatives ranked the top five business education publications as (1-2 tie) *The Delta Pi Epsilon Journal* and *NABTE Review,* (3) *Journal of Business Communication,* (4) *Journal of Vocational Education Research* (now known as *Career and Technical Education Research*), and (5) NBEA *Yearbooks.* Table 1 lists publications that National Business Education Association members might access when conducting business education research.

In addition, business educators researching career and technical education topics may find useful publications from outlets such as the National Centers for Career and Technical Education Research.

The reputation of a business education periodical, as reflected in rankings, is influenced by a variety of factors. One is the rigor that the periodical demands of all who publish within its pages. Another is the type of review process the periodical uses. Blind peer review with multiple reviewers and editorial oversight is widely perceived to be more stringent than editorial review alone, especially if that review is done by one person. The credentials and reputations of periodical editors and reviewers are also considerations, as are the credentials and reputations of authors who regularly publish in that periodical. Even periodical longevity influences rankings, with older, well-established periodicals that have withstood the tests of time generally being more highly regarded than newer periodicals that are seeking their niches among business education practitioners.

Understanding the Research Cycle

The research cycle is composed of eight basic elements: the research questions supported by theory, the literature review, the study design, the instrumentation and pilot testing, the data collection, the data analysis, the findings, and the generalizations.

Table 1. *Some Potentially Useful Business Education-Related Publications to Consider When Conducting Research*

A B C Blue Book: US and Canadian Business Publications
AERA SIG (Business Education Computer Information Systems Research) Proceedings
Arizona Business Education Association Journal
Association for Business Communication Conference Proceedings
Balance Sheet
Business Communication Quarterly
Business Education Digest
Business Education Forum
Canadian Business and Current Affairs—Business
Canadian Business and Current Affairs—Education
Career and Technical Education Research
The Delta Pi Epsilon Fall Conference Book of Readings
The Delta Pi Epsilon Journal
EBIT: Educators of Business and Information Technology
Educational Technology Research and Development
Georgia Business Education Association Journal
Human Resource Development Quarterly
Human Resource Development Review
The Information Management Journal
Information Resources Management Journal
Information Systems Management
Information Technology, Learning, and Performance Journal
International Journal of Information Management

Journal for Global Business Education
Journal of Applied Research for Business Instruction
Journal of Business Communication
Journal of Business and Training Education
Journal of Career and Technical Education
Journal of Computer Information Systems
Journal of Consumer Affairs
Journal of Database Management
Journal of Economic Education
Journal of Education for Business
Journal of End User Computing
Journal of Global Information Management
Journal of Global Marketing
Journal of Marketing Education
Journal of Organizational Behavior Management
Kentucky Business Education Association Journal
Management Communication Quarterly
NABTE Review
NBEA Yearbooks
Ohio Business Technology Educator
Ontario Business Educators' Association Newsletter
Performance Improvement Quarterly
The Review: The Journal of the International Society for Business Education
Techniques
THE Journal (Technological Horizons in Education Journal)
Training
Training and Development
Wisconsin Business Education Journal

Research questions supported by theory. A researcher's curiosity often spurs research endeavors. Statements that begin with "I wonder if . . . " could serve as the basis for research studies. Research endeavors stem from questions about the relationship between at least two variables (Wunsch, 1991). Once questions have been identified, a researcher reviews the business education-related literature to determine what has been written about the topic of the research question. If the research question has already been rigorously investigated and the findings are still current, then the research question will not be pursued. If the research question has not been rigorously investigated, or if the findings are not current, the research question will be pursued.

Literature review. The literature review is a critical component of the research cycle. Boote and Beile (2005) asserted that "a researcher or scholar needs to understand what has been done before, the strengths and weaknesses of existing studies, and what they mean. A researcher cannot perform significant research without first understanding the literature in the field" (p. 3). A careful researcher conducts a thorough review of the literature, taking care to use the most current sources available (Wilhelm & Kaunelis, 2005). An appropriate literature review provides a theoretical foundation as well as documents the compelling need for conducting the study.

The time span for the literature review varies, depending on the topic under investigation. Generally speaking, if the topic is one that changes rapidly, such as computer software, a ten-year time span would be warranted; if the topic is one that changes slowly, such as ethical business behavior, a significantly longer time span would be warranted.

Study design. The nature of the research question influences the type of research conducted, and thus, the design of the study. The study design also includes the sample selected and its size (see Bartlett, Higgins, & Kotrlik, 2001; Wunsch, 1986). Regarding the reporting of sample size, Wunsch (1991) recommended this wording:

> The sample size of 100 was selected from a population of 300. This sample size provides an error level of plus or minus 8 percent and a probability level of .95 that the sample data represent the population (pp. 3-4).

A prudent researcher protects the identity of the research subjects or informants and follows the human subjects requirements of the institution, including its Institutional Review Board (IRB), and the funding agency. To that end, an ethical researcher obtains informed consent from research participants (Blaszczynski, 1998; Pyrczak, 2003).

Instrumentation and pilot testing. The research instrument is crafted according to the principles of good survey or interview protocol design. Care must be taken by the researcher to ensure that research items are clearly constructed and not leading or biased. The sequencing of items is also important so that the instrumentation is logical and nonredundant. The researcher should pilot test the instrument to ensure suitability for the desired purposes with a group who possesses the identical or nearly same characteristics as in the targeted sample group (Blaszczynski & Green, 1999; Pyrczak, 2003). Based on feedback from those involved in the pilot testing, the researcher makes necessary additions, deletions, or clarifications before the survey instrument or interview protocol is used to collect study data.

Data collection. The data collected needs to be both representative of the sampled group and valid and reliable (Wunsch, 1991). Representative means that the data were obtained from participants who display the same characteristics as the larger population to which the findings can be generalized. Valid data are data needed to answer the research question (Wunsch, 1991). Reliable data are data that would be identical or at least very similar to what was obtained if the study were to be repeated (Fink, 2005; Girden, 2001; Nardi, 2003). Obtaining a sufficient usable response rate is critical for any researcher. He or she will need to use appropriate follow-up techniques to generate a representative response from a sufficient number of participants to ensure validity and reliability in responses, be they from mailed or e-mailed surveys, Web-based collection methods, or interviews (Blaszczynski, 2003).

Data analysis. Research questions that ponder a relation "between and among variables will require data to be statistically analyzed, which in turn will require interpretation" (Wunsch, 1991, p. 2). Quantitative statistical analysis goes beyond presenting ranges, calculating averages, and using Likert-type scales to measure opinion; it involves uncovering relationships between and among study variables. Data analysis is accomplished using software packages. For example, basic statistics can be generated using Microsoft Excel. More advanced statistical applications require more sophisticated software such as the Statistical Package for the Social Sciences (SPSS) or SAS. Qualitative data analysis is accomplished by hand, by creating a customized database, or by using software packages such as AskSam or Ethnograph (O'Connor, 2002).

Findings. The findings from a research study answer the question "What?" (Dauwalder, 2000, p. 7). The researcher should discuss the findings in light of the study research questions, hypotheses, or objectives (Delta Pi Epsilon, n.d.). The researcher should also discuss how the findings relate to the research of others.

Generalizations. The generalizations apply study findings to a larger population than the research study sampled and/or reveal social patterns and processes. If research is to make a significant contribution, then it must be generalizable beyond the studied group. "The relative value of what we read, listen to, and discuss is dependent upon the significance and applicability of the results" (Wunsch, 1991, p. 1). Perhaps the greatest power of research is that its findings apply to the larger community of practice in business education (Lambrecht, 2003).

Evaluating Study Components

When evaluating study components, focus on the major evaluation checklist items, including such things as the title; the abstract; the introduction, need for the study, and hypotheses or research questions; the literature review, the research design, methodology, and data collection; the findings; and the discussion, conclusions, and recommendations.

Evaluation checklists. Consumers of research studies should realize that a number of useful checklists for evaluating research studies are available. For examples, see American Psychological Association (APA), 2001; Blaszczynski & Green, 1999; Delta Pi Epsilon, n.d.; Fink, 2005; and Pyrczak, 2003. These checklists ensure that research consumers think about the most important factors as they assess the rigor and contribution of research studies. For instance, regarding the introduction, Blaszczynski and Green (1999) suggested that research evaluators consider the degree to which the introduction gives background to understand the problem; states the problem, quandary, or perplexity under investigation; establishes a need for and the importance of the research; and provides a clear research purpose and related research questions or hypotheses. A thoughtful comparison and contrast of multiple research studies with one of these checklists will help both novice and skilled research reviewers do a better job of sorting out which research studies are more credible and less credible.

Title. The title of a research study should concisely but precisely describe the focus of the study. In fact, the American Psychological Association (2001), whose style manual is used by almost all business education publications, recommends that the study title be about 10 to 12 words in length. Any acronyms appearing in the title should be written out in their entirety (Pyrczak, 2003).

Abstract. An abstract captures the essence of the conducted research and helps research consumers determine if the research study is relevant and useful for their purposes. While traditional abstracts have grouped all study information together, typically in one paragraph, structured abstracts, which are increasingly popular in the social sciences literature, use headings to divide the information into categories that allow research consumers to make direct comparisons from one study to another (Miech, Nave, & Mosteller, 2005; Scott & Blaszczynski, 2005).

Introduction, need for study, and hypotheses or research questions. The introduction sets the stage for the research and provides its context. The introduction should identify the specific problem being investigated and build a compelling case with cited literature why that problem is important and merits further study (Blaszczynski & Green, 1999; Fink, 2005; Pyrczak, 2003). The hypotheses, which are tentative answers to questions under investigation, or research questions, which are questions that describe the topics under investigation, identify the focal points of the study. To minimize confusion among readers of the study, the researcher should define key terms (Pyrczak, 2003).

Literature review. The literature review cites the most relevant related studies, and if the study methodology is new or controversial, the relevant literature about that methodology as well. The following are some potentially useful questions to ask when assessing the literature review. How selective is the literature review? How current is the cited literature? Are older cited studies considered to be classic studies in the discipline? Did the researcher clearly differentiate among research, theory, and opinion? Is the literature review sequenced from the more general to the more specific information (Pyrczak, 2003)?

Research design, methodology, and data collection. The researcher should use a defensible research design that is clearly explained. The researcher should also carefully explain the study methodology so that others could replicate the study if they desired to do so. The researcher ought to collect the data through the use of well explained procedures and appropriate instrumentation. The sampling technique of the researcher should attempt to provide a representative sample so that the findings of the study are generalizable to a larger population than was studied (Pyrczak, 2003; Wunsch, 1991). The researcher must avoid the fatal flaws of research, especially using an inadequate sample size (Blaszczynski & Green, 1999; Pyrczak, 2003; Wunsch, 1991) and failing to follow up with nonrespondents (Blaszczynski, 1998).

Findings. The researcher should relate study findings to the hypotheses or research questions that are presented earlier in the research reporting (Pyrczak, 2003). The researcher must report research results without displaying bias. Both positive and negative findings should be reported to maintain objectivity (Dauwalder, 2000). The levels of statistical significance used by the researcher should be reported (Blaszczynski, 2003; Blaszczynski & Green, 1999), as should effect sizes (Girden, 2001; Lipsey & Wilson, 2001; West, 1990).

Discussion, conclusions, and recommendations. The researcher should make reference to the hypotheses or research questions for contextual purposes as he or she engages in discussion, draws conclusions, and offers recommendations. Further, the conclusions and recommendations should be discussed in terms of the cited literature (Pyrczak, 2003). No new reference sources should be introduced by the researcher in the discussion, conclusions, and recommendations (Dauwalder, 2000). Two common errors made by the researcher are making unsupported conclusions and recommendations and presenting restated research findings as conclusions (Dauwalder, 2000). The researcher ought to provide specific study implications and future research recommendations (Pyrczak, 2003). The researcher should make two types of recommendations: recommendations for specific action(s) to be taken and recommendations for additional research (Blaszczynski & Green, 1999).

Thus, to assess business education research effectively, business educators must understand assessment procedures commonality for teachers, researchers, authors, and reviewers; evaluate research outlets; understand the research cycle; and evaluate study components.

IMPLEMENTING BUSINESS EDUCATION RESEARCH FINDINGS

This section discusses implementing business education research findings at various instructional levels.

Secondary Level

Rader (2005) compared state and national business education standards in a nationwide study. She found that 39 of the 50 states had specific content standards for programs involving business education. Twenty-three of the states with standards had standards that were somewhat similar, very similar, or identical to the National Business Education Association's *National Standards for Business Education*. Secondary business educators and business teacher educators, as well as state department of education personnel, can use this research information as a guide for developing their instructional programs in business education and for evaluating those programs. Further, this research information facilitates the providing of equal educational opportunities for students through relatively consistent content standards from one state to another state and the improving of business education student performance regardless of location.

Chadd and Anderson (2005) surveyed teacher-coordinators and worksite mentors of Illinois high school work-based learning programs about the mentors' knowledge of teaching work skills to students in work-based learning programs and the training provided to the worksite mentors. They found no statistically significant difference in knowledge about teaching among worksite mentors based on training attendance. Informal training was most often provided by teacher-coordinators to inform worksite mentors about work-based learning program procedures. Worksite mentors who were untrained reported that training was not available, while worksite mentors who were formally trained rated that instruction highly. This research tells office occupations and marketing educators, among other career and technical educators, that for worksite learning to be as good as or better than traditional classroom learning, worksite mentors need training from teacher-coordinators that expands worksite mentors' techniques and abilities to develop new work skills in students.

Community College Level

Kilcoyne and Redmann (2005) conducted a regional study of administrative support workers who belonged to the International Association of Administrative Professionals (IAAP) in East Texas, Louisiana, and Mississippi. The study purpose was to find out the perceived importance of job skills, related categories, and tools that were needed to perform their jobs successfully. Study outcomes included an ordering of job skills in terms of relative importance and reporting of such things as software used, office technology used, and the like. This research information is most applicable at the community college level, where the majority of administrative support workers are trained, although is does have value at the secondary school and college and university levels as well. The research findings provide insight into what administrative support workers in the studied area and possibly elsewhere are doing and how they are doing it, which is important rich information for designing new administrative support programs and modifying existing ones to ensure that information systems graduates meet the real needs of the business community.

College and University Level

Scott and Blaszczynski (2005) surveyed students in six intact sections of the core business communication course at a Western state university about their perceptions of a traditional abstract and a structured abstract with embedded headings regarding reading ease, information value, reading speed, and usefulness in deciding whether to read the related article. The researchers found that the students preferred the structured abstract over the traditional abstract in terms of reading ease (65% vs. 35%), information value (70% vs. 30%), reading speed (55% vs. 45%), and usefulness in deciding to read the related article (70% vs. 30%). This research, which is applicable at the college and university levels in business communication- and research-related courses, suggests that because today's students are receptive to structured abstracts, which are increasingly used in the research and academic worlds, teachers of business communication and research courses should expand their course content to include the teaching of structured abstracts.

All Instructional Levels

Groneman (2005) used data-mining techniques to compare the content of online want ads from a Web site in 2000 and again in 2004 to help information systems educators assess which skills for new information technology workers should be emphasized or de-emphasized. She found that the ranking of information technology (IT) skills listed in the ads did not significantly change between 2000 and 2004, although there were notable changes in the programming/scripting, database skills, operating systems, desktop publishing, and groupware categories. This research can be used by business educators at all instructional levels who prepare information technology workers, since it focuses attention on the information technologies being demanded in the marketplace. This information can be used to identify the IT skills most in demand, thereby informing curricular choices about what to emphasize or de-emphasize in offered courses and instructional programs.

Thus, business educators at all instructional levels—secondary, community college, and college and university—can make major use of business education research to shape and to improve the instruction that they deliver.

SUMMARY

Business educators should realize the importance of research and research assessment. They need to be able to find the business education literature using available research tools and an appropriate literature search process. Business educators should assess business education research by understanding research assessment procedures commonality for all types of business educators, evaluating research outlets, understanding the research cycle, and evaluating research study components. By comprehending and applying these principles of research assessment, business educators at all instructional levels are ready to use research findings to enhance the quality of the instruction that they deliver to diverse audiences at various instructional levels.

REFERENCES

American Psychological Association. (2001). *Publication manual of the American Psychological Association* (5th ed.). Washington, DC: Author.

Bartlett, J. E., Higgins, C. C., & Kotrlik, J. W. (2001). Selecting an appropriate sample size for conducting survey research. In *Book of readings, 2001 Delta Pi Epsilon national conference* (pp. 143-148). Little Rock, AR: Delta Pi Epsilon.

Beghetto, R. (2003). Scientifically-based research: *ERIC Digest.* Retrieved October 14, 2005, from First Search database.

Blair, R. B., & Balachandran, M. E. (2002). Faculty perceptions of business education journals. *The Delta Pi Epsilon Journal, 43*(3), 190-204.

Blaszczynski, C. (1998). Conducting ethical business education research. *The Delta Pi Epsilon Journal, 40*(4), 202-213.

Blaszczynski, C. (2003). Strategies for credible data reporting and presentation. *The Delta Pi Epsilon Journal, 45*(2), 77-86.

Blaszczynski, C., & Green, D. J. (1999). Strategies for writing quantitative and qualitative research articles. *The Delta Pi Epsilon Journal, 41*(4), 204-211.

Blaszczynski, C., & Scott, J. C. (2003a). The business education literature: Going, going, gone? *NABTE Review, 30,* 23-28.

Blaszczynski, C., & Scott, J. C. (2003b). The researcher's challenge: Building a credible literature review using electronic databases. *Information Technology, Learning, and Performance Journal, 21*(2), 1-8.

Boote, D. N., & Beile, P. (2005). Scholars before researchers: On the centrality of the dissertation literature review in research preparation. *Educational Researcher, 34*(6), 3-15. Retrieved October 10, 2005, from http://www.aera. net/publications/?id=331

Chadd, J., & Anderson, M. A. (2005). Illinois work-based learning programs: Worksite mentor knowledge and training. *Career and Technical Education Research, 30*(1), 25-45.

Clyde, L. A. (2005). The basis for evidence-based practice: Evaluating the research evidence. Online conference proceedings. World Library and Information Congress: 71th IFLA General Conference and Council, "Libraries – A voyage of discovery," Oslo, Norway, August 14-18, 2005. Retrieved October 7, 2005, from http://www.ifla.org/IV/ifla71/ papers/050e-Clyde.pdf

Dauwalder, D. P. (2000). Formulating sound conclusions and recommendations. *The Delta Pi Epsilon Journal, 42*(1), 6-13.

Davis, O. L., Jr. (2003). Editorial: The need to ponder results. *Journal of Curriculum and Supervision, 18*(3), 197-199.

Delta Pi Epsilon. (n.d.). Delta Pi Epsilon national conference research proposal evaluation form. Retrieved December 14, 2005, from http://www.dpe.org/pdf/ NatConf-ResearchCriteria.pdf

DuFrene, D. D., Shane-Joyce, M. P., & Zimmer, T. M. (1990). Quality perceptions of journals for business education professionals. *NABTE Review, 17,* 38-42.

Fink, A. (2005). *Conducting research literature reviews: From the Internet to paper* (2nd ed.). Thousand Oaks, CA: Sage Publications.

Girden, E. R. (2001). *Evaluating research articles from start to finish* (2nd ed.). Thousand Oaks, CA: Sage Publications.

Groneman, N. (2005). Trends in IT skills needed by businesses from 2000-2004 with implications for IT curricular offerings. *NABTE Review, 32,* 42-47.

Hostetler, K. (2005). What is "good" education research? *Educational Researcher, 34*(6), 16-21.

Kilcoyne, M. S., & Redmann, D. H. (2005). Administrative support occupations skills inventory: Implications for information systems graduates. *NABTE Review, 32,* 62-68.

Lambrecht, J. (2003). Guest editorial. *The Delta Pi Epsilon Journal, 45*(1), 1-2.

Lipsey, M. W., & Wilson, D. B. (2001). *Practical meta-analysis.* Thousand Oaks, CA: Sage Publications.

Miech, E. J., Nave, B., & Mosteller, F. (2005). The 20,000 article problem: How a structured abstract can help practitioners sort out educational research. *Phi Delta Kappan, 86*(5), 396-400.

Nardi, P. M. (2003). *Doing survey research: A guide to quantitative methods.* Boston: Pearson.

O'Connor, B. N. (2002). Qualitative case study research in business education. *The Delta Pi Epsilon Journal, 44*(2), 80-90.

Pyrczak, F. (2003). *Evaluating research in academic journals: A practical guide to realistic evaluation* (3rd ed.). Los Angeles: Pyrczak Publishing.

Rader, M. H. (2005). A comparison of state and national standards for business education. *NABTE Review, 32,* 10-15.

Scott, J. C. (2003a). Conceiving and building a sustainable research program. *The Delta Pi Epsilon Journal, 45*(1), 3-16.

Scott, J. C. (2003b). Lifelong professional development. In M. H. Rader (Ed.), *Effective methods of teaching business education in the 21st century,* (pp. 314-326). Reston, VA: National Business Education Association.

Scott, J. C., & Blaszczynski, C. (2005). Business students' perceptions about structured versus traditional abstracts. In *Book of readings, 2005 Delta Pi Epsilon national conference* (pp. 43-48). Little Rock, AR: Delta Pi Epsilon.

Software & Information Industry Association. (2004, February). What the words mean: Help for understanding SBR from the Software & Information Industry Association. Retrieved October 14, 2005, from http://www.thejournal.com/ magazine/vault/ aritcleprintversion.cfm?aid=4684794

West, L. J. (1990). Distinguishing between statistical and practical significance. *The Delta Pi Epsilon Journal, 32*(1), 1-4.

Wilhelm, W. J., & Kaunelis, D. (2005). Literature reviews: Analysis, planning, and query techniques. *The Delta Pi Epsilon Journal, 47*(2), 91-106.

Wunsch, D. R., (1986). Survey research: Determining sample size and representative response. *Business Education Forum, 40*(5), 31-34.

Wunsch, D. R. (1991). How to evaluate research as a research consumer. *Instructional Strategies: An Applied Research Series, 7*(3), 1-6.

Assessment for Teacher Certification/Licensure

Michael L. McDonald
Western Kentucky University
Bowling Green, Kentucky

Dennis LaBonty
Utah State University
Logan, Utah

Richard C. Lacy
California State University, Fresno
Fresno, California

The goal of preparing competent business employees and economically literate citizens is important and begins with highly qualified business teachers. To assure that our business teacher education programs are developing highly qualified teachers, the qualifications of business teachers must be scrutinized and assessed. The question this chapter addresses is how business teacher candidates and practicing business teachers are currently assessed.

In the United States of America, the responsibility for setting standards and assessing the qualifications of teachers rests with the states. In addition, business education programs in the U.S. territories and the overseas programs that are represented by the International Society for Business Education (ISBE) determine their own methods of assessing business teacher candidates. Describing how all business education candidates are assessed would be an extensive task. In this chapter, a sampling of three states is used to describe the assessment of business teacher candidates, including the impact of No Child Left Behind (NCLB) as it influences the assessment process for business education. Each state reporting here represents a different region of the National Business Education Association (NBEA). Although differences will surely exist in other states, territories, and countries, the sampling should offer general characteristics of assessments of business education candidates and teachers.

TEACHER CERTIFICATION IN KENTUCKY

The purpose of this section is to explain Kentucky's assessment for business education teacher licensure and required business subject matter competence. This will be accomplished by describing the Kentucky teacher preparation program, the PRAXIS subject assessment, the routes to licensure, alternative routes to teacher certification, and the impact of the No Child Left Behind (NCLB) Act of 2001.

Teacher Preparation Program

Business and marketing education teachers in Kentucky are certified to teach grades 5 through 12. Certification is based upon the completion of an accepted four-year teacher preparation program that includes student teaching and testing when applicable. The approval of teacher education programs rests with the Education Professional Standards Board (EPSB).

The EPSB oversees the education profession and is the standards and accreditation agency for Kentucky teachers and administrators and for programs of education at colleges and universities. The EPSB does not prescribe course requirements for particular teacher education programs. Each teacher education program submits a folio describing its prospective program for approval by this board. All teacher education programs are reviewed to determine if they meet the Kentucky New Teacher Standards for Preparation & Certification. The teacher education program must show that prospective teachers are prepared to design and plan instruction, create and maintain a learning climate, implement and manage instruction, assess and communicate learning results, reflect and evaluate teaching and learning, collaborate with colleagues, parents, others, and engage in professional development. Additionally, teachers must demonstrate knowledge of content in their subject area and the implementation of technology (Education Professional Standards Board, 2006).

The approved folio for the business and marketing education program at Western Kentucky University lists the required courses that provide the subject area expertise for teaching business and marketing courses at middle school, high school, or area technical centers. The required courses in the business and marketing specialization component include Accounting (financial and managerial), Macroeconomics, Computer Applications, Personal Finance, Organization and Management, Basic Marketing Concepts, Principles of MIS, Word Processing, Desktop Publishing, Law or Legal Environment, Business Communications, Office Systems, Office Employee Training, and a Business and Marketing Education Seminar (Western Kentucky University, 2002).

Kentucky requires a recommendation from the certification official at the college/university (where applicants complete their initial teacher preparation program and student teaching) regarding the specific teacher preparation program completed, the grade level(s), the degree level, and the completion date of the program. All applicants must submit the following for certification:

- Official transcripts of all graduate and undergraduate coursework

- Verification of full-time classroom teaching experience at the appropriate grade level(s)

- Passing score on the PRAXIS II Subject Assessment test for the area of certification

- The Principles of Learning and Teaching test score for appropriate grade range

- Verification of completion of teacher preparation program (Education Professional Standards Board, 2006).

Praxis II: Subject Assessment

The PRAXIS II test measures knowledge of specific subjects that K-12 educators will teach, as well as general and subject-specific teaching skills and knowledge. There are Subject Assessments, Principles of Learning and Teaching (PLT) Tests and Teaching Foundations Tests. (Educational Testing Service, 2006). Business and Marketing Education candidates in Kentucky must score a minimum of 590 on the Business Education PRAXIS II exam. There is no exam for Marketing Education. According to a representative at PRAXIS (personal communication, March 1, 2006), 44 states and the Virgin Island require the PRAXIS exam for teacher certification.

Routes to Licensure

Kentucky teacher certification involves three rank levels and a state-prescribed internship. The rationale for multiple levels is to encourage teachers to continue their education and update their skills.

Rank III/ Kentucky Teacher Internship Program (KTIP). After meeting the educational requirements for teacher certification and upon beginning their first teaching position, candidates enter the Kentucky Teacher Internship Program (KTIP) and become interns. After successfully completing the one-year internship, candidates receive a four-year Rank III certification. The following are requirements of the Rank III certification:

- A bachelor's degree leading to a provisional teaching certificate

- An official college transcript of the rank change

- Verification by the certification officer at the institution where the candidate completed the rank change

After two years of teaching at the Rank III level, the teacher must have completed one-half of the requirements for Rank II (Education Professional Standards Board, 2006).

Rank II/ (KTIP). To continue in a teaching career in Kentucky, teachers must obtain the Rank II certification, which includes the following requirements.

- A master's degree to enhance the professional competency of the initial teaching certification; add a certification area not covered by the initial certificate; or advance professionally to a higher position, OR

- A 32 semester-hour non-degree Education Planned Fifth-Year Program (graduate level); OR the Kentucky Continuing Education Option (Education Professional Standards Board, 2006).

Rank I/ (KTIP). Teachers in Kentucky must obtain the Rank II certification to continue their careers. However, a Rank I certification is *not* required. This rank change may be obtained for salary increases. The requirements for a Rank I certification follow:

- Thirty semester hours of approved graduate credit in addition to Rank II; OR

- Sixty semester hours of approved graduate credit including a master's degree; OR

- National Board for Professional Teaching Standards Certification; or the Kentucky Continuing Education Option (Education Professional Standards Board, 2006).

Alternative Routes to Teacher Certification

Another method business education candidates may follow to become certified in Kentucky is the use of alternative routes. This method is primarily for candidates who did not follow the traditional education route in becoming certified. These candidates usually do not have degrees in education but have exceptional work and/or educational experiences. Kentucky has seven alternative route options (Education Professional Standards Board, 2006).

The most popular alternative route used in Kentucky is the university-based route. Candidates follow the guidelines of the state-approved university program. According to the Kentucky Educational Professional Standards Board (Education Professional Standards Board, 2006), 14 universities in the state have approved programs. The program at Western Kentucky University (WKU) is one of those state-approved programs.

Applicants for alternative admission to the College of Education and Behavioral Sciences at WKU are expected to demonstrate that they are qualified to pursue graduate study in rigorous academic programs with undergraduate GPA and Graduate Record Examination (GRE) scores that meet the university's minimum standards for acceptance to the graduate studies program. In addition, the applicant must submit a professional portfolio that contains a record of vocational attainment and recognition; a statement of goals indicating commitment to pursue graduate education; letters of support from instructors, co-workers, or work supervisors; scholarly papers and/or projects; and any other supportive materials (Western Kentucky University, 2003).

The Impact of No Child Left Behind (NCLB)

The No Child Left Behind Act (NCLB) of 2001 did not have a substantial impact on Kentucky's education system. The state had already enacted legislation and provisions that met most of the NCLB requirements. "Kentucky already had goals for proficient student performance, baselines, and a support system for schools in assistance" (Kentucky Department of Education, 2006). Modifications were made to assessments to make federal accountability decisions. Kentucky had adopted and implemented goals that are shared with those of NCLB. One example, the Commonwealth Accountability Testing System (CATS) was designed to improve teaching and student learning in Kentucky. CATS includes the Kentucky Core Content Test, a nationally norm-referenced test, writing portfolios and prompts, and the alternate portfolio for students with severe to profound disabilities.

The Commonwealth of Kentucky has two entities monitoring and upgrading education. The Kentucky Department of Education (KDE) provides resources and guidance to Kentucky's public schools and districts as they implement the state's K-12 education requirements. The department also serves as the state liaison for federal education requirements and funding opportunities.

In Kentucky the EPSB has set high standards for college and university programs approved to prepare business and marketing education teachers in the Commonwealth. These standards align with national NCLB requirements. Further, this board implemented seven alternative routes to teacher certification for individuals who wish to teach now, but did not take the traditional education route to teacher certification.

TEACHER CERTIFICATION IN UTAH

The purpose of this section is to explain Utah's assessment for business education teacher licensure. This will be accomplished by discussing Utah's business education state standards, routes to licensure, the PRAXIS II assessment in Utah, and the impact of No Child Left Behind (NCLB).

Business Education State Standards

Utah has state specialists who are responsible for establishing state standards for five distinct business-related content areas. These content areas are business education, economics and entrepreneurship, keyboarding, information technology, and marketing education. The business education endorsement includes subject areas of accounting, banking and finance, business communications, business information technology, business law, business management, and business math. The information technology endorsement is very technical. It includes the certification areas of Certified Novell Administrator (CAN), Cisco Certification Networking Associate (CCNA), Microsoft Certification Professional (MCP), A+ (Computer Repair/Maintenance), Occupational Computer Programming, Networking+, and Multimedia. Both the business education and information technology endorsements have separate and distinct state specialists who are responsible for establishing and assessing teaching endorsement programs. Most Utah postsecondary business teacher education programs qualify for content areas in business education, economics and entrepreneurship, and keyboarding; however, only two prepare teachers for selected areas of Information Technology endorsements.

The twenty-four state business education standards, which were revised in 2000, address business education teacher education program guidelines such as student teaching and advisement; internships; teaching methodology; student and professional organizations; knowledge base content including accounting, communication, economics, management, information systems and technology, marketing, entrepreneurship, finance, international business related practices, business law, and business mathematical computations. The fourteen marketing education standards, similar to those in business education, address pedagogical skills and marketing content specifically.

These two sets of teacher program standards are reviewed by the state specialist from each of the CTE (Career and Technical Education) subject areas. The teacher program standards, along with the institutional requirements, are designed to prepare business teachers and marketing teachers to teach courses related to these subject areas in the 6-12 grade levels.

Routes to Licensure

There are two routes to licensure in Utah—a traditional route and an alternative route. The traditional route contains Level 1 and Level 2 licensure requirements. Licensure information specifically related to business and marketing education is available through the Internet (Utah Business Education Licensing, 2006 and Utah Marketing Education Licensing, 2006).

Level 1 License. The traditional method is followed by individuals seeking an Educator License Level 1. It is available to individuals who graduate with a business education degree from a postsecondary institution that has an approved business teacher education program. Each of the higher education institutions recommend their graduates for licensure, and the Utah State Office of Education (USOE) Educator Licensing Bureau grants the license. A Level 1 license is issued for only three years. The higher education institutions that offer business teacher education, as of the writing to this chapter, are Southern Utah University, Utah State University, Utah Valley State College, and Weber State University. The degree programs at these schools comply with the twenty-four state business education standards.

Furthermore, each institution sets graduation requirements for students in their programs. These requirements vary. At Utah State University, for example, students must complete an application in order to be accepted into the College of Education. Items that are checked on this entry application include completion of English, math, and science courses; passing a writing exam, passing a speech and hearing exam, and submitting to an FBI criminal background check. All students must graduate with a minimum 2.75 GPA.

Level 2 License. After a teacher completes at least two successful years of teaching, the school district recommends that teacher to the USOE Educator Licensing Division for an Educator License Level 2. A Level 2 license is issued for only five years, and must be renewed every five years by providing proof of 100 Educator Licensing points.

Education licensing points are called "Professional Development Points." Teachers receive points for a variety of activities (Utah State Office of Education, 2006). There are ten categories of acceptable license renewal activities from which teachers can earn points. Three of the ten categories include complete college or university coursework, attend in-service professional development, and attend acceptable conferences or workshops. Upon reaching the 100 points, teachers are recommended by their districts for a Level 2 license.

Alternative routes to licensure. A second method to business teaching licensure in Utah is through Alternative Routes to Licensure (ARL). ARL is a program for individuals who have a bachelor's degree or higher but lack teacher preparation (Utah.gov., 2006) Qualified candidates are eligible to teach in an accredited secondary school (middle school, junior high school, high school). They must have a degree major in a subject taught in Utah secondary schools. University degrees and degree majors are verified through original transcripts that document the degree, the major, and the year conferred. ARL only accepts degrees and transcripts from institutions of higher education that have been accredited. The following is a list of acceptable accrediting organizations: (1) Middle States Commission on Higher Education, (2) New England Association of Schools and Colleges, (3) North Central Association Commission on Accreditation and School Improvement, (4) Northwest Commission on Colleges and Universities, (5) Southern Association of Colleges and Schools, (6) Western Association of Schools and Colleges: Senior College Commission, (7) National Council for Accreditation of Teacher Education NCATE, and (8) Teacher Education Accreditation Council TEAC.

In addition, the ARL program allows participants to teach in an accredited Utah school on a temporary license (in years two or three of the program), while they are satisfying licensure requirements. ARL participants, who complete the program, receive a Level I license for Secondary Education (Grades 6-12). Additionally, there are ARL programs for Early Childhood Education (Kindergarten) and Elementary Education (Grades 1-8).

Career and Technical Education (CTE) has eight content areas for candidates to enter an ARL program. State specialists administer and advise these programs. The program areas under CTE are agriculture, business, economics, family and consumer science, engineering, marketing, technology, and trades & industry.

PRAXIS II Subject Assessment Test

Utah is in its initial stage of implementing PRAXIS II assessment tests, and has been in the process of establishing passing scores in all subject areas. Business education is one of those subject areas. Utah State Board of Education personnel have initiated a plan to establish a passing score. This plan involves waiting until 30 teachers from various colleges and universities complete the test. A committee will review the 30 exam scores to determine a benchmark passing score. Until the benchmark passing score is established, teachers who complete the PRAXIS II subject assessment test with a score above 650 automatically will be considered "Highly Qualified," which satisfies the requirement for No-Child-Left-Behind. Teachers who score below 650 will be placed in a category known as "Temporary." This category of teachers will be reviewed after the passing score is established. The current national medium for the business education content exam is a score of 650; therefore, Utah is starting out with a passing score of 650.

Furthermore, ARL teacher candidates must also complete the PRAXIS II content tests. This is accomplished in Step 5 of the six-step ARL licensing process. In step 5, ARL candidates are required to take the PRAXIS Content Area Tests for assessment purposes.

Currently in Utah, there is only one PRAXIS II content test for business education and no test for marketing education, with no plans to develop one. Business and marketing education graduates and ARL candidates only have to complete the business content test.

The Impact of No Child Left Behind (NCLB)

NCLB requires specific standards in order to meet the Highly Qualified (HQ) requirement of the federal law in Section 1119 of the Elementary and Secondary Education Act as defined in Section 9101(23). NCLB addresses only certain core subjects: English, reading, language arts, mathematics, science, foreign language, civics and government, economics, art, history, and geography. In Utah, NCLB is an add-on to the current state licensing standards for endorsements and renewals. A teacher may become permanently Highly Qualified (HQ) by passing a content test or accumulating a major equivalency in an endorsement that is required to teach an assigned class. Content tests include subject content related to specific discipline areas. For example in business education, the content test includes questions directed at several business and consumer areas including accounting, marketing, economics, information systems, and keyboarding. Other teaching disciplines such as physical education, language arts, and others have content specific questions for graduates from those programs. Utah is using the PRAXIS II subject assessment tests to assess teacher content knowledge.

As of July 1, 2005, all students who graduate from a Utah accredited business education program must submit that they have taken a PRAXIS II subject assessment test. Currently, business education graduates and ARL business teacher candidates are required to take the PRAXIS II test for business even though a content test of any type for business education is not listed in NCLB for "Highly Qualified" status. Consequently, it is too early to tell if the PRAXIS II content area test is adequately assessing the traditional business or marketing education entering teachers or the ARL teacher candidates.

While it is clear that there is assessment of business and marketing teachers from higher education institutions and ARL teacher candidates, further determination of business education teaching quality likely will be evident when a passing score is assessed and teachers apply their teaching skills and content in the classroom.

Business teacher education licensure in Utah is available through two routes—a traditional university program route and an alternative route. The traditional route based on business education standards contains two levels known as Level 1 and Level 2. The alternative route is more complicated than the traditional route, but it is available for individuals who have professional business experience and desire to become public school teachers. Recently the state has implemented NCLB requirements into the licensure process. This is being accomplished through content area assessment testing in both the traditional and alternative routes.

TEACHER CERTIFICATION IN CALIFORNIA

The intent of this section is to describe the business teacher education certification process in California that includes the SB (Senate Bill) 2042 credential, state standards for business education, routes to licensure, and alternative paths to certification. In addition, the impact of No Child Left Behind (NCLB) for business teacher certification will also be addressed.

SB 2042 Credential

In 1998, the California Commission on Teacher Credentialing (CCTC) launched an extensive standards and assessment development effort designed to improve the preparation of K-12 teachers. In 1999, that effort resulted in the passage of SB 2042, Commission-sponsored legislation. The SB 2042 credential is a two-tier credential with specific requirements for each tier. The first tier is the Five-Year Preliminary Credential and the second tier is the Professional Clear Credential. In California, candidates obtain either a multiple-subject credential to teach in grades K-6 or a single-subject credential to teach in grades 7-12. The latter is discipline specific; that is, business, English, math, science, social science, etc. (Induction Manual – A Credential Application Processing Guidebook for Commission-Approved Induction Programs, 2004).

State Standards for Business Education

Currently there are 16 standards of quality and effectiveness that guide business teacher preparation in California. These 16 standards pertain to (1) Program Philosophy and Purpose, (2) Administrative Systems and Support, (3) Computer/Information Systems, (4) Marketing, (5) Accounting, (6) Macroeconomics, (7) Microeconomics,

(8) Business Management, (9) Legal Environment, (10) Entrepreneurship, (11) Quantitative Analysis, (12) Diversity and Equity in the Program, (13) Coordination of the Program, (14) Student Advisement and Support, (15) Assessment of Subject Matter Competence, and (16) Program Review and Development.

In 2005, the CCTC convened business educators from throughout California to update and revise these standards. Therefore, in 2007, each collegiate business teacher education program will need to be re-approved again. The first 10 standards are now common to all disciplines, i.e., all subject matter programs have these same 10 standards. These are (1) Program Philosophy and Purpose, (2) Diversity and Equity, (3) Technology, (4) Literacy, (5) Varied Teaching Strategies, (6) Early Field Experience, (7) Assessment of Subject Matter Competence, (8) Advisement and Support, (9) Program Review and Evaluation, and (10) Coordination. The following 6 standards specifically relate to business. These are (11) Business Management, (12) Accounting and Finance, (13) Marketing, (14) Information Technology, (15) Economics, and (16) Business Environment and Communication.

Routes to Licensure

To teach business education at the secondary level (7-12) in California, candidates must graduate from a college/university that has a subject-matter competency program in business teacher education that has been approved by CCTC. Currently, there are three approved collegiate business teacher education programs in California: California State University, Fresno; California State Polytechnic University, Pomona; and Humboldt State University. Several other paths to certification are also available that will be discussed. These programs must currently comply with the 16 standards for teaching business adopted by the CCTC in 1996 (California Commission on Teaching Credentialing, 1999).

In California all business single subject programs are fifth-year programs. That is, candidates complete a bachelor's degree in business and then complete the course-work for the preliminary single-subject credential in business education as a fifth-year course of study after the bachelor's degree has been earned. This fifth-year program also includes an English Learner's Authorization so candidates are able to teach English language learners more effectively.

The preliminary credential is issued for five years and is not renewable. Candidates for this credential who complete their teacher preparation through a Commission-accredited program must be recommended through their college/university credential office. During the five-year period, candidates must work toward a Professional Clear Credential by completing one of three options. Option 1 requires candidates to complete a Commission-approved SB 2042 Professional Teacher Induction Program through an approved school district, county office of education, college/university, consortium or private school. Option 2 requires candidates to complete a Beginning Teacher Support and Assessment (BTSA) Program and Commission-approved course work. Option 3 requires candidates to complete a fifth year of study at a California college/university with a Commission-accredited teacher education program. All three options include advanced work in health education, law, methods, computer technology, English learners, and requirements for providing educational opportunities to special populations in the regular classroom.

The Professional Clear Credential is valid for five years. Then every five years, candidates must complete an additional 150 hours of professional development work that may include additional collegiate coursework, attending conferences or workshops, providing service in a leadership role, or conducting educational research. (Requirements for the Professional Clear Credential, SB 2042, 2005).

The California Commission on Teacher Credentialing maintains a Web site with current information pertaining to licensure including information on subject matter authorizations, supplementary authorizations, and credential program administration (California Commission on Teacher Credentialing, 2005).

Alternative Paths to Certification

Alternative paths to certification in California include four options: The California Subject Examination for Teachers (CSET) exam; Transcript evaluation for individuals who are completing a credential from an institution in California (that institution does not have a CCTC approved subject matter program); supplementary authorizations; and individuals who hold an out-of-state credential.

California Subject Examination for Teachers (CSET). The first alternative path to certification requires candidates to pass the California Subject Examination for Teachers (CSET). Presently, there are 30 different CSET examinations and business is 1 of these 30. The CCTC allows candidates to complete a Commission-approved subject-matter program or pass the CSET exam. Individuals in California that complete any single-subject subject program or pass the CSET exam in their discipline are considered Highly Qualified (HQ) under NCLB. If candidates complete a subject-matter program, then the CSET is not required. In addition, if candidates pass a CSET exam in a selected teaching area, then completing a single-subject program is not required. Upon successful completion of either the exam or subject matter program, candidates are able to enter a Commission-approved teacher education program. As a result, those who pass the CSET exam may enter a teacher education program at any college/university in California and obtain a credential to teach business, even though that institution may not offer an approved business teacher education program.

The CSET exam, developed with the assistance of National Evaluation Systems, replaces the PRAXIS exam. The CSET exam has objective and written response components for each of the following three subtests: (1) Business Management and Marketing, (2) Accounting, Finance and Economics, and (3) Information Technology,

Business Environment, and Communication. All secondary and postsecondary standards including the CSET exam were aligned to ensure the continuity of standards (California Subject Examinations for Teachers, 2006).

Transcript evaluation. A second alternative path to certification is for those who have earned a business degree from a college/university that does not have a CCTC-approved subject matter program. In business these individuals may have their transcripts evaluated by one of the three approved business subject-matter programs in California to determine if they have met subject matter equivalency. Subject matter equivalency means that one has completed essentially the same business coursework that is required from one of these three CCTC approved programs. If not, additional coursework is required. When subject-matter equivalency is met, the candidates can pursue a single-subject credential from any college/university in California that grants a teaching credential (Induction Manual, 2004).

Supplementary authorizations. A third alternative path is for one to obtain a supplementary authorization. California grants supplementary authorizations to teach in additional disciplines other than one's single-subject discipline. For example, if a candidate has a single subject credential in English, then that candidate could teach business subjects by completing an introductory subject authorization to teach business in grades 9 or below by completing either 20 semester units (or 10 upper-division units) of business coursework in addition to a business methods course. This introductory authorization must include courses in business management, business marketing or introduction to business, computer concepts and applications, economics, business communications or business English, and accounting. Also, candidates can obtain a supplementary authorization to teach in grades 12 or below by completing either 20 semester units (or 10 upper division units) in one of the following specific content areas: (1) accounting (including finance), (2) computer concepts and applications, (3) economic and consumer education, (4) marketing/entrepreneurship, and (5) office technologies, word processing, and business communication in addition to a business methods course (Supplementary Authorization Guidebook, 2005).

Out-of-state credential. The fourth alternative path to certification is for those who currently hold a credential outside of California. Teachers who complete their elementary or secondary teacher preparation outside of California may apply directly to CCTC for their initial credential. This preliminary credential is issued for a maximum of five years. Individuals have five years to complete the requirements and qualify for the Professional Clear, and the requirements are similar to those who have obtained the preliminary credential in California. The education code requires that individuals earn a degree from an accredited institution in order for the degree to be acceptable for certification purposes. The accrediting associations that the Commission recognizes are as follows: (1) Middle States Commission on Higher Education, (2) New England Association of Schools and Colleges, (3) North Central Association

Commission on Accreditation and School Improvement, (4) Northwest Commission on Colleges and Universities, (5) Southern Association of Colleges and Schools, and (6) Western Association of Schools and Colleges.

Since 1999 the SB 2042 credential has established new standards for teacher certification in California designed to improve the preparation of K-12 teachers. SB 2042 is a two-tier credential. The first tier is the Five-Year Preliminary Credential and the second tier is the Professional Clear Credential. In California, a business single subject credential is a fifth-year program. First, candidates earn a bachelor's degree and then earn a teaching credential during a fifth year of study. Candidates may either complete an approved CCTC subject matter program, the equivalent of an approved CCTC subject matter program, or pass the CSET examination in their discipline to teach in California.

SUMMARY

This chapter offers readers a "snapshot" or sample of the methods used to deter-mine the quality for certification of business teachers in three different states. Several similarities and one difference were revealed.

Five similarities were reported in each of the three state programs described in this chapter. Each state reported a requirement that potential business teachers following the traditional education route graduate from a university program that is aligned with state-approved business education standards and NCLB stipulations for the highly qualified designation. A professional content examination is required by each state. Each state utilized a multilevel certification process to evaluate the qualifications of existing teachers. Existing business teachers are required to advance in certification levels requiring continuing education and/or professional development to remain current in their field in order to continue their teaching careers. Each state makes accommodations for candidates who did not follow the traditional education route in becoming certified. Each state has an alternative route program that utilizes standardized exams (PRAXIS or CSET) to attempt to evaluate alternative certifica-tion candidates.

A primary difference reported was that one state (California) does not require business teacher candidates to pass the PRAXIS II Subject Assessment test. Instead, candidates are required to pass the California Subject Examination for Teachers (CSET). Other states, territories, and countries will probably have differences in their methods of evaluating the credentials of business teacher candidates. This chapter offers a sample of credentialing assessment procedures from three states for those interested in this subject to compare and contrast with the systems used in other states.

REFERENCES

California Commission on Teacher Credentialing. (1999). *Business teacher preparation in California: Standards of quality and effectiveness for subject matter programs, handbook for teacher educators and program reviewers.*

California Commission on Teacher Credentialing. (June 2004). *Induction manual – a credential application processing guidebook for commission-approved induction programs.*

California Commission on Teacher Credentialing. (March 2005). *Credential information.* Retrieved March 3, 2006 from http://www.ctc.ca.gov/credentials/manuals.html.

California Subject Examinations for Teachers. (2006). *CSET Web site.* Retrieved March 3, 2006 from http://www.cset.nesinc.com/.

Education Professional Standards Board. (2006). *Certification/educator preparation.* Retrieved January 9, 2006 from http://www.kyepsb.net/.

Educational Testing Service. (2006) *The Praxis Series web site.* Retrieved September 6, 2006 from http://www.ets.org.

Kentucky Department of Education. (February 23, 2006). *KY Department of Education Web site.* Retrieved March 3, 2006 from http://www.education.ky.gov/KDE.

Requirements for the Professional Clear Credential, SB 2042. (2005). Retrieved August 17, 2006 from http://www.omsd.k12.ca.us/teacher/indreq.pdf#search=%22professional%20clear%20credential%20ca%22.

Supplementary Authorization Guidebook. (February 2005) *California Commission on Teacher Credentialing.* Retrieved March 13, 2006 from http://www.ctc.ca.gov/credentials/manuals-handbooks/Supplement-Auth.pdf

Utah.gov. (2006). *Licensing routes.* Retrieved March 3, 2006 from http://www.rules.utah.gov/publicat/code/r277/r277-503.htm#T4.

Utah State Office of Education. (2006). *Marketing education: Utah Marketing Education Licensing.* Retrieved August 6, 2006 from http://www.usoe.k12.ut.us/ate/marketing/licensing.html.

Utah State Office of Education. (2006) *Educator licensing.* Retrieved March 3, 2006 from http://www.schools.utah.gov/cert/require/renewal/PD_categories.htm.

Utah State Office of Education. (2006). *Business education: Utah Business Education Licensing.* Retrieved September 6, 2006 from http://www.usoe.k12.ut.us/ate/business/belicenses/bematrix.htm.

Western Kentucky University (WKU). (2002, February). *Department of Middle Grades and Secondary Education.* Retrieved January 9, 2006 from http://edtech.wku.edu/~wkuncate/business/business.doc.

Western Kentucky University (WKU). (2003, November). *College of Education and Behavioral Sciences: Policy on alternate admissions to graduate study.* Retrieved January 9, 2006 from http://edtech.wku.edu/programs/AlternateAdmission.htm.

Program Evaluation in Business Education

Judith J. Lambrecht
University of Minnesota
St. Paul, Minnesota

Peter F. Meggison
Massasoit Community College
Brockton, Massachusetts

The vitality of any education program depends on providing evidence that the program is accomplishing its mission. This mission has both stable and changing elements, as program leaders respond to both social mandates and their own professional judgments about what students need. While change may be inevitable, systematic program evaluation is a key tool for assuring that the right types of changes are made to ensure program quality (Lynch, 2004). This chapter examines the goals of program evaluation within the context of business education programs. The overall goals of program evaluation will be progressively illustrated by showing specific examples of these goals in business program documents, the recurrent attention to these goals in informal and formal evaluation practices, the impact of current legislative and cultural mandates, and finally examples of the ways that business programs can implement program evaluation in ongoing practices.

GOALS OF PROGRAM EVALUATION
The chief goals of program evaluation in business education are to enable a department to improve the quality of its program, to increase the program's effectiveness, and to strive constantly for excellence. As an ongoing process, program evaluation improves program quality by asking three fundamental questions about the worth of the enterprise being examined (Alkin & Christie, 2004):

1. Are the goals reasonable and appropriate (Goal Accountability)?

2. Are the procedures for accomplishing those goals reasonable and appropriate (Process Accountability)?

3. To what extent have the established goals been achieved (Outcome Accountability)?

These business examples will be used to illustrate some fundamental ideas about program evaluation, since business education as a field draws on a long history and body of ideas related to what program evaluation can do and what methods do it effectively.

Business Education Accountability Standards

Business education accountability standards from state curriculum standards documents show how business programs address the three types of evaluation questions presented at the outset: Goal Accountability, Process Accountability, and Outcome Accountability. To illustrate the structure of evaluation models, examples from business education standards documents are presented in Table 1. For the complete texts of state standards in Table 1, see the Web sites in each state, as follows: Wisconsin: www.dpi.wi.gov/cte/pdf/bitcurrguide.pdf; Minnesota: www. children.state.mn.us/mde/Academic_ Excellence/Career_ Technical_Education/ Forms_Resources/index.html; and Texas: http://www.tea.state.tx.us/teks/.

Goal Accountability

The excerpt in the far left column of Table 1 from the *Wisconsin Business and Information Technology Curriculum Planning Guide* (2005) addresses the question of whether goals are reasonable and appropriate. The Wisconsin Guide illustrates well-documented rationales for the program standards presented in this document. A standard is presented followed by a rationale for that standard.

Process Accountability

The excerpt in the middle column of Table 1 from the Minnesota Department of Education (2004), *Career and Technical Education Standards and Measures,* addresses the question of whether the procedures for accomplishing stated goals are reasonable and appropriate. This Minnesota document illustrates a focus on program elements or instructional processes, those characteristics which need to be visible as available to students (See CTESM).

Outcome Accountability

The third column of Table 1 is an excerpt from the Texas Knowledge and Skills (TEKS) and addresses the question of the extent to which established goals been achieved. The Texas standards illustrate the outcome expectations required in one course.

Table 1. *Excerpts from State Business Curriculum Models: Three Types of Accountability*

Goal Accountability Are the goals reasonable and appropriate?	Process Accountability Are the procedures for accomplishing those goals reasonable and appropriate?	Outcome Accountability To what extent have the established goals been achieved?
Wisconsin Wisconsin Business and Information Technology Curriculum Planning Guide (2005) **Rationale for Program Standards** <u>QUALITY EDUCATOR</u> <u>(1 of 8 Stds)</u> There is an increasing body of research that supports the assertion that teacher and teaching quality are the most powerful predictors of student success. **Standard 1** – *The business educator is high qualified and appropriately certified to teach all corresponding business and information technology courses within a business program.* **Rationale for Standards 1, 2, and 3** The first step to ensuring that business educators in every Wisconsin classroom are highly qualified is to make sure that they hold the appropriate certification to teach all corresponding business and information technology courses within a business and information technology program. Certification alone, however, is not enough. Research suggests that it is what teachers know and are able to do in the classroom that most influences student learning (Burmaster, 2002).	**Minnesota** Minnesota Department of Education (2004), *Career and Technical Education Standards and Measures* **BUSINESS & MARKETING EDUCATION** <u>STANDARD 1 (out of 9 Stds)</u> The Local Education Agency (Business and Marketing Education Program) will provide learners with opportunities to gain employability, interpersonal, and career skills. These skills will enhance the learner's opportunity to: A. Be a willing and motivated life long learner; B. Be a productive and contributing member of society; C. Understand how career areas impact local, national, and global economies; D. Be prepared to articulate high school credits to postsecondary educational opportunities; and E. Be employable. Curricula will include components that develop management skills, specific job-entry skills, career education, lifelong learning, and related applied academic skills required for employment in one or more of, but not limited to, the following Business, Marketing, and Entrepreneurial Education program areas: Business, Marketing and Entrepreneurship will include components to develop task management skills of the Secretaries Commission on Achieving Necessary Skills (SCANS), occupational knowledge, career development, positive work ethics and integrated academic skills necessary to become economically self-sufficient and productive members of society.	**Texas** Texas Knowledge and Skills (TEKS) **§120.43. Banking and Financial Systems (One-Half Credit).** (a) **General requirements**. This course is recommended for students in Grades 11-12. (b) **Introduction**. Students develop a foundation in the economical, financial, technological, international, social, and ethical aspects of business to become competent consumers, employees, and entrepreneurs. Students incorporate a broad base of knowledge that includes the legal, managerial, marketing, financial, ethical, and international dimensions of business to make appropriate business decisions. (c) **Knowledge and skills**. (1) The student evaluates the role of money in the modern economy. (2) The student identifies the principal functions of financial institutions. (3) The student utilizes the services of banking and financial institutions for loans, savings, and investing. (4) The student compares business financing opportunities with conventional or government options. (5) The student assesses the differences in mortgage transactions. (6) The student identifies the economic theories and financial forces that influence international business.

PROGRAM EVALUATION MODELS

It can be helpful to notice that the three fundamental goal questions raised by program evaluation are always present, whether stated explicitly or not. The three questions can be seen as part of ongoing informal assessments of programs, as well as part of formal program evaluation models. Two major models will be described, the CIPP (Context, Input, Process, and Product) model and the Kirkpatrick model. These general models are implicitly part of practical applications of program evaluation within business programs.

CIPP Model

Program evaluation will be more successful if business educators choose a conceptual framework to represent their thinking about the influences on their program, the components to be examined, and the kinds of evidence they will accept to illustrate the ongoing processes or ultimate attainments. A commonly used model is the CIPP model developed in the 1970s by Stufflebeam (Finch & Crunkilton, 1999) and regarded as a helpful way to look at an education system. The following are the four types of evaluation included in the CIPP model:

1. *Context*

   - deals with whether to offer a curriculum

   - decides on parameters (focus, goals, and objectives)

   - corresponds to question of Goal Accountability.

2. *Input*

   - determines what resources and strategies will be used to achieve curriculum goals and objectives.

3. *Process*

   - determines what effect curriculum has on students in school

   - examines intermediate progress

   - makes changes to align an program with expectations

   - is similar to *formative assessment* in purpose

4. *Product*

   - examines curriculum's effects on former students

   - makes decisions about program continuation or re-focusing

   - judges final outcomes of program in relation to original expectations (similar to summative assessment)

- views evaluation as evaluation research (when an experimental design is used)

- compares outcomes of different programs/processes.

As an example of a "decision-oriented" evaluation model, Stufflebeam's CIPP model has been widely used. A key purpose of program evaluation is to aid decision makers in allocating resources (Alkin & Christie, 2004), and Stufflebeam's model uses both formative and summative information to enable stakeholders to establish an accountability record and make decisions. Current recommendations for using the CIPP model have extended the definitions of the elements to break the final P, *Product*, into impact, effectiveness, sustainability, and transportability evaluations, indicating the dynamic nature of this often-used model (Stufflebeam, 2002). The CIPP model has also been linked to a national set of standards for conducting program evaluations, *The Program Evaluation Standards* (Joint Committee for Education Evaluation, 1994). Space does not permit discussing these standards here, but persons interested in exploring ideas about evaluation should examine this document.

Kirkpatrick Model
The CIPP model has also been compared with another well-known evaluation model commonly used in industry training settings, Kirkpatrick's (1994) levels of evaluation or assessment. The following are Kirkpatrick's four evaluation levels:

Level 1 – Reaction

- determines how participants react to a program or course

- considered a process evaluation (participants express their attitudes toward program/course components)

- example: student course evaluation surveys for industry workshop or school courses

Level 2 – Learning

- focuses on skills, knowledge or attitude changes after program/course participation

- suggests change, e.g., pre- and post-test assessment models and formal measures of outcomes

- example: paper/pencil tests administered throughout a course and performance assessment at end

- n.b.: It is becoming increasing important for learning assessment to focus on meaningful, business-like activities called "projects." The extensive materials development by Indiana business teachers represent such complex learning activities coupled with learning assessment (Indiana Department of Education, 2006).

Level 3 – Behavior

- examines performance changes of course/program participants after leaving instruction and returning to work or other social engagements
- assumes learning is intended to transfer beyond the classroom
- assumes behaviors observable or measurable in other settings validate course/program success
- examples: (1) a large-scale project evaluating different types of online technology training. Employees were followed into their work settings and asked to complete performance tasks similar to those completed in training sessions to learn computer applications (Boyle, Kolosh, L'Allier, & Lambrecht, 2003). (2) the follow-up survey mentioned at the end of this chapter
- n.b.: This level of assessment examines performance at work after instruction is completed and is affected by the type of contact teachers/trainers have with their students after they move beyond formal education.

Level 4 – Results

- looks broadly at overall outcomes of a curriculum by looking at ultimate effects. (In a corporation, the results may be greater profits, more efficient service, or greater return on investment. In a school, the results may be the number of students passing certification exams or obtaining employment in specified areas.)
- n.b.: This evaluation is an extension of evaluation in the job setting, but it looks further at the impact of this performance on the larger organization. Since institutional/ corporate results are affected by many factors, not just education or training, it is particularly challenging for business educators or industry trainers to present program assessment at Level 4.

The CIPP Model and the Kirkpatrick Models have been compared by Finch, Crunkilton, & Crunkilton (1999, p. 279) as shown in Table 2 that follows.

Table 2. *Application of Kirkpatrick Evaluation Levels to CIPP Evaluational Elements*

CIPP Evaluation Elements	Kirkpatrick Evaluation Levels			
	Reaction	Learning	Behavior	Results
Context	+	0	0	-
Input	+	+	0	-
Process	0	+	+	-
Product	0	0	+	+

Range is from greater (+) to less (-) application.

LEGISLATIVE AND CULTURAL MANDATES

Current cultural and political changes have heightened attention to the two ends of the evaluation spectrum—decisions about the context or goals that are to be chosen and judgments about the product or outcomes that result from educational or training interventions. Rojewski (2002) makes the following statement about the legislative emphasis on accountability and the four core outcome areas targeted by program evaluation:

> Accountability has become a hallmark of educational reform initiatives and has not escaped reform efforts in career and technical education. Perkins III legislation requires that states develop evaluation systems to assess four core indicators of student performance, including academic and vocational achievement, program completion (e.g., high school graduation or postsecondary degree or certificate), successful transition from high school to postsecondary education and/or employment, and accessibility and equity (Rojewski, 2002, p. 45).

The traditional outcome assessment measures—job and college placement rates— still dominate the criteria used to evaluate the effectiveness of career and technical education programs (Rojewski, 2002). These are product assessments, and the focus is on results beyond the immediate classroom. In order to attain these far-reaching goals, the entire business program needs to work together, with the entire school, and also with other educational institutions to which students transfer in developing well-articulated programs that cumulatively lead to student success. If new, legislated ideas related to educational reform are to become identified with quality business programs, such as the idea that academic and vocational content should be integrated, quality process and product evaluation practices are needed to document the expected positive impact (Stasz, 1999).

The impetus for the focus on long-term goals like college attendance and eventual employment stem from cultural mandates, namely economic and technological changes, compelling all educators to recognize the need for higher-level skills, greater depth of understanding, and the ability of students to continue to learn and continually deal with open-ended, ill-structured problems. Reports such as *Standards for What? The Economic Roots of K-16 Reform* (Carnevale & Desrochers, 2003) include the following generalizations about trends affecting educational planning, ending with the need for accountability for matching educational and economic needs:

- For most Americans, education and training through and beyond high school is now a necessary condition (not just the most advantageous or desirable route) for developing skills required by most well-paying jobs.

- With the retirement of the baby boomers and increases in jobs requiring college-level knowledge and skills, the nation faces a prospective shortage of workers needed for economic growth and competitiveness.

- In the knowledge economy, the educational prerequisites for individual opportunity and mobility, economic growth, social justice, civic and cultural participation, and national and state economic competitiveness are converging.

- A major challenge will be to achieve accountability for education at all levels through high standards while, at the same time, maintaining the flexibility of educational organizations and individuals that is correctly credited with much of the nation's past economic and educational success (Carnevale & Desrochers, 2003, p. vi).

The nature of higher standards mentioned in the fourth generalization above has been summarized in many places, including several standards documents related specifically to business education to be described in the second half of this chapter. If business education is to have a place in current educational reform efforts, programs need to provide evidence that includes attention to broad standards areas. In condensed form, the standards to be assessed through outcome evaluation, also called product evaluation, are the following:

- Developing higher levels of functional academic skills

- Developing general employability skills

- Developing creative problem-solving abilities

- Having more realistic career aspirations

- Having an understanding of technology related to career majors

- Possessing a sample of representative skills related to career majors (Pucel, 2001, p. 151).

The above list can be said to represent general outcome expectations. Specific examples illustrate how business education has answered the three fundamental evaluation questions—specifying reasonable goals, specifying how to accomplish valued goals, and specifying how outcomes will be assessed.

PROGRAM IMPROVEMENT PROCESSES

Several steps, as part of the program evaluation process, can be undertaken in order to bring about improvement. Evaluation should be conducted, preferably, with the involvement of local program staff that know the program best and have the most to gain by the results (Levesque, Bradby & Rossi, 1996). Some aspects of a program will be stronger than others, and it is through a process of program evaluation that a program's weaknesses can be identified and remediated. Self-regulation, therefore, becomes a key component in ongoing improvement of the business education program, since the most effective curriculum improvement is initiated and implemented by the classroom teacher. As the three fundamental evaluation questions imply, program evaluation is a multifaceted issue for the business educator. Specific examples are provided below of how business educators can examine their programs on several dimensions of program quality, namely: program goals; curriculum; student organizations; staff; community resources; facilities, software, and equipment; and instructional materials. Lastly, the common program practice of student follow-up will be described as a special assessment practice directed toward program evaluation.

Program Goals

Local control of schools is a long-established American education value, and business education programs are no exception. Effective business education programs are the outgrowth of considerable attention being given to the make up of the student population and the community in which the institution is located. Years ago Roman (1966) pointed out:

> Ultimately, the most effective curriculum work is done at the local level. State and national curriculum study may provide the superstructure, but in order to reach the real curriculum objective—the pupil in the classroom—local educators must reshape, adjust, and often originate ideas and concepts that ensure the process a reasonable chance of success (p. 5).

From a practical standpoint, however, program objectives and standards are usually developed at the state level and are intended for use by local school systems. In current times, this is often the result of federal legislation. Specifically, the Carl Perkins Act and Title 1 (for economically disadvantaged students) force local school systems to develop performance standards for evaluating student competency by specific career clusters. These standards are filtered into the local systems through the state. In turn, the state standards are often the outgrowth of national recommendations.

Program standards are the foundation for all other activities. The *Wisconsin Business and Information Technology Curriculum Planning Guide* (2005) has already been featured as an excellent source for teachers interested in program evaluation and improvement, in that it provides a rationale for each of the standards in the curriculum. For a list of all 20 of Wisconsin's standards in eight major categories that can be implemented on a continual basis, view the *Guide's* Web site at http://dpi.state.wi.us/pubsales/stw_1.html.

Curriculum

The *National Standards for Business Education* (2001) utilizes a developmental approach in a curriculum model for elementary schools, middle/junior high schools, secondary schools, and two-year postsecondary colleges. Eleven business education content areas indicate achievement standards and performance expectations in accounting, business law, career development, communication, computation, economics and personal finance, entrepreneurship, information technology, international business, management, and marketing. Recent research by Rader (2005) showed that of the 39 states that adopted specific content standards for business education, 46%

were somewhat similar, very similar, or identical to the NBEA standards. The Minnesota Frameworks for Career and Technical Education (Minnesota Department of Education, 2004) are an example of aligned of state standards with the NBEA standards.

Each of the 11 content areas in the *National Standards for Business Education* can be evaluated as part of the overall curriculum improvement process in order to ascertain areas where improvements can be made. With technological improvements continuing at a rapid pace, those involved with curriculum evaluation in business courses must recognize the ongoing suitability of the content of the individual courses. Integration of the soft-skills, ethics, international concepts, as well as technological concepts, need to be fused into course offerings—those with general educational value, as well as those with an occupational thrust.

For students in a business career cluster, the individual student's program of studies should follow a meaningful sequence. Upon graduation, the student should possess enough marketable skills to accept an entry-level position in the occupation for which he or she has prepared or to pursue postsecondary education. From a general education standpoint, business offerings must include "common core" learning in consumer and economic business information in order to prepare all students for participation in the American free enterprise system.

Teachers in business programs need to work cooperatively to establish and implement curriculum and program clusters and to establish and utilize standards for assessment. Teachers themselves need to revise the curriculum as student needs and workplace trends warrant.

Student Organizations

Student organizations provide an excellent vehicle to extend learning beyond the formal classroom. While schools attempt to provide instruction in various facets of emerging technology that students will encounter in the workforce, the rapidity of change makes this an impossible task in even the most technologically advanced school systems. By encouraging engagement in the business community through both employment and class projects, business student organizations deliver a sound mechanism through which students can become acquainted with technology, software, and hardware that they may not encounter in their school experiences.

Another positive benefit student organizations provide is the opportunity for students to learn to compete, a scenario difficult to replicate in the typical classroom setting. Competitive events, usually considered an integral part of student organizations, showcase student abilities in various aspects of the business curriculum. Students participating in student organizations are also given numerous opportunities for leadership training, personal development, and social responsibility, in addition to continued enhancement of specific business skills (PCBEE Statement 30, 1982).

The effectiveness of student organizations can be assessed by the extent to which the extra-class activities of the student organization supplement and compliment the goals and objectives of the program by providing optimum learning activities for the students.

Staff

Business educators, especially at the 5-12 instructional levels, are licensed by standards established in each state. Guidelines for the licensing of business teachers have been established by the *Business Teacher Education Curriculum Guide and Program Standards* (National Association for Business Teacher Education, 2005). Beyond the initial preparation of teachers, school systems are increasingly concerned about the continued professional development of its teachers. In fact, a portion of Perkins funds are specifically earmarked for this purpose; and individual professional development plans are required in many states. These plans include a yearly individual progress report to the school's administrator outlining the steps the teacher has taken to ensure advancement and improvement, sometimes a requirement for recertification. Relevant work experience is often required as a component of the professional development process to ensure that real-world situations augment classroom presentations. Sometimes this can be accomplished through job shadows and externships.

Perkins funds also enable teachers to become members of professional associations and to participate in conferences and seminars to upgrade their skills and to learn of new developments in both business and education. In the multifaceted area of technology, formal and informal course work becomes imperative for the business teacher. Professional growth and development, therefore, becomes a lifelong process for the business teacher, since the expectation is that the business teacher will continue to learn throughout his or her career.

Community Resources

Unlimited opportunities exist for the business teacher to become engaged with the community to enhance learning. Primary among these is the opportunity to use businesspersons to suggest improvements in the school's program. These businesspersons meet regularly with the business faculty to advise on job preparation, placement opportunities, and course content. Advisory board members frequently will describe the qualifications necessary for applicants to fill initial business positions and the minimum standards that are acceptable for employment.

In addition, advisory board members can provide placement opportunities for students. This can be accomplished through internship programs (Kosek, 2006) as well as actual job placement upon graduation. Field trips to local businesses can often be arranged by members of the advisory board, whereby the community becomes an extension of the business classroom.

An advisory board should also assist the department with developing an effective mission statement. The statement should include specific declarations that describe what the students should know and what they should be able to do once they finish the program.

Advisory boards of this nature are required in programs that are funded through the Perkins Act. These advisory boards can be an outstanding medium for implementing and expanding the goals of the business education program. If the members of the group are selected wisely, they can offer sage advice to those involved with program improvement.

Surveys of local businesses can be used to obtain occupational information relative to the types of positions that are available in the community which, in turn, can be used to plan or revise the business curriculum. Occupational surveys can also be used to determine job components such as the kind and type of software and equipment used in the community, the activities and duties of an employee's typical day, and other recommendations that may be used to improve the business curriculum.

Press releases to local newspapers showcasing students' accomplishments and modifications within the business department are another way to keep the community—and parents and local businesses in particular—up-to-date and in touch with the business program. A complete guide to the effective establishment and maintenance of advisory committees is available from the Pennsylvania Department of Education (Pennsylvania Department of Education, Bureau of Career and Technical Education, 2003).

Facilities, Software, and Equipment

In these days of rapidly changing technology, designing facilities and selecting software and equipment are perennial challenges for the business teacher. Effective departments establish a specific strategy and plan for acquiring, replacing, and upgrading equipment and software. While it is not recommended that schools necessarily adopt new versions of software immediately after they are released, an attempt should be made to utilize the software and equipment that is commonly used in the community.

Instructional Materials

In-depth examination of instructional materials, particularly the textbook, is essential; for without excellent instructional materials, the implementation of established curriculum guidelines and the realization of standards becomes a futile effort. Although program standards and objectives should not be based on a textbook, in many situations, the textbook does become the curriculum. The danger in this is that the textbook or supplementary materials become simply a venue for assignments or the completion of problem-based projects. Students become robotic in situations such as these, since decision-making is removed. This frequently leads to complaints that students are merely being assigned busywork!

There is no dearth of materials available for instruction in nearly all the business subjects. In addition to the instructional aids offered by major publishing companies, other useful materials—in both print and electronic form—are available from software vendors; business, governmental, and professional associations; civic groups; and private industry groups. Textbook adoption practices vary within the United States. Textbook selection should involve multiple individuals, but teachers who will use the textbook should be given first consideration.

Factors to consider in selecting textbooks and related materials primarily involve the selection of appropriate content for the course being considered. The nature of the contents, both general and specific, is important, since it should parallel the standards and objectives that have been set out for the course. Other factors to consider include the reading level; illustrations; authorship; sturdiness; copyright; cost; appearance; and supplementary materials which may be available both online and in hard copy such as test banks, software presentations, workbooks, and instructor's manuals. Online support in the form of help lines is essential for many of today's classroom resources, especially in the area of technology.

In order to ensure utmost objectivity in textbook selection, evaluative criteria should be developed to serve as a guide in the decision-making process. A useful guide, *Middle School and High School Business, Marketing and Information Technology Textbook/Instructional Materials Review Form*, is available from the Indiana State Department of Education at http://www.doe.state.in.us/olr/textbook/pdf/05-BMITReviewForm.pdf.

Follow-Up

Educators at all levels of instruction today are besieged with pressures to measure the effectiveness of their programs. If administered properly, the follow-up study can be one of the most useful devices in assessing the outcomes of the business program. Interpretation of the findings from the follow-up study will help deal with the issue of accountability as well as offer sound suggestions for curriculum improvement and revision. For continuance of Perkins funding, follow-up activities are absolutely essential.

The follow-up study is a means of ascertaining how well graduates of a particular program are prepared for their intended careers. The remarks of the graduates can serve to confirm the need for continuation of existing practices, eliminate various other practices, or even add new programs or courses of study in order for the educational institution to better meet the needs of its constituents. When responses are tabulated in terms of numbers and percentages, brief job descriptions and opinions, this information can serve as a motivating factor to students currently enrolled in a particular course of study to pursue their career aspirations.

The process of conducting a follow-up study can also serve as an effective means of public relations. Taxpayers—both employers and employees—are impressed with the attempt of the school to improve its product, the graduate working in the community. Employers, too, appreciate that the school is interested in evaluating the graduates of the business program.

The result of follow-up studies should be made public and the information shared with other educators who are involved with the same type of students as those surveyed in the particular study. Educators who find it difficult, either because of lack of time or lack of money, to conduct this type of research will find the completed research of others helpful in improving their own curricula.

A useful follow-up survey instrument that can be modified to meet the needs of one's own school situation is available from the authors by e-mailing them at jlambrec@umn.edu or pmeggison@massasoit.mass.edu. Samples of a cover letter, follow-up letter, and follow-up post card are also included.

SUMMARY

The program improvement process always brings about change, and change always requires resources—either new resources or those shifted from other places. Business programs can make, and have made, justifiable claims for resources when they can answer three essential accountability questions: 1) Are the goals reasonable and appropriate? 2) Are the procedures for accomplishing those goals reasonable and appropriate? and 3) To what extent have the established goals been achieved? Answers to these fundamental questions lead to the development of ongoing programs which are regularly reviewed to ensure that program improvement is an ongoing process.

By effectively examining the curriculum, student organizations, staff, community resources, facilities, instructional materials, and follow-up studies, program evaluators will have at their disposal the resources upon which to base change. In turn, business programs will have the resources to provide quality instruction when they can continually demonstrate they are doing the right things—*and doing them well.*

REFERENCES

Alkin, M. C., & Christie, C. A. (2004). An evaluation theory tree. In M. C. Alkin, (Ed.), *Evaluation Roots: Tracing theorists' views and influences* (pp. 12-65). Thousand Oaks, CA: Sage Publications.

Boyle, S. L.T., Kolosh, K., L'Allier, J., & Lambrecht, J. J. (2003, Fall). Thomson NETg's blended-learning model: The next generation of corporate and school-based learning, *The Delta Pi Epsilon Journal, 45*(3), 145-161.

Burmaster, E. (2002). *Wisconsin oral communication assessment educators' guide.* Madison, WI: Wisconsin State Superintendent Department of Public Instruction.

Carnevale, A. P., & Desrochers, D. M. (2003). *Standards for what? The economic roots of K-16 reform.* Washington, D.C.: Educational Testing Service.

Finch, C. R., Crunkilton, J. R., & Crunkilton, J. (1999). *Curriculum development in vocational and technical education: Planning, content, and implementation* (5th ed.). Boston: Allyn & Bacon.

Indiana Department of Education. (2006). *Business, marketing, and information technology course descriptions, contentsStandards, and performance expectations.* Office of Career and Technical Education, Indiana Department of Education. Retrieved August 17, 2006, from: http://www.doe.state.in.us/octe/bme/curriculum/contentstandards.htm

Indiana Department of Education. (2005). *Middle school and high school business, marketing and information technology textbook/instructional materials review form.* Office of Career and Technical Education, Indiana Department of Education. Retrieved August 17, 2006, from: http://www.doe.state.in.us/olr/textbook/pdf/05-BMITReviewForm.pdf.

Kirkpatrick, D. I. (1994). *Evaluating training programs: The four levels.* San Francisco, CA: Berrett-Koehler.

Kosek, S. (2006). A coordinator's advocacy for success. *Business Education Forum, 60*(4), 27-29.

Levesque, K., Bradby, D., & Rossi, K. (1996). Using data for program improvement: How do we encourage schools to do it? Retrieved fromhttp://ncrve.Berkeley.edu/CenterFocus/CF12. html

Lynch, R. (2000). *New directions for high school career and technical education in the 21st century* (Information Series No. 384). Columbus, OH: ERIC Clearinghouse on Adult, Career, and Vocational Education.

Minnesota Department of Education. (2004). *Frameworks for career and technical education.* St. Paul, MN: Adult and Career Education, Minnesota Department of Education.

Minnesota Department of Education. (2004). *Career and technical education standards and measures.* St. Paul, MN: Adult and Career Education, Minnesota Department of Education.

National Association for Business Teacher Education. (2005). *Business teacher education curriculum guide & program standards* (2nd ed.). Reston, VA: Author.

National Business Education Association. (2001). *National standards for business education: What America's students should know and be able to do in business.* Reston, VA: Author.

Policies Commission for Business and Economic Education (PCBEE). (1982). *This we believe about the role of student organizations in business education.* (Policy Statement No. 30). Cincinnati, OH: Southwestern Publishing Company.

Policies Commission for Business and Economic Education (PCBEE). (1997, October). *This we believe about the professional development of business teachers.* (Policy Statement No. 60). Reston, VA: National Business Education Association.

Policies Commission for Business and Economic Education (PCBEE). (2002). *This we believe about the role of business education in financial education.* (Policy Statement No. 69). Reston, VA: National Business Education Association.

Pennsylvania Department of Education, Bureau of Career and Technical Education. (2003). *Establishing and operating effective local advisory committees.* Retrieved July 27, 2006, from http://www.pde.state.pa.us/career_edu/lib/career_edu/ Local_Adv_Manual.pdf

Pucel, D. J. (2001). *Beyond vocational education: Career majors, tech prep, schools within schools, magnet schools & academies.* Larchmont, NY: Eye on Education.

Rader, M. (2005). A comparison of state and national standards for business education. *NABTE Review, 32,* 10-15.

Roman, J. (1966). The business curriculum. *Monograph 100.* Cincinnati: South-Western Publishing Company

Rojewski, J. W. (2002). *Preparing the workforce of tomorrow: A conceptual framework for career and technical education.* Columbus, OH: National Dissemination Center for Career and Technical Education, The Ohio State University

Sanders, J. R., et al. (1994). The *program evaluation standards: How to assess evaluations of education programs* (2nd ed.). (Joint Committee on Educational Evaluation). Newbury Park, CA: Sage Publications, Inc.

Stasz, C. (1999, May). *Assessing the quality of vocational education in high schools.* Paper presented during an independent advisory panel meeting of the National Assessment of Vocational Education, Washington, DC: Rand. Retrieved from http://www. ed.gov/rschstat/eval/sectech/nave/stasz.html

Stufflebeam, D. L. (2002). *CIPP evaluation model checklist.* Retrieved from http://www. wmich.edu/evalctr/checklists/cippchecklist.htm

Texas Knowledge and Skills (2004). *Banking and financial systems TEKS,* §120.43. Houston, TX: University of Houston Curriculum Dissemination Center.

Wisconsin business and information technology curriculum planning guide. (2005). Retrieved February 12, 2006, from http://dpi.wi.gov/cte/pdf/bitcurrguide.pdf